LANGUAGE AND LITERA(

Dorothy S. Strickland, FOUNDI
Donna E. Alvermann and María Paula G
ADVISORY BOARD: Richard Allington, Kathryn Au, E
Anne Haas Dyson, Carole Edelsky, Mary Juzwik, Susan Ly

Reading With Purpose: Selecting and Using
Children's Literature for Inquiry and Engagement
ERIKA THULIN DAWES, KATIE EGAN CUNNINGHAM,
GRACE ENRIQUEZ, & MARY ANN CAPPIELLO

Black Immigrant Literacies: Intersections of Race,
Language, and Culture in the Classroom
PATRIANN SMITH

Core Practices for Teaching Multilingual Students:
Humanizing Pedagogies for Equity
MEGAN MADIGAN PEERCY, JOHANNA M. TIGERT, &
DAISY E. FREDRICKS

Bringing Sports Culture to the English Classroom:
An Interest-Driven Approach to Literacy
Instruction
LUKE RODESILER

Culturally Sustaining Literacy Pedagogies:
Honoring Students' Heritages, Literacies, and
Languages
SUSAN CHAMBERS CANTRELL, DORIS WALKER-DALHOUSE,
& ALTHIER M. LAZAR, EDS.

Curating a Literacy Life:
Student-Centered Learning With Digital Media
WILLIAM KIST

Understanding the Transnational Lives and
Literacies of Immigrant Children
JUNGMIN KWON

The Administration and Supervision of Literacy
Programs, 6th Edition
SHELLEY B. WEPNER & DIANA J. QUATROCHE, EDS.

Writing the School House Blues: Literacy, Equity,
and Belonging in a Child's Early Schooling
ANNE HAAS DYSON

Playing With Language: Improving Elementary
Reading Through Metalinguistic Awareness
MARCY ZIPKE

Restorative Literacies:
Creating a Community of Care in Schools
DEBORAH L. WOLTER

Compose Our World: Project-Based Learning in
Secondary English Language Arts
ALISON G. BOARDMAN, ANTERO GARCIA, BRIDGET
DALTON, & JOSEPH L. POLMAN

Digitally Supported Disciplinary Literacy for
Diverse K-5 Classrooms
JAMIE COLWELL, AMY HUTCHISON,
& LINDSAY WOODWARD

The Reading Turn-Around with Emergent
Bilinguals: A Five-Part Framework for Powerful
Teaching and Learning (Grades K-6)
AMANDA CLAUDIA WAGER, LANE W. CLARKE,
& GRACE ENRIQUEZ

Race, Justice, and Activism in Literacy Instruction
VALERIE KINLOCH, TANJA BURKHARD,
& CARLOTTA PENN, EDS.

Letting Go of Literary Whiteness:
Antiracist Literature Instruction for White Students
CARLIN BORSHEIM-BLACK
& SOPHIA TATIANA SARIGIANIDES

The Vulnerable Heart of Literacy:
Centering Trauma as Powerful Pedagogy
ELIZABETH DUTRO

Amplifying the Curriculum: Designing Quality
Learning Opportunities for English Learners
AÍDA WALQUI & GEORGE C. BUNCH, EDS.

Arts Integration in Diverse K–5 Classrooms:
Cultivating Literacy Skills and Conceptual
Understanding
LIANE BROUILLETTE

Translanguaging for Emergent Bilinguals: Inclusive
Teaching in the Linguistically Diverse Classroom
DANLING FU, XENIA HADJIOANNOU, & XIAODI ZHOU

Before Words: Wordless Picture Books and the
Development of Reading in Young Children
JUDITH T. LYSAKER

Seeing the Spectrum: Teaching English Language
Arts to Adolescents with Autism
ROBERT ROZEMA

A Think-Aloud Approach to Writing Assessment:
Analyzing Process and Product with Adolescent
Writers
SARAH W. BECK

"We've Been Doing It Your Way Long Enough":
Choosing the Culturally Relevant Classroom
JANICE BAINES, CARMEN TISDALE, & SUSI LONG

Summer Reading: Closing the Rich/Poor
Reading Achievement Gap, 2nd Edition
RICHARD L. ALLINGTON & ANNE MCGILL-FRANZEN, EDS.

Educating for Empathy:
Literacy Learning and Civic Engagement
NICOLE MIRRA

Preparing English Learners for College and Career:
Lessons from Successful High Schools
MARÍA SANTOS ET AL.

Reading the Rainbow: LGBTQ-Inclusive Literacy
Instruction in the Elementary Classroom
CAITLIN L. RYAN & JILL M. HERMANN-WILMARTH

Educating Emergent Bilinguals: Policies, Programs,
and Practices for English Learners, 2nd Edition
OFELIA GARCÍA & JO ANNE KLEIFGEN

Social Justice Literacies in the English Classroom:
Teaching Practice in Action
ASHLEY S. BOYD

Remixing Multiliteracies: Theory and Practice from
New London to New Times
FRANK SERAFINI & ELISABETH GEE, EDS.

Culturally Sustaining Pedagogies: Teaching and
Learning for Justice in a Changing World
DJANGO PARIS & H. SAMY ALIM, EDS.

continued

For volumes in the NCRLL Collection (edited by JoBeth Allen and Donna E. Alvermann) and the Practitioners
Bookshelf Series (edited by Celia Genishi and Donna E. Alvermann), as well as other titles in this series,
please visit www.tcpress.com.

Language and Literacy Series, *continued*

Choice and Agency in the Writing Workshop
FRED L. HAMEL
Assessing Writing, Teaching Writers
MARY ANN SMITH & SHERRY SEALE SWAIN
The Teacher-Writer
CHRISTINE M. DAWSON
Every Young Child a Reader
SHARAN A. GIBSON & BARBARA MOSS
"You Gotta BE the Book," 3rd Edition
JEFFREY D. WILHELM
Personal Narrative, Revised
BRONWYN CLARE LAMAY
Inclusive Literacy Teachings
LORI HELMAN ET AL.
The Vocabulary Book, 2nd Edition
MICHAEL F. GRAVES
Reading, Writing, and Talk
MARIANA SOUTO-MANNING & JESSICA MARTELL
Go Be a Writer!
CANDACE R. KUBY & TARA GUTSHALL RUCKER
Partnering with Immigrant Communities
GERALD CAMPANO ET AL.
Teaching Outside the Box but Inside the Standards
BOB FECHO ET AL., EDS.
Literacy Leadership in Changing Schools
SHELLEY B. WEPNER ET AL.
Literacy Theory as Practice
LARA J. HANDSFIELD
Literacy and History in Action
THOMAS M. MCCANN ET AL.
Pose, Wobble, Flow
ANTERO GARCIA & CINDY O'DONNELL-ALLEN
Newsworthy—Cultivating Critical Thinkers, Readers, and Writers in Language Arts Classrooms
ED MADISON
Engaging Writers with Multigenre Research Projects
NANCY MACK
Teaching Transnational Youth—
Literacy and Education in a Changing World
ALLISON SKERRETT
Uncommonly Good Ideas—
Teaching Writing in the Common Core Era
SANDRA MURPHY & MARY ANN SMITH
The One-on-One Reading and Writing Conference
JENNIFER BERNE & SOPHIE C. DEGENER
Critical Encounters in Secondary English, 3rd Edition
DEBORAH APPLEMAN
Transforming Talk into Text—Argument Writing, Inquiry, and Discussion, Grades 6–12
THOMAS M. MCCANN
Educating Literacy Teachers Online
LANE W. CLARKE & SUSAN WATTS-TAFFEE

WHAM! Teaching with Graphic Novels Across the Curriculum
WILLIAM G. BROZO ET AL.
Critical Literacy in the Early Childhood Classroom
CANDACE R. KUBY
Inspiring Dialogue
MARY M. JUZWIK ET AL.
Reading the Visual
FRANK SERAFINI
ReWRITING the Basics
ANNE HAAS DYSON
Writing Instruction That Works
ARTHUR N. APPLEBEE ET AL.
Literacy Playshop
KAREN E. WOHLWEND
Critical Media Pedagogy
ERNEST MORRELL ET AL.
A Search Past Silence
DAVID E. KIRKLAND
The ELL Writer
CHRISTINA ORTMEIER-HOOPER
Reading in a Participatory Culture
HENRY JENKINS ET AL., EDS.
Teaching Vocabulary to English Language Learners
MICHAEL F. GRAVES ET AL.
Bridging Literacy and Equity
ALTHIER M. LAZAR ET AL.
Reading Time
CATHERINE COMPTON-LILLY
Interrupting Hate
MOLLIE V. BLACKBURN
Playing Their Way into Literacies
KAREN E. WOHLWEND
Teaching Literacy for Love and Wisdom
JEFFREY D. WILHELM & BRUCE NOVAK
Urban Literacies
VALERIE KINLOCH, ED.
Bedtime Stories and Book Reports
CATHERINE COMPTON-LILLY & STUART GREENE, EDS.
Envisioning Knowledge
JUDITH A. LANGER
Envisioning Literature, 2nd Edition
JUDITH A. LANGER
Artifactual Literacies
KATE PAHL & JENNIFER ROWSELL
Change Is Gonna Come
PATRICIA A. EDWARDS ET AL.
Harlem on Our Minds
VALERIE KINLOCH
Children, Language, and Literacy
CELIA GENISHI & ANNE HAAS DYSON
Children's Language
JUDITH WELLS LINDFORS
Storytime
LAWRENCE R. SIPE

Reading With Purpose

Selecting and Using Children's Literature for Inquiry and Engagement

Erika Thulin Dawes, Katie Egan Cunningham,
Grace Enriquez, and Mary Ann Cappiello

Foreword by Xenia Hadjioannou

TEACHERS COLLEGE PRESS
TEACHERS COLLEGE | COLUMBIA UNIVERSITY
NEW YORK AND LONDON

To the book creators who bring beauty, wonder, hope, and joy to classroom bookshelves.

Published by Teachers College Press,® 1234 Amsterdam Avenue, New York, NY 10027

Copyright © 2024 by Teachers College, Columbia University

Cover design by Holly Grundon / BHG Design. Cover illustration by Freepik.

All rights reserved. No part of this publication may be reproduced or transmitted in any form or by any means, electronic or mechanical, including photocopy, or any information storage and retrieval system, without permission from the publisher. For reprint permission and other subsidiary rights requests, please contact Teachers College Press, Rights Dept.:tcpressrights@tc.columbia.edu

Library of Congress Cataloging-in-Publication Data

Names: Dawes, Erika Thulin, author. | Cunningham, Katie Egan, 1978– author. | Enriquez, Grace, author. | Cappiello, Mary Ann, author.
Title: Reading with purpose : selecting and using children's literature for inquiry and engagement / Erika Thulin Dawes, Katie Egan Cunningham, Grace Enriquez, and Mary Ann Cappiello.
Description: New York : Teacher's College Press, [2023] | Series: Language and literacy series | Includes bibliographical references and index. | Summary: "Reading With Purpose provides teaching ideas, narratives from diverse classrooms, student work samples, reflective questions, and recommendations for recently published children's and young adult literature"—Provided by publisher.
Identifiers: LCCN 2023023011 (print) | LCCN 2023023012 (ebook) | ISBN 9780807768501 (paper : acid-free paper) | ISBN 9780807768518 (hardcover : acid-free paper) | ISBN 9780807781807 (ebook)
Subjects: LCSH: Interdisciplinary approach in education—United States. | Curriculum planning—United States. | Language arts—Correlation with content subjects—United States. | Content area reading—Study and teaching (Elementary)—United States. | Content area reading—Study and teaching (Middle school)—United States.
Classification: LCC LB2806.15 .D38 2023 (print) | LCC LB2806.15 (ebook) | DDC 375/.001—dc23/eng/20230715
LC record available at https://lccn.loc.gov/2023023011
LC ebook record available at https://lccn.loc.gov/2023023012

ISBN 978-0-8077-6850-1 (paper)
ISBN 978-0-8077-6851-8 (hardcover)
ISBN 978-0-8077-8180-7 (ebook)

Printed on acid-free paper
Manufactured in the United States of America

Contents

Foreword *Xenia Hadjioannou*	ix
Acknowledgments	xi
Introduction	1
Who We Are: The Classroom Bookshelf Story	3
Why This Book?	4
Purposes for Reading	5
Using This Book	6

PART I: PURPOSES FOR SELECTING AND USING BOOKS

1. A World of Purpose in the Pages of Books	11
Classroom Story: If I Were a Book	11
What Matters Most	13
Braided Purposes: The Reader, the Text, the Context	16
Many Books, Many Purposes	21
Purpose Matters: A Community of Readers	22
2. Center Care for Ourselves and One Another	25
Classroom Story: Nurturing Care	25
Why Center Care?	28
Why Now? Supporting the Whole Child	29
Centering Care: Understanding Ourselves and Connecting to Others	31
Selecting Books That Center Care to Teach and Reach the Whole Child	38

3. Connect to the Past to Understand the Present — 40
Classroom Story: The Value of Knowing the Past — 40
Why Connect to the Past? — 42
Why Now? Barriers and Bridges — 43
Connecting to the Past — 45
Selecting Books That Connect to the Past to Better Understand the Present — 55

4. Closely Observe the World Around Us — 57
Classroom Story: Idea Making and Learning to Look Closely — 57
Why Closely Observe? — 58
Why Now? The Climate Crisis and Disconnect With the Natural World — 59
Close Observation: Strengthening Our Connection to Our World — 61
Selecting Books That Inspire Close Observation to See the World in New Ways — 73

5. Cultivate Critical Consciousness — 75
Classroom Story: Raising Critical Consciousness Across the Curriculum — 75
Why Cultivate Critical Consciousness? — 77
Why Now? Agency, Equity, and Justice in an Ever-Changing World — 79
Cultivating Critical Consciousness: Creating a Better World for All — 84
Selecting Books That Cultivate Critical Consciousness Toward Creating a Better World for All — 91

PART II: AN INVITATIONS APPROACH TO ENCOURAGE PURPOSEFUL READING

6. Invitations to Use Books to Center Care for Ourselves and One Another — 95
Text Sets — 95
Content Connections and Disciplinary Literacies — 96

	Critical Literacies	97
	Reading Process	98
	Visual Literacies	99
	Writing Development	100
	Multimodal Response	100
	Social-Emotional Learning	102
7.	**Invitations to Use Books to Connect the Past to the Present**	**107**
	Text Sets	107
	Content Connections and Disciplinary Literacies	108
	Critical Literacies	111
	Reading Process	112
	Visual Literacies	112
	Writing Development	113
	Multimodal Response	114
	Social-Emotional Learning	115
8.	**Invitations to Use Books to Closely Observe the World Around Us**	**116**
	Text Sets	116
	Content Connections and Disciplinary Literacies	117
	Critical Literacies	119
	Reading Process	120
	Visual Literacies	121
	Writing Development	122
	Multimodal Response	124
	Social-Emotional Learning	125
9.	**Invitations to Use Books to Cultivate Critical Consciousness Toward Creating a Better World**	**127**
	Text Sets	127
	Content Connections and Disciplinary Literacies	128

Critical Literacies	131
Reading Process	132
Visual Literacies	133
Writing Development	133
Multimodal Response	135
Social-Emotional Learning	136

In Closing — 138

References — 139
    Children's Books — 149

Index — 157

About the Authors — 164

Foreword
Readers, Literature, and Purpose Matter

"We need a moment. We are having a mind shift!," a group of preservice teachers told me as I approached them for a conference while our children's literature class was reviewing entries on The Classroom Bookshelf for picturebooks they had just read. After some more discussion and furious note-taking, they were ready to talk. The entry had surprised them, they explained, compelling them to think beyond traditional comprehension questions and activities. "We had never imagined that there could be this many possibilities with a single picture book," they mused before beginning to share the fresh ideas the entry ignited for their upcoming curriculum planning assignments.

The Classroom Bookshelf has for years been a respected resource for children's book reviews and instructional inspiration for teachers and teacher educators. This book's four contributors channel the expertise, commitments, sensibilities, and teaching artistry that characterizes their long-standing collaborative work into a title that collegially invites readers to consider the *purpose* and the whys of their teaching of literacy. "Purpose matters," they assert. "Why we read matters as much as what we read. Why we choose books matters as much as what we do with them" (p. 1). At a time when decision-making regarding what students read in class and through school libraries is under increased scrutiny and deliberate narrowing, and when the whys of literacy instruction are obscured under curricular mandates and exhaustively directive instructional programs, a book that centers purposefulness is critically important. Being clear about why we pick the books we bring to our students and why we pursue certain tracks in our teaching is not only vital in clarifying our instructional awareness and strengthening the exactness of our teaching, but it also enriches our students' experience of a coherent environment of literacy learning and fortifies our capacity to articulate, and if needed defend, our choices.

After framing "the transaction of reader, text, and context as a set of braided purposes, together creating a unique reading experience for each reader in a classroom" (p. 16), the authors list and substantiate four core purposes that have guided their book selections over the years: centering care to understand ourselves and one another, exploring and connecting to the past to inform our present and reach to the future, closely observing and re-seeing the world, and nurturing critical consciousness for reimagining and reshaping it. The authors consider each of these purposes in individual chapters in Part I, carefully exploring key aspects and untangling complexities. Each chapter in this first part concludes with an invitation to readers to locate one or more books that can serve the purpose examined, and then visit the corresponding chapter in Part II where they are treated to a menu of delectable teaching invitations that create opportunities for students to engage with literature deeply and purposefully.

Reading this book feels like sitting with a gentle, erudite mentor, who is at the same time generous with their insight and recommendations, as well as trusting of our capacity to make deft instructional choices for our particular literacy contexts. Because of that trust, readers are afforded insight into the authors' commitments and priorities through robust, yet readable, theoretical explanations, compellingly illustrated through rich examples of books and of classroom practice across grade levels and school communities. They are also offered scaffolded invitations to reflect on their own practices and decision-making processes through checklists and questionnaires that can make visible patterns and potential biases and offer pathways for constructive shifts.

Beyond demonstrating genuine respect for the teachers who are the envisioned readers of the book, the text also radiates esteem for young people, recognizing them as individuals with histories, preferences, intentionality, and agency in positioning themselves toward the world and toward the books with which they engage. Young people are acknowledged as meaning creators, idea makers, and action takers, who are capable of dealing with complexity, who can pursue shared understandings of trauma and build compassion, who can ask and investigate questions of the social and physical world, and who can envision and enact change.

This is a book that will send readers to library shelves and bookstores and will prompt furious writing in notebooks and on sticky notes, brimming with fresh new ideas about how to recognize and honor the students in our classrooms and how to center purposefulness in our invitations to them to read and think about literature. These ideas may constitute a mind shift, or they may be an elaboration and reinforcement of existing dispositions and practices. Either way, they are bound to inspire some magnificent teaching with literature.

—Xenia Hadjioannou
Associate professor of language and
literacy education, Penn State University,
Berks Campus
President of the Children's Literature
Assembly of NCTE

Acknowledgments

This book represents a decade of reading, writing, thinking, and talking together. It is also a celebration of the bonds children's literature has fostered in us through the joys and sorrows of life. We are grateful to have learned alongside each other the past decade and for the friendship we have found in one another.

Special thanks to our children, who offer levity and light and who have shown us that imagination and books can be tools for dreaming big: Will, Clara, Jack, Matthew, Ana, Eva, and Ella. We would also like to thank our spouses and family members, who provided us with support, patience, and encouragement throughout this writing project: Bill, Chris, Karin, Jim, Mike, and Tim. To Barbara Kiefer, Marjorie Siegel, Maureen Barbieri, Pam Allyn, Margery Staman Miller, Ruth Vinz, Stephanie Jones, and the late Larry Sipe—thank you for kindling our love of books and teaching. Thank you to Emily Spangler, Susan Liddicoat, and the team at Teachers College Press for believing in this book and the potential it has to do good in the world. Finally, our deep gratitude goes to Dana Frantz Bentley, Amanda Goodman, Mr. K. (aka Ted Krupman), Olivia Petraglia, Nicole Corneau, Jessica Della Calce, Tory Munsell, Paige Schale, Kate Allen, and Orla Higgins-Averill—educators extraordinaire, who welcomed us into their classrooms and reinforced our belief that teaching is one of the most amazing, difficult, and important professions in the world.

Introduction

"Literature is a place for imagination and intellect, for stretching the boundaries of our own narrow lives, for contextualizing the facts of our nonfictions within constellations of understanding that we would not be able to experience from the ground, for bringing our dreams and fictions into detail, clarity, and focus. Books allow us a bird's-eye view of our own lives, and especially how our lives relate to those lives around us." (Myers, 2013, para. 11)

As teacher educators and literacy professors, our work with teachers and students is all about helping readers find and engage with books that enrich their inner lives and provide them with encounters with worlds outside their own. We listen to teachers and students as they describe their reading and their purposes for reading and we seek to expand the possibilities. We spend time in elementary and middle school classrooms and talk to teachers about the capacity of reading to change students' lives. We notice the students who find themselves belonging between the pages of a book and who readily read for a variety of purposes. And we engage with students who are still searching for the joy that comes from a rich reading life. We seek to develop classrooms where students see the purposes and practices of their home languages and literacies valued and where their conceptions of the purposes and practices of literacy are expanded and made more inclusive—classrooms where diversity, equity, inclusion, and belonging are central to literature-based learning.

Collectively, we have worked as classroom teachers, literacy specialists, literacy supervisors, and teacher educators. When we write about books and learning with and through books, we hold in mind the children and young adults we have encountered across our careers as well as the aspiring and experienced teachers whom we meet in our university classrooms. Our teaching and learning experiences are diverse, yet we share a fundamental belief about literacy instruction: Purpose matters. Why we read matters as much as what we read. Why we choose books matters as much as what we do with them. This book is about making the purposes that drive book selections deliberate and visible. Our intention in writing this book is to share our lenses for book selection and curriculum development and to offer a framework for teachers' own choices and lesson planning.

While our work is framed by the broadest questions—*Why do we read? Why do we teach? What do we hope to accomplish through classroom interactions?*—this professional text zooms in on answers to these more specific questions:

- *Why and how do teachers choose the books to use in their classrooms?*
- *What do teachers hope their students will do with books?*
- *What roles do teachers want books to play in the lives of their students?*

By being deliberate about book choices and what students are asked to do with books, teachers can equip students with a sense of the many purposes that drive reading practices, ensuring they view books as:

- a site for learning more about themselves and others through reading and discussion;
- a source of various perspectives on histories and the human experience;
- socially constructed objects that represent worldviews that may resonate with or contradict their own worldviews; and
- models, launching points, or foils for their own writing and rewriting of their worlds.

What is it that books give us exactly? In the opening quote, Caldecott Honor Medal and Coretta Scott King Award–winning author/illustrator Christopher Myers describes the transformative power of literature in all genres. By reading we can come to know, understand, reflect upon, and rewrite the histories of ourselves, our communities, and our world. Countless teachers, researchers, and scholars have pursued that question in order to motivate students to become lifelong readers. Researchers have systematically examined the cognitive, linguistic, physiological, and emotional impact reading has on our brains; the affective, creative, and agentive influences reading has on our bodies; as well as the social and cultural power reading has on our daily lives. Curriculum developers have devised primers, basal readers, and systematic phonics, vocabulary, and comprehension programs. But, still, we witness some students finding joy in the pages of books and others turning away from books as a possible source of comfort, affirmation, or growth.

For decades, reading-comprehension curriculum has emphasized skills and strategies based on proficient-reader research; that is, research on what readers do successfully with automaticity. We want all students to read with accuracy, fluency, and purpose. This is important research that helps teachers identify reading behaviors in students and then design instruction for strategic approaches to growth. Yet, reading programs and curricula have attempted to narrowly define what books give us into discrete skills often taught in isolation, like finding the main idea or identifying character traits void of content connections or personal meaning. As adult readers, we have never picked up a book and been motivated to read in this way. And when students are observed closely, neither are they.

Introduction

In writing this book, we acknowledge the importance of proficient-reader research. But we also challenge teachers to balance instruction about *how* to read (also known as strategy instruction) with instruction on *why* we read with deep consideration of *what* we read. With a deeper understanding of what books give us as humans and the content that propels us to think about ourselves and the world, teachers can make reading something students *choose* to do rather than something they *have* to do. We align ourselves with French novelist Marcel Proust, who describes the heart of the reading act as going beyond the wisdom of the author to discover one's own (Proust & Ruskin, 2011) and with education professor emerita Rudine Sims Bishop (1990), who asserts: "Literature transforms human experience and reflects it back to us, and in that reflection we can see our own lives and experiences as part of the larger human experience" (p. ix). We want all students to have the feeling that reading changed their life and that it supported them to be more fully human in the world.

WHO WE ARE: THE CLASSROOM BOOKSHELF STORY

From our mutual love of children's literature and our belief that literature-based classrooms spark transformative experiences for learners, we created The Classroom Bookshelf, an open-source site for teachers. This collective, digital resource is all about the power of books and the possibilities they hold for inspiring, galvanizing, and engaging learners. Our blog arose out of our desire to model for our undergraduate and graduate students the ways we would be using new children's and middle-grade literature if we still had our own K–8 classrooms and to showcase the ways in which we use literature with teacher research partners.

So, what do we do that makes The Classroom Bookshelf different from what is already out there? We read widely and we read closely. We sit in library stacks with our piles of books and our sticky notes and notice language that grabs our attention, characters that challenge us, and new ways authors and illustrators are reinventing what a book can be. We think about how young readers will process the words and illustrations. We imagine critical conversations that can take place and inquiries that can be ignited. We read book reviews from the teams at *School Library Journal, Kirkus Reviews,* and *The Horn Book*. Oftentimes, books grab our attention right away, and we want to tell the world about them. We ask ourselves that if we were using this book in a classroom, in what ways we could use it to honor the natural curiosity and compassion of young people with the belief that books have the power to change lives.

For over a decade, we have posted weekly entries on The Classroom Bookshelf about a recently released work of children's or young adult literature along with teaching invitations to help teachers engage their students in meaningful and memorable learning through literature. However, we recognize there are limitations to our process of selecting texts for the blog, as well as for this book. In making decisions about which books to center, we inevitably leave other selections unrecognized. We recognize the power and privilege we have in sharing books and that we are limited by our own experiences and identities. In selecting books, we strive to keep the learners with whom we have worked at the forefronts of our minds—children with a wide range of cultural, social, academic, linguistic, and emotional experiences. We know the texts we recommend need to be similarly varied so that each child has reading material that motivates, intrigues, and inspires. Keeping our readers in mind, we select books for their quality, their complexity, and their utility (Cappiello & Dawes, 2014). We also strive to spotlight books across genres, including fiction, narrative nonfiction, expository/nonnarrative nonfiction, and poetry. Additionally, we are committed to our shared belief that we need more diverse representations of society on classroom bookshelves. As such, we aim to select books that include characters from different cultural and linguistic backgrounds authored and illustrated by culturally and linguistically diverse authors.

We also consider whether the book tells a compelling story; includes a character with whom students can identify or from whom they can learn; helps children to better understand the social or scientific dimensions of their world; or inspires children to think like historians, mathematicians, or scientists. In addition, we look closely at the language of the text. What kind of writing is this? Is it lyrical, informative, playful, evocative, clever? We consider the content and language in relation to the developing readers in our classrooms. How has the author used language to make the content more accessible? What do readers need to know to access and comprehend this particular text?

Finally, we consider how teachers will use the text. Is it a text they would want all of the readers in the class to experience through a read-aloud? Does the text offer an opportunity to extend or reinforce content knowledge for small groups of readers in the class? Will the text appeal to a subset of readers who will enjoy a lively discussion in a literature circle? Or might this be the perfect book to offer an individual reader because it is so well matched to their personal interests. We believe that you can make powerful text choices for your students precisely because you are the ones who know your students best.

WHY THIS BOOK?

This book sprang from our partnership with one another and our partnerships with new and veteran teachers. It also sprang from our observations of the ways literature could transform the lives of young people when we prioritize purpose with books day-by-day all year long.

We realized we had some ideas about books that could not be accomplished in a blog post. We wanted to guide teachers toward expanding curricular and instructional possibilities through concrete, actionable ideas for engaging their students with books.

We also bear witness to teachers inundated with external demands and increasingly scripted curriculum. We have experienced new demands on teachers' time and flexibility in the context of a pandemic. We believe teachers are, by definition, curriculum creators regardless of whether they craft their own units and lessons or whether they are handed them. The world of children's and young adult literature continues to evolve, offering myriad pathways for supporting the inner reader and creator in every student. Yet, knowing about recent titles and planning how to use them can be challenging. This is the space in which we do our work: supporting teachers to think deeply about *why* and *how* they might use a particular text in the classroom.

This book is a place to start intentionally building reading experiences for students that broaden the possibility that every student will experience a range of purposes and practices for using books. This book is a resource to turn to for inspiration, titles, and practical ideas about how to use books in meaningful and innovative ways. With thousands of children's and young adult books published each year, it can be hard to know where to begin. This book is here to help. Whether you have the latitude to build your classroom curricula around children's literature or whether you are seeking to augment and deepen a prescribed curriculum, we hope this book will inspire you to explore new ways of bringing children's books into your daily interactions and discussions.

PURPOSES FOR READING

This book originated in a discussion we had about how and why we each select the works of children's literature that we write about on The Classroom Bookshelf. We were not surprised to notice that although we each pick books for deeply personal reasons that define who we are as teachers and individuals and that help us understand our complex engagements with books, those reasons also overlap. Across the four of us, we saw that we often select books because we want students to *care about* themselves and others; to *connect* to the past and understand why it matters in the present and for the future; to *closely observe* and to cherish the natural world; and to *cultivate critical consciousness* of the power dynamics in our society, seeking stories that represent a broad range of human histories and experiences.

Combined, our four purposes offer a framework for incorporating children's literature across the school day and across the curriculum. We know that experiences shaped by these purposes for reading invite children to see their worlds in new and critical ways. When students read for these purposes, they are positioned as learners and as activists. Reading is no longer a passive activity, something they do in school, but instead it is a way of engaging with the world; with questions, ideas, and actions; and with diversity, equity, inclusion, and belonging.

Our reasons for selecting books show us that not all reading experiences are the same even if we are reading the same book. A champion for the power of readers' experiences and responses to texts, Louise Rosenblatt (1978/1994) notes that "the reading of a text is an event occurring at a particular time in a particular environment at a particular moment in the life history of the reader" (p. 20). Rosenblatt also asserts that readers respond to text along a continuum of *aesthetic*—affective, emotive, and qualitative—to *efferent*—factual, analytical, logical, and quantitative—stances, both appreciating the artistry of a book and learning from the information it contains. Readers can use both stances while reading the same text, and readers can use both stances with any genre. Thanks to our collaboration, we are able to imagine more possibilities for using books in classrooms because of our different experiences with books. Our reasons for why we choose books helped shape the way we structured this book—to explore four purposes: Center Care for Ourselves and One Another, Connect to the Past to Understand the Present, Closely Observe the World Around Us, and Cultivate Critical Consciousness.

In school and in life, we read for many purposes and within many contexts. Teachers can harness the potential of individual reading transactions and support students to engage more deeply with any text they are reading. Our four purposes create a middle ground between traditional classroom goals for reading (e.g., to acquire information, to understand literary genres, to mine a mentor text), a student's personal transactions with the text, and the wider world around us. When we read in social studies, we do not have to limit our reading to historical information. We read to connect with the people of the past and the present, to consider their lives in relation to our own. When we read in language arts, we do not just focus on understanding how the genre of fiction operates, but to learn more about how we humans can care for one another. When we read in science, we are not reading just to understand a theory, but to see the natural world with a new set of lenses, to observe the interconnectivity of all living and nonliving things. In all the reading we do, we can cultivate a critical consciousness, asking ourselves whose experiences are represented and how and whose are missing. Just as Rosenblatt's stances can be used within the same text, so too can our purposes. We can ask students to read to care and closely observe, or to connect and cultivate a critical consciousness.

USING THIS BOOK

In *How Reading Changed My Life*, Anna Quindlen (1998) writes, "In books I have traveled, not only to other worlds, but into my own. I learned who I was and who I wanted to be, what I might aspire to, and what I might dare to dream about my world and myself" (p. 6). Our greatest hope with this book is that teachers be inspired to dream about the world of their classroom in new ways with books and students at the center. We hope the books and classroom ideas we share spark feelings of purpose and engagement for your students and for you.

The chapters in Part I focus on the value of reading in a learning community and of honoring students' reading purposes, practices, and preferences. Chapter 1 specifically considers what matters most in selecting and using children's literature and introduces our framework of purposes with consideration for the text, the reader, and the context. Chapters 2–5 are each dedicated to a specific way students can connect with books to read and keep reading for the four purposes discussed above. The Part II chapters provide a collection of books and teaching invitations meant to exemplify our framework of purposes. Drawing from our blog entries, we share teaching invitations for supporting all students to experience books with a range of purposes for broadening their experiences with the "word and the world" (Freire & Macedo, 1987).

Across this book, we have intentionally shared a collection of books that together represent a mosaic of human diversity and experience. In doing so, we hope you and your students experience what multiple award-winning author Walter Dean Myers (2014) did as a reader when he writes, "Every book was a landscape upon which I was free to wander" (para. 3). And in that wandering, we hope you and your students recognize which landscapes call out to you, and which ones don't. What matters is that such wandering and exploration through books is purposeful and meaningful for each of us.

Part I

PURPOSES FOR SELECTING AND USING BOOKS

In Part I, we explore our framework of purposes for selecting and using children's books in the classroom. Chapter 1 is intended to prompt reflection on how we select books for classroom use, keeping the students in the classroom at the forefront of our choices. Chapters 2–5 are each focused on a specific reason why we read and the ways students might find purpose in books. These core chapters all begin with a classroom story and include research and theoretical orientations that support the framing of the chapter. The core chapters also help you consider examples of books that are well matched to the purpose described and provide criteria you can hold in mind as you select books for that purpose. The philosophical underpinnings for our book selection process can be applied to the countless books published in the future.

Chapter 2 on care offers support for the ways in which books can support the social and emotional lives of students. We posit that books that are emotionally transporting offer us portals for growing in self-awareness and compassion for others to become critically minded, global citizens of the world. Chapter 3 on connection is designed to support students to connect the past with their world today and with their future selves. In this chapter, we also consider the ways in which democracy is under threat around the globe and how books can help build a better, more free and just world. Chapter 4 on closely observing the world offers guidance on how to support students to see the world in front of them with new eyes, identifying patterns, understanding interdependency, and appreciating beauty, while also acknowledging human impact on our environment. Books can help students understand our natural world, the ways it is at risk, and how they can take action to help. Chapter 5 on cultivating critical consciousness highlights the thread of equity, diversity, inclusion, and justice running through all the other chapters and purposes, advocating books as a site for social, cultural, and political awareness and as tools in a social justice–oriented curriculum. As you read these chapters, you likely will note examples of overlap among the purposes; for example, a title explored in Chapter 3 also appears in Chapter 5. This overlap is also intentional. Although each purpose is distinct and rich, they are interconnected and held together by our overarching purpose of reading words to make the world a better place for all.

CHAPTER 1

A World of Purpose in the Pages of Books

CLASSROOM STORY: IF I WERE A BOOK

When coauthor Katie visits classrooms in September, she brings a small book that invites curiosity when children see it in her hand. *If I Were a Book* is written and illustrated by a Portuguese father-and-son duo, José Jorge Letria and André Letria (2011). Each page weaves together art and prose that captures the magic and wonder of books. Hearing the eponymous refrain, "If I were a book . . . ," students lean in closer to find out what new idea will come with each turn of the page:

> *If I were a book, I'd be an endless journey.*
> *If I were a book, I'd share my deepest secrets with my readers.*
> *If I were a book, I'd be in no hurry to reach the words "the end."* (n.p.)

Seated on the carpet, many students nod their heads in agreement. Some laugh out loud. Others smile when they see the clever graphic illustrations that extend each line of text. A fan favorite is the image of a book on a leash to accompany the statement "If I were a book, I'd be your best friend" (n.p.). At the end of the book, Katie hands out clipboards and pencils and students jot down and illustrate their own "If I were a book" statements. Pencils scribble down the first thoughts that come to mind. Many rival the author with their creativity affirming the myriad ways books give us so much more than just words on the page:

> *If I were a book, I'd want to have cookie crumbs in my spine and dog-ears on my pages.*
> *If I were a book, I'd want to be passed from friend to friend.*
> *If I were a book, I'd rest on your lap after you fell asleep dreaming of my stories.*

But there are those who, trusting the assurance they received, reveal some telling statements about their relationships with books:

If I were a book, I'd never be opened.
If I were a book, I'd be lost on the shelf.
If I were a book, I'd be bored with myself.

As teachers, we want all children to imagine if they were a book, what they would do for their readers and the world. When students craft their own "If I were a book" statements we gain a quick, informal assessment that reveals what students believe about books. We learn about the connections or disconnections students have to books. Their statements reveal their longings and greatest hopes for what books can do for them. They also potentially reveal fears and anxieties based on their own reading autobiographies and relationships with books. We have found that "If I were a book" statements gathered at the beginning of the year give us insights that can shape our book talks, individual student book conversations, and reading conferences for weeks to come. Engaging in this activity yourself can also lend insight, and we invite you to use the following questions as a guide:

- What do your "If I were a book" statements reveal about what matters most to you as a reader and teacher of readers?
- Does your reading autobiography reveal deep connections to books, or did you find yourself disconnected from books, searching for greater purposes for reading?

Although literacy scholars and researchers have expanded the definition of reading and texts, largely in response to 21st-century developments in technology and communication, we recognize that books continue to harness power in the classroom. Furthermore, teachers have tremendous influence on students' relationship to books. Nathanson et al. (2008) found that teacher education students who reported they had a teacher who shared a love of reading in elementary school were more likely to be enthusiastic readers all those years later. Similarly, Burgess et al. (2011) found that teachers with specific and broad knowledge of children's literature were most likely to use effective literacy practices in their daily teaching. Teachers who are readers not only share their passion, but perhaps because of their engagement with the texts they read, also enact teaching practices that support more than a love of reading.

We open this chapter with an invitation to explore your own reading preferences and practices in order to build an awareness of how these preferences may influence your selection of books in the classroom. In the sections that follow, we suggest a close look at the preferences, practices, and purposes of the readers in your classroom and invite you to consider the implications for book selection in curriculum design and in your classroom library, especially toward goals of diversity, equity, inclusion, and belonging. We conclude the chapter by inviting you to think about the classroom context and by sharing our framework of purposes for using children's books across the curriculum.

WHAT MATTERS MOST

What matters most when a teacher is confronted with the reality that a child dislikes reading? Katie's brother, Jimmy, did not like to read in school settings, although he had a rich reading life at home where he enjoyed reading baseball card manuals, the sports section of the local newspaper, and his *Calvin and Hobbes* collection. When he was in 5th grade, Jimmy leaned over to his friend before a reading lesson and said that reading "sucked." His teacher did not take that pronouncement well. Jimmy was one of many children who think many of the books they read in school are irrelevant and disconnected from their realities and the world around them. He simply had the courage to say it out loud.

Fast-forward 30 years and Katie's oldest son Jack is sitting on the classroom rug in 3rd grade. The mini-lesson is focused on how readers identify text structures, and Jack raises his hand to ask a question that has been on his mind: *Why are we learning this?* Thankfully, he is not reprimanded but is met with gratitude by his teacher who appreciates his question as an opportunity to better express the purpose of the lesson. We find in our observations and partnerships with teachers in classrooms that many children are left wondering: Why are we learning this? They just might not have the courage or the language to express this human need for meaning and purpose. One of our intentions in writing this book is to help teachers consider some of the many reasons to read and to talk about books, and to share with their students how books can serve as guideposts at different times in life.

When we start the school year with books that frame literacy as the language of possibility, we start to build a classroom culture that says we can all find meaningful purpose in books. Literacy theorists Paolo Freire and Donald Macedo (1987) illuminated our understanding of reading with their assertion: "Reading does not consist merely of decoding the written word or language; rather, it is preceded by and intertwined with knowledge of the world" (p. 29). Our lived experiences and encounters in the world provide the foundations for understanding what words mean when we eventually learn how letters and sounds make up those words. But we do not just use our lives and worlds to make meaning of the words we read. Reciprocally, we also use words to make sense of our lives and our worlds. In this sense, we acknowledge the incredible power that reading has to help us work toward change. As Freire and Macedo (1987) explain, engaging in reading is "an act of knowing and of creating" and "reading the word is not preceded merely by reading the world, but by a certain *writing* or *rewriting* it" (pp. 34–35). That dynamic is central to their understanding of the purpose of reading, and it drives us to help students find and sustain meaningful purposes for engaging with books.

Ultimately, what we hope students find is that books can help them make sense of and promote growth and positive change in their lives and worlds. Sustaining the feeling of meaningful purpose in a world of books is one of the most pressing roles literacy teachers have so that students choose to read of their own volition. The deceptively simple fact is human beings were never born to read (Wolf,

2018). The acquisition of literacy is one of the most incredible achievements of humankind. What we read, how we read, and why we read changed us as a species (Deheane, 2009; Wolf, 2018). And each book we read continues to change us individually and as a society throughout our lives.

What Is Your Purpose for Reading?

Some adults had childhoods where access to books was never in question, and sometimes they preferred the company of characters in books to the company of those around them. Others had childhoods filled with books they never wanted to read and actively avoided reading. Yet others grew up in book deserts (Neuman & Moland, 2019) where they longed for books and cherished every book that came into their hands. And some had neither access to books nor any firm models that showed them how books could provide a steady source of possibility in their lives. We assert it is a child's right to feel a sense of belonging and purpose within a world of books, and as teachers, we can guide young readers to find and name purposes for reading that help them see what is possible. Take a moment to think about your past experiences with books (see Figure 1.1).

Figure 1.1. *Reflecting on Your Own Experiences With Books*

Thinking About Your Past Experiences With Books
- Think back to the books that made you feel differently about yourself.
- Think about the books that made you see someone else in your life in a new way.
- Think about the times you spent in childhood lost in a book.
- Think about a time you did not like reading.
- Think about the books that felt disconnected from your experiences and understanding of the world.
- Think about the books that seemed to celebrate one view of the world and silence or completely omit other, equally legitimate, ways of viewing the world.

Your reading experiences shape the way you read the world. They also shape the instructional decisions you make in your classroom. The books you gravitate toward for read-alouds, incorporate across the subject areas you teach, and recommend to students in your conferences with readers are shaped by your reading past. This book is designed to help you think in new and purposeful ways as you make decisions about the books you read with students to engage their hearts and minds.

What Are Your Reading Practices?

We teach young people with a range of tastes, interests, experiences, and identities. If we want to provide students with a range of options in independent and curricular-based reading, we need to seek out books they will enjoy. In doing so, we must avoid trying to turn them into miniversions of ourselves, or worse, referring to them as reluctant or struggling readers simply because we do not offer them the books they are genuinely interested in reading. Before we build a reading community with our students, we need to affirm our purposes for reading and we need to know the reading preferences and practices we bring into that community. Consider how the answers to the questions in Figure 1.2 can help you to see new areas you might want to try out when reading. We can all continue to grow and strengthen our reading practices, and modeling experimentation can be an important part of our instructional approaches.

Take some time to review and reflect on your answers to these questions, perhaps sharing them with a colleague. What do you notice about your reading preferences and practices? How might these preferences and practices influence your book choices in the classroom?

Figure 1.2. *Reflecting on Your Own Reading Practices*

Thinking About Your Own Practices

What do you like and dislike when reading? Why? How does that shape your reading practices? Consider the following questions:

Genres
- What genres did you enjoy reading as a child? What genres do you continue to enjoy? What do you enjoy about your preferred genres?
- What genres did you avoid reading as a child? Do you still? What do you dislike about the genres you avoid?
- What genres have you never really been exposed to? What barriers have prevented you from experiencing these genres?

Authors
- Who are your favorite authors? What is it you enjoy about their writing?
- What authors have you given up on or not enjoyed? What is it about their writing style you did not like?

Topics
- What topics have you always loved to read about? Why?
- What topics would you like to read about if you could find the right books?
- What topics are you pretty confident you do not enjoy reading about? Why?

Formats
- Do you prefer short stories to novels?
- Do you prefer graphic fiction or nonfiction to straight verse?
- Do you prefer audio books, ebooks, or print books?
- Do you prefer short digital nonfiction to book-length nonfiction and informational texts?
- Do you prefer reference books (guidebooks, atlases, how-to books) to verse nonfiction?

BRAIDED PURPOSES: THE READER, THE TEXT, THE CONTEXT

In the Introduction, we shared a quote that illustrates literary and literacy scholar Louise Rosenblatt's (1938) Transactional Theory of Reader Response. She argued it was the live exchange between a reader and a text that generated meaning. This construct contradicted previously held models of reading that positioned the reader as a decoder of the meaning intended by the text's author. Rosenblatt posited that a reader's experiences and purposes for reading led them to construct a unique and situated meaning of the text. However, the same can be said of a text's influence on the reader, as each experience with text can create new understandings for the reader. She calls this interplay a "transaction," emphasizing the mutual impact the text and reader have on one another, as well as the unique sense of meaning that interplay produces. In 2001, the authors of the influential RAND review of research on reading comprehension framed reading comprehension as the interaction of the text, the reader, and the activity all situated in sociocultural context, highlighting the many dynamics that influence comprehension (Snow, 2002). Scholars have since expanded and deepened Rosenblatt's theory to show that reader response is also rooted in a reader's cultural identities and practices (Brooks & Browne, 2012; Dávila, 2015); impacted by classroom norms, materials, and practices (Coleman, 2021); and felt and expressed through the body and in multiple modalities (Enriquez, 2016; Enriquez & Wager, 2018; Lewis & Dockter Tierney, 2011). Even the physical materiality of a text (think: book cover image, thickness, scent, notes in the margins, screen size, page swipe or button click, etc.) can influence the ways readers make meaning of what they read (Enriquez, 2022; Myers, J., 2014). In other words, the distinct assortment of identities, lived experiences, prior knowledge, emotions, sociocultural context, values, and assumptions of each individual reader combines with the author's intention and materiality of the reading material to create meaning of the text.

We view the transaction of reader, text, and context as a set of braided purposes, together creating a unique reading experience for each reader in a classroom. This model is powerful to us because it recognizes the importance of each component of the braid:

- **Reader**—The diversity and individuality of each reader in the classroom, each bringing particular identities, experiences, perspectives, values, and goals to the reading of a text
- **Text**—The perspectives of the author and illustrator of the text, as well as the content and materiality of the text, each bringing a particular worldview and purposes for composing to the creation of a text
- **Context**—The purposes and goals held in mind by the teacher for using the text in the classroom as well as the relationships and culture of the classroom environment

Through these braided purposes, reading in the classroom becomes an act of collaboration and a site of possibility. Teachers and students explore and compare the meanings they construct from reading texts together; collaborating to understand, to critique, to build new meaning, new ideas, new inquiry; and to compose and create new texts. Reading books together is both purpose-driven and purposeful.

Because each student brings a unique set of identities, experiences, and prior knowledge to our classrooms, it is vital to take the time to learn who they are, what interests them, what their strengths are, and for what purposes they engage in reading. In the sections that follow, we offer some examples of learning about the students we teach, reflecting on the texts we share with them and any possible bias around them, and establishing the classroom contexts we hope will nurture students' meaningful transactions with books.

Thinking Purposefully About the Readers in Your Classroom

Of course, finding purpose in books means something different to each reader. If you have ever been in a book club, you know you might be moved to tears by a book that other people struggled to finish. Or that the language that enchanted you in one book left other readers feeling left out, bored, and disappointed. Today's classrooms are filled with diverse individuals. To support those varied readers as they develop their reading identities and abilities, we must be mindful about what we ask students to do with books—and which books—across the school day and throughout the year. Much of our thinking about books is done in community—within our classrooms, teaching teams, school communities, and the local, national, and international children's book community.

Beyond affinity or disaffinity for a book, teachers should consider the critical issue of representation in books. Children's literature and literacy scholar Rudine Sims Bishop (1990) asserted the multiple purposes and possibilities that books offer:

> Books are sometimes windows, offering views of worlds that may be real or imagined, familiar or strange. These windows are also sliding glass doors, and readers have only to walk through in imagination to become part of whatever world has been created and recreated by the author. When lighting conditions are just right, however, a window can also be a mirror. . . . Reading, then, becomes a means of self-affirmation, and readers often seek their mirrors in books. (p. ix)

Statistics bear out our observations that Black, Indigenous, Native, Latinx, Asian, and other historically minoritized populations rarely find their life experiences reflected in the texts offered to them in educational settings. And when they do, too often they are included in superficial and stereotypical ways. As teachers, how can we rethink our obligations as teachers of readers in order to prioritize windows, mirrors, and sliding doors for all of our students, understanding the nuances of their individual identities? We all find ourselves drawn to a book in our own ways for our own purposes. How can we be more consciously aware of the purposes for which we select books in our classrooms?

Countering Book Bias

Because we know two people can approach the same book and find a different meaning and purpose for it, we often have to step back from our own feelings about books to honor the feelings students have about books. Teachers who help students find purpose in books know the books in their classroom library intimately and are able to say, "If you like ____, you might also like ____." Building those book associations for students can be a big source of inspiration.

We all have biases of all kinds. And some people carry the weight of battling the bias of others every day. As literacy education consultants Christine Hertz and Kristine Mraz (2018) explain, "having bias is like needing glasses, but not realizing it. Once we get an eye exam, and see how different the world looks when calibrated with others, we notice when the world becomes blurry again" (p. 20). In our classrooms and with our book selections, our unexamined biases can turn children away from reading altogether with the assumption that the books and characters they are interested in are undervalued or do not count. Children can also turn away from books, like Katie's brother Jimmy did, when classroom practices don't support students to see purpose in reading.

One day, coauthor Grace sat down with 8th-grader Derrick to find out what kind of books he was interested in reading. As a Black adolescent from a working-class urban neighborhood, Derrick had faced the negative stereotypes and assumptions about low-income Black boys and their reading skills throughout his life and was viewed by teachers as a "struggling reader." And yet, rather than accept those beliefs, he pushed back against them, enthusiastically launching into his love for reading manga (comics and graphic novels originally created in Japan). When Grace asked if he ever had opportunities to read those in school, he shook his head and replied, "No. 'Cause really the school only like[s]—the Board of Ed—America so they don't really bring graphic novels in that much. . . . It's like a comic book, but it's a book version, you know? I see it as reading" (Enriquez, 2013, p. 39). Derrick's response indicated his keen awareness of the bias around books that exist in schools. More important, he saw that his authentic and passionate purpose for books was dismissed, contributing to the myopic view that he "struggled" with reading. Take a moment to consider what biases about reading you may bring unconsciously to the classroom (see Figure 1.3).

Just as we transmit attitudes about what behaviors are "appropriate" for classrooms, we transmit ideas about which books are valued in school and about sanctioned purposes for reading. We all also have biases toward characters that look, act, and live like us. Into adulthood, we still find ourselves identifying with characters that remind us of ourselves. When left unexamined, our biases can shape our read-aloud selections and book recommendations to students, and

Figure 1.3. *Reflecting on Book Biases*

Thinking About Your Own Practices

Below are some of the biases about books that we have heard over the years in the schools and communities we have worked with:

- Novels are more important than graphic books.
- Award-winning books are for everyone.
- Slang and intentional misspellings have no place in books.
- Toilet humor is inappropriate in a book read for school.
- We only find mirrors in characters that look like us.
- Windows are more important than mirrors.
- Fiction makes for a stronger read aloud.
- Nonfiction is boring but we just have to get through it.
- My students cannot handle this content.

Do any of these sound familiar to you? Think about the biases you might have toward books. Are there others you might have encountered? How might those biases impact the way your students interact with books?

---

sometimes those biases can miss the meaningful, purposeful reading practices of students.

So how do we counter our implicit biases? First, take stock of your classroom library and read-aloud selections. In the world of children's literature, much work needs to be done to publish books that represent the diverse society we live in. While we cannot eliminate bias, including book bias, we can actively work to make space for voices of underrepresented cultural and linguistic groups, and we can make our book selections more purposefully. We also may typecast readers unintentionally based on their social location, just as Derrick's teachers did throughout much of his schooling. Jerry Craft (2019) reminds us in his Newbery Award–winning graphic novel, *New Kid,* that teachers and librarians make assumptions about the types of books students will love based on their race, neighborhood, native language, religion, and gender. In *New Kid,* Miss Brickner assumes that Maury will love *The Mean Streets of South Uptown* (a fictional title), a gritty tale of survival about a boy growing up in poverty without a father because Maury is African American. Maury hands the book back to her letting her know that his dad is the CEO of a Fortune 500 company. This poignant moment in *New Kid* reminds us that we need to interrogate our own unconscious biases about matching readers with texts and the unintended harm we may cause in the process.

Examining Your Classroom Library

When coauthor Mary Ann began teaching 8th grade in New Hampshire, she brought in several hundred books that comprised her personal collection. Matching books and students was challenging. Most of her students did not see themselves as readers. Many said they had never actually finished a book before. Even with a well-stocked school library down the hall, they struggled to find books without Mary Ann's one-on-one support. When one student complained about the confusing rows of book spines, Mary Ann could only agree. Without a list, she herself often felt helpless at the public library.

The next morning, she brought in a stack of plastic bins, and over the next few days, student volunteers worked together to group the books by topics and subtopics, and sometimes by genre. As this work progressed, more students became interested in the process. Two things happened as a result: Students began to find books independently and to identify all the holes in Mary Ann's collection. *Why don't you have any sports books? Where are the mysteries? I want to read about animals.* Sheepishly, she realized her collection was based on *her* reading interests, not *theirs*.

One of the most important and effective moves we can make as teachers to counter book bias is to take an inventory of the books we share with our students, whether for whole-class, small-group, or independent reading instruction (see Figure 1.4). That inventory can reveal important information about what we are privileging in terms of content and purposes for reading, and it can reveal where the books we offer disconnect with our students' actual lived experiences and purposes for reading (Jones & Clarke, 2007). Knowing your readers well and diversifying your classroom library to better match their interests and needs are

---

Figure 1.4. *Conducting a Classroom Library Inventory*

Thinking About Your Own Practices

Consider the following questions when taking stock of your classroom library and the books you regularly use in your instruction:

- Whose lives are reflected in the books in your classroom library? Whose are left out?
- Are the stories on your shelves told by authentic authors?
- Do you include books published in your students' home languages?
- What inferences would someone outside your classroom make about your students based on the books you have?
- How are you balancing your use of window, mirror, and sliding-glass-door books across your teaching? (Bishop, 1990; Wager et al., 2019)
- What content areas are covered across the books? Do they represent a variety of topics within those content areas as well? For example, are your books about animals limited to those primarily found in North America? Do your books about the Civil Rights Movement only focus on Martin Luther King, Jr., and Rosa Parks?
- Is there a balance among genres represented across the books in your classroom reading? What genres are missing?
- Is there a balance of diverse identities in terms of protagonists or biographies? If so, is the identity of the character the primary driver of the storyline or simply a detail about the character?
- Does the diversity represented in books reinforce stereotypes? Do the books available to students make varied experiences and intersectional identities available?

important aspects of the larger picture of building a classroom community that forefronts learning through books, conversations about books, and a broad range of purposes for reading.

MANY BOOKS, MANY PURPOSES

As explained in the Introduction, while we have blogged about books over the last decade, we have noticed patterns in our book selection and in the teaching invitations we offer to our readers. We think of these patterns as pedagogical, professional, and even personal purposes for sharing books with students and using them in our teaching. All of these purposes can be found within each book we blog about, but books may lean more prominently toward one or two primary purposes. In the chapters that follow, we will elaborate on four purposes.

Center Care for Ourselves and One Another

The books read in childhood are a rehearsal for experiences later in life. Books and the conversations that books inspire are a transformative tool to help students show grace to themselves, to seek points of connection and belonging with others, and to rethink the world they live in to imagine a better one. In Chapter 2, we focus on how books can support students to care more deeply about themselves and others. We posit ways in which books and the conversations that surround them can emotionally transport students, expanding their hearts in the process. In particular, we focus on the role of books with diverse, inclusive, and equitable representations of society. Emphasizing a critical view of care, we offer suggestions for teaching toward compassion as an active, questioning stance to disrupt deficit thinking about who has value, who can be trusted, and who is worthy of love. This chapter will guide you to select and use books to support students to care for themselves and others, thanks to the enticing storylines, evocative illustrations, and compelling characters.

Connect to the Past to Understand the Present

Philosopher George Santayana (2011) wrote, "Those who cannot remember the past are condemned to repeat it" (p. 172). Without an understanding of the past, our understanding of the present remains limited. It is like looking at a tree with no knowledge of the roots and soil underneath that have nourished it. Or damaged it. We cannot time travel. But we can read historical fiction and nonfiction.

When historical fiction is done right, readers can experience the events of the past as if they are a participant. They connect to characters, as they see themselves in others. A similar vicarious experience occurs when reading nonfiction or biography. When we read the words of others left to us through primary source documents and artifacts, the past whispers—or sometimes shouts—to us. When young people read about the perseverance and stamina of a historical figure—famous or otherwise—entwined in conflicts of a previous generation, they can see themselves and others. Chapter 3 will guide you through a process of supporting students to experience the past through literature, to carry that knowledge with them to better understand the present, and to work toward a more just future.

Closely Observe the World Around Us

Young children are natural observers of the world around them. Sights, sounds, smells, touch, and taste sensations all provide opportunities for wondering, experiencing, and learning. Books can be vehicles to sustain students' natural curiosity and to develop observation skills and lenses to inspire an even closer look. Now more than ever, as we seek solutions to improve human caretaking of the natural world, books that bring that world into clearer focus serve as pathways to the kinds of inquiry and invention that will serve to bring our relationship with nature into greater balance. Chapter 4 will guide you to select and use books that launch close observation, pattern recognition, inquiry, appreciation, and mindfulness.

Cultivate Critical Consciousness

Chapter 5 surfaces a thread running through the previous three chapters—that is, the core belief that books reflect various ideologies and understandings about the world, asking us to contemplate how we uphold, challenge, and subvert them in our teaching. Framing literacy as reading both the word and the world (Freire & Macedo, 1987), we surface how the ways we use and make meaning of books stem from our sociocultural identities, lived experiences, knowledge, values, and assumptions. With a lens toward critical literacies—the socioculturally situated view of literacy and text (Shor, 1999)—this chapter also asks us to consider how our ideologies and understandings could influence the selection and discussion of diverse works of children's books.

We use what we know about readers, a diverse range of texts, and these purposes for text selection to construct classroom learning contexts in which books spark deep conversations and rich learning experiences. This approach to curriculum development and community building features diverse representations, strives toward equity, and fosters inclusion. Chapter 5 will guide you through a process of selecting books that support students to cultivate a critical consciousness as they engage with books and one another.

PURPOSE MATTERS: A COMMUNITY OF READERS

Imagine walking into a 1st-grade classroom. You immediately notice the myriad ways books are valued as tools for learning. Topically and thematically related books are displayed cover out along whiteboard ledges and on freestanding book displays. The classroom tables hold collections of books in cardboard magazine holders. A cozy reading corner is framed by bookshelves filled with baskets of books. In this library, you also will find a collection of bound student-authored books. These are popular selections during independent reading time. Looking at the classroom walls, you will see charts that demonstrate the ways the teacher and their students read books as writers: One chart lists the lively verbs students noticed in April Pulley Sayre's photo essay *Being Frog* (2020) while another lists the character traits of Rachel Carson gleaned from Laurie Lawlor's picture book biography, *Rachel Carson and Her Book That Changed the World* (2012). One wall displays a collection of student-composed poetry inspired by their reading of Nicola Davies's illustrated collection, *Outside Your Window: A First Book of Nature* (2012).

In this classroom, books and related texts are an integral part of all aspects of the day. While following the guidelines of the state curriculum frameworks, the teacher selects both fiction and nonfiction titles to explore themes and topics in language arts, math, science, and social studies. Students experience several read-alouds a day, read together in small groups, and have time to read on their own, books of their own choosing. Books are viewed as sources of information, vehicles for entertainment, and as a means for connecting with each other. This is a classroom community built on books, a place where students find purpose with language, literacy, and learning.

Listening in on the conversations that occur in this book-rich classroom, you hear how talk about books connects with talk about other kinds of texts. These 1st-graders and their teacher are learning about interdependent relationships in the natural world at the same time they are learning about self-expression through poetry and the art of nonfiction writing. More broadly, they are reinforcing a sense of stewardship in the natural world and understanding how the communicative arts can be used as a tool to learn and express evolving understandings and to advocate for change. While they have read a broad array of books, they also have read newspaper and magazine articles, watched short videos in which nature scientists and conservationists describe their work, and listened to podcasts like NPR's *Wow in the World*.

When we consider the role books can play in a learning community that has as its foundation in reading, writing, creating, and conversation, we approach and select books with purpose. Books written for children and young adults are unique texts—they are carefully crafted works of art. Combined with additional texts of all types, genres, and modalities (articles, podcasts, video, artwork, performances), books offer an opportunity to stretch the classroom discourse far beyond the confines of a textbook or curriculum package in a way that is meaningful to their individual and communal purposes for reading and learning.

What matters most, then, is not whether a classroom library is filled with award-winning books or whether a beloved book from your own childhood is included in the curriculum. Rather, what matters most is that we as teachers help students identify and articulate the kinds of books that catch their attention, the roles they see books playing in their lives both in and outside of school, and the purposes and goals they hope to achieve in reading particular books. And in that vein, we share as diverse a selection of books as possible with them, in all content areas, in all of our pedagogical structures, and in all aspects of our work with them.

When coauthor Erika worked as a literacy supervisor, she had the opportunity to collaborate with elementary teachers and reading teachers to reshape the Title I–funded summer reading intervention program. Traditionally, this program, which served students labeled as "struggling," focused on skills-based remedial instruction. Students used workbooks and leveled texts. Erika and the teachers believed student engagement could be increased through a focus on inquiry and nonfiction writing. Students read engaging nonfiction texts, examined and discussed the characteristics of nonfiction genres, and had the opportunity to compose in those genres on topics of their choice. What happened was significant. Teachers noted that students were excited to come to the program, were more engaged and more successful reading texts, asked lots of questions about the content they were reading, and approached the goal of composing nonfiction texts with enthusiasm. The students in this program were assessed before the summer program and after the summer program. Results showed not only had they avoided the "summer slump," they had grown as readers. Why did this happen? We believe it was because the students were engaged in purposeful reading and writing. The books they experienced were ones they were eager to learn from. The writing they were asked to do was driven by their own choices of topics in which they had interest. To support their writing, they had discussed high-quality, engaging texts that could then serve as models for their own writing. They were reading with purpose!

This book is intended to offer you a framework for creating meaningful and memorable experiences for students to engage purposefully in reading books. Identifying and nurturing students' purposeful engagement with books is not a one-day event. This chapter has challenged you to reflect honestly and openly and to confront (if necessary) how your own literacy autobiography is shaping your classroom and the reading experiences of your students. Think about your purposes for reading. What are the book experiences that have meant the most to you? Why? In what ways have you, because of something you read, been inspired to center care, to connect with the past, to closely observe the world, or to cultivate your critical consciousness? The chapters that follow will help you discover new reasons to read, new book recommendations, and many ways to invite your students to deepen their purposes with books for years to come.

CHAPTER 2

Center Care for Ourselves and One Another

A book, too, can be a star, a living fire to lighten the darkness, leading out into the expanding universe.

—Madeleine L'Engle, *A Wrinkle in Time*

CLASSROOM STORY: NURTURING CARE

Walking into Ted's 3rd-grade classroom in a suburb outside New York City, students lean in to listen to another chapter of Newbery Medal–winner *The One and Only Ivan* by Katherine Applegate (2012). Part of the book's charm is Applegate's choice of first-person narration from the point of view of Ivan, a silverback gorilla, who is one of the main attractions at the Exit 8 Big Top Mall. While the book is fictional, Ted's students know that Applegate was inspired by the true story of a gorilla also named Ivan who lived in a similar situation for 27 years. Composed of a series of short, but observational sentences, Ivan's story is both believable and shocking. The simplicity of Ivan's voice makes his captivity all the more heartbreaking.

Ted's students have followed Ivan's thoughts, feelings, and reactions throughout the story. They have strong opinions about Ivan, the other imprisoned animals, and animal cruelty. What seems to capture their hearts the most is the passing of Stella, an older elephant, who dies from what may have been a treatable injury. The injustice, cruelty, and greed of Mack, the mall owner, stirs the class and some students speak up with disbelief and outrage:

Student 1: "I can't believe Mack's heart was so cold."
Student 2: "What will happen to Ruby now that Stella is gone? Stella was like a mother to her. It's the saddest thing I've ever heard."
Student 3: "I couldn't watch the animals suffer like that. Mack should go to prison for this."
Student 4: "Stella was so wise. So gentle and kind."

Student 1: "I really don't believe in caging animals. I've never really liked going to zoos, and I don't think I could go to them after this."

Their conversation shuffles between responses to the story and the injustice of animal cruelty writ large. Through this conversation, we can see that Ted's students are changed by Ivan's emotions and intelligence. They are changed by Stella's death. They are changed by each other's reactions and feelings. Reading this book together has given them clear-eyed realism that hope and heartbreak often live side by side. They are realizing that life is never the same when we lose those we love. They are learning to challenge systems of oppression rooted in power and privilege—in this case, the containment of animals for entertainment. In reading *The One and Only Ivan* with his students, Ted trusts them to navigate the challenging and emotional content in the text. In doing so, he intentionally makes space for the 8- and 9-year-olds in his class to hone their collective moral imagination as they work together for a more interdependent and just world (Campano, as cited in Dutro, 2019). Through their experiences as readers, speakers, and listeners, his students are learning what it means to care wholeheartedly about something outside of yourself.

Across the globe in Laos, Olivia's 3rd-grade students are engaged in a literature-infused investigation into care starting with deepening care for themselves. They began this inquiry by reading the Charlotte Huck Award–winning picture book *I Am Every Good Thing* by Derrick Barnes (2020). After a read-aloud of the book, Olivia's students created self-portrait collages (see Figure 2.1), which express parts of their identities with accompanying "I am" statements, including:

I am the turning of a page.
I am an artist.
I am as happy as a dog getting new toys.
I am the sun bulging with energy shining to my core bringing sunshine to the world.

Charlotte Huck Award winners are selected by the National Council of Teachers of English (n.d.) awards committee to honor works of fiction that "transform children's lives by inviting compassion, imagination, and wonder" (para. 1). These were precisely the goals Olivia had in selecting *I Am Every Good Thing* to launch this investigation into care from a place of affirmation and joy. The artwork and writing her students created in response to the book were designed to help them look inside their hearts, affirm their strengths, and come to know one another's gifts, aspirations, and contributions.

Ted and Olivia select and use children's literature to purposefully center care in their literacy instruction. They understand that the teaching of essential literacy skills and strategies, such as growing word knowledge, making inferences, or monitoring comprehension, must be coupled with helping their students build

Figure 2.1. *Third-Grade Self-Portraits Created After Reading* I Am Every Good Thing *(Barnes, 2020)*

the kinds of knowledge that will sustain them as humans. Kiefer and Tyson (2010) remind us of the potential books have to shape us when they write, "We all have memories of certain books that changed us in some way—by disturbing us, by affirming some emotion we know but could never shape in words, or by revealing to us something about human nature" (p. 3). Ted and Olivia understand this important truth about the power of literature, thereby making their text selections all the more purposeful.

One of their primary goals as teachers, and specifically as teachers of reading, is that their students expand their capacity to care for themselves, others, and the world around them through the impactful experiences they have with books. To do that, the reading selections Ted and Olivia make help their students acknowledge their genius and joy (Muhammad, 2020, 2023). But, they also understand that children often know how hard the world is and that literature can provide an antidote to the unbearable truths they are coming to recognize as they experience rejection, lose loved ones, and bear witness to racism, sexism, homophobia, xenophobia, and any number of abuses that erode our humanity and dignity (Dutro, 2019). In their interactions with children each day and in sharing meaningful works of children's literature with them, Ted and Olivia are reminded that "the hard stuff of life reverberates" (Dutro, 2019, p. 1). As teachers, they help their students navigate life through the loving, sophisticated, hopeful lens of story. After all, "children see beauty where there is ugliness; they are hopeful when adults have given up" (Kiefer & Tyson, 2010, p. 4). In this way, the text selections they make offer students reasons to remain hopeful that there is good in the world and that they have the power to create change and fight injustices despite how uncertain so many things might seem. Teaching with literature, then, is about more than developing the intellectual or analytical skills of students; rather, teaching with literature calls for moral imagination and an ethic of care (Hilder, 2005; Noddings, 2012).

WHY CENTER CARE?

As seen in Ted and Olivia's classrooms, books have the potential to become windows to our interior worlds and the larger world outside ourselves—sometimes at the same time. In her Newbery Medal acceptance speech for *Flora and Ulysses: The Illuminated Adventures* (2013), author Kate DiCamillo explains that authors "are working to make hearts that are capable of containing much joy and much sorrow, hearts capacious enough to contain the complexities and mysteries and contradictions of ourselves and of each other. We are working to make hearts that know how to love this world" (2014, para. 43). Nearly 70 years earlier, E. B. White expressed a similar sentiment in his correspondence with a reader of *Charlotte's Web* (1952): "All that I hope to say in books, all that I ever hope to say, is that I love the world" (Elledge, 1986, p. 300). As teachers and teacher educators, we intentionally seek out books for instruction that have the potential to push against readers' hearts, so that our students are more capable of loving themselves, others, and the world. Our text selections are not haphazard; rather, we place enormous importance on selecting books with intention—with care.

Yet, we recognize that purposefully selecting texts to deepen students' capacity for care is not without risk. It requires emotional vulnerability and a willingness to center stories that address the joyful and the hard parts of life. Etymologically, the word *care* comes from the Old High German *cara,* meaning grief or lament. Caring, then, is inherently about being there alongside those experiencing sorrow. The texts and teaching ideas we recommend in this chapter invite into our learning spaces "our deepest sorrows, raw moments, the jagged edges, and the tender spots" (Dutro, 2019, p. 8). We want to clarify, though, that by recognizing and rendering care as inherently connected to grief and trauma, we do not embrace cynicism or despair; rather, we support a culture of "reciprocal love" (Dutro, 2019; hooks, 2001; Jackson et al., 2014; Watson et al., 2014) and "critical hope" (Duncan-Andrade, 2009).

Great works of children's literature have long trusted young readers with the juxtaposition of the beautiful with the tragic. In *Charlotte's Web* (1952), E. B. White gently prepares readers for Charlotte's death when Charlotte affirms for Wilbur that he will live:

> You will live to enjoy the beauty of the frozen world, for you mean a great deal to Zuckerman and he will not harm you, ever. Winter will pass, the days will lengthen,

the ice will melt in the pasture pond. The song sparrow will return and sing, the frogs will awake, the warm wind will blow again. All these sights and sounds and smells will be yours to enjoy, Wilbur—this lovely world, these precious days. (pp. 163–164)

Contemporary picture book authors continue to place faith in the capacious hearts of young readers as seen in books like *Joy* by Corinne Averiss (2018) in which a young girl named Fern goes on a hunt to bring joy back into her Nanna's life, and in *Bear Island* by Matthew Cordell (2021), in which a young girl, Louise, mourns the passing of her beloved dog, Charlie, by venturing to a nearby island to find her strength again. These authors and those we feature in this chapter understand that children's hearts can hold both joy and sorrow and that, in fact, both are essential for living a happy life. In centering care as an essential purpose for selecting and using children's literature, we draw from authors and literacy scholars who reconceptualize trauma as a source of connection, reciprocity, knowledge, and literacy engagement (Dutro, 2019; Muhammad, 2020, 2023).

We know this work takes courage. By bravely centering care in your classrooms through literature, you will support students to ask big, life questions like: "Who am I? What might I become? What is this world in which I find myself? How might it be changed for the better?" (Edmundson, 2004, p. 5). This chapter is intended to guide you to select and use books to nurture and deepen care in your students' lives, so their experiences and perspectives are honored, and so that they come to appreciate others with greater compassion, understanding, and love.

WHY NOW? SUPPORTING THE WHOLE CHILD

We believe the books children encounter in childhood help them make sense of the world around them as well as their place in it and that they serve as rehearsals for experiences they may have later in life. In this section, we explain why centering care to support the whole child in front of us is essential, if not urgent, in our literacy instruction. We begin by offering guidance on how literature serves as a gateway to social and emotional learning (SEL)—widely understood as essential to student well-being. We conclude this section with consideration of the profound collective loss that children around the world have encountered as a result of the COVID-19 pandemic. This trauma will have an incalculable impact on students and teachers for years to come, making the vulnerable hearts of literacy learners (Dutro, 2019) all the more important in the selection and use of children's literature.

Social and Emotional Learning Through Literature

In the wake of the COVID-19 pandemic, many schools are realizing what we should have known all along: "that relationships are critical for learning, that students' interests need to be stimulated, and their selves need to be recognized" (Mehta, 2020, para. 20). One way these priorities are being actualized in schools is through social and emotional learning. The Collaborative for Academic, Social, and Emotional Learning (2023) defines SEL as "the process through which children and adults understand and manage emotions, set and achieve positive goals, feel and show empathy for others, establish and maintain positive relationships, and make responsible, ethical decisions" (n.p.). Studies have found that effective SEL has the potential to influence students' social, emotional, and academic skills, both short-term and long-term, to form healthy relationships, demonstrate higher levels of engaged citizenship, and experience less emotional stress (Durlak et al., 2011; Jones et al., 2011).

The urgency of integrating social and emotional learning with academic learning has never been more pressing. In the United States, approximately 35 million children—that is nearly half of all children—have experienced serious adverse childhood experiences such as parental divorce or separation, violence among adults in the home, living with someone who has a substance abuse problem, and economic hardship, including difficulty to afford food and housing (Child and Adolescent Health Measurement Initiative, 2021).The high prevalence worldwide of depression and anxiety among young people, declines in life satisfaction, and the potential synergy between learning and positive emotion all point to the need for school experiences that support the well-being of students. There is now substantial evidence from well-controlled research that literature studies integrating SEL can increase resilience and positive emotion, engagement, and meaning (Seligman et al., 2009).

While SEL has received increased attention, it has placed greater demands on teachers to consider how to integrate SEL into academic content. Literature-based instruction, in particular, provides rich opportunities for reflecting on the connections between our thoughts, feelings, and actions, taking on someone else's perspective, and using language and writing to better understand ourselves and others. As Kirkland (2019) explains, if we are committed to teaching toward equity and inclusion as an essential purpose of literacy learning, "we have to respond to non-cognitive social–emotional aspects of literacy learning, as greater than 80% of learning literacy deals with things beyond mental ability or intellectual capacity" (p. 11).

Despite its research base, SEL has been called into question in recent years. Growing fears about the indoctrination of children and misconceptions about the teaching of critical race theory in schools have led to sharp increases in the censorship of books in schools and local libraries. Friedman and Johnson (2022) of PEN America found that in the first 9 months of 2022, bans occurred in 138 school districts with a combined enrollment of nearly 4 million students across 32 states. They argue these bans are not spontaneous responses by individual, concerned parents; rather they reflect a growing, organized movement demanding censorship of certain books and ideas as a central part of their mission. During our writing of this book, more books have been banned in more schools in more states, making our purposes for text selection and our use of children's literature all the more urgent if we are to reach and teach the whole child.

Trauma, Loss, and Hope

In centering care as an essential purpose for selecting and using children's literature, we recognize that loss is always present in our classrooms and that trauma is a powerful pedagogy (Dutro, 2019). At the time of writing this book, there have been over 6 million deaths worldwide due to the COVID-19 pandemic. Research reported by the National Institute of Health in the fall of 2022 found that over 8 million children lost a parent or caregiver due to the pandemic (Hillis et al., 2022). Decades of research has also shown that inequity and racism are also the cause of trauma inside and out of school (Bryant-Davis & Ocampo, 2005; Howard, 2013). Literacy scholars have long studied the impact of traumatic experiences on students' literacy learning experiences in school, and questions continue to be explored by literacy scholars seeking to understand how the realities of extra word loss and trauma impact children's resilience, moral courage, and literacy learning experiences (Dutro, 2011, 2019; Falter & Bickmore, 2018; Jones, 2012; Lewis Ellison, 2014; Wissman & Wiseman, 2011).

While shared understanding of trauma and its impact on literacy learning continues to evolve, we are weary of what Duncan-Andrade (2009) refers to as "false hope"—that is, hokey hope, mythical hope, and hope deferred—which are often perpetuated through the use of didactic children's literature. We advocate instead for literature selections and teaching ideas that foster long-term, sustainable, audacious hope. This kind of hope cultivated through literature-based instruction fosters the moral outrage of young people and affirms their inherent goodness without ignoring the trauma or erasing the loss children have encountered.

CENTERING CARE: UNDERSTANDING OURSELVES AND CONNECTING TO OTHERS

Books can be tools to help students better understand themselves, to grow their connections with others, to embrace moments of joy, and to make meaning out of pain, loss, fear, disruption, and injustice. But what should be considered when selecting children's literature for these purposes? In this section, we offer three objectives for selecting and using books to center care: (1) to deepen comprehension and connection through emotionally transporting texts, (2) to center realistic characters to represent a more diverse, inclusive, and equitable world, and (3) to focus on compassion instead of empathy to help students develop responsibility for the world outside themselves.

The Power of Emotionally Transporting Texts

The transformative power of stories to change our hearts and our minds—one of the great gifts of reading—is now confirmed by neuroscience. Stories that are emotionally compelling engage more of the brain and are more easily remembered even weeks later if they capture and hold our attention and transport us into the narrative (Bal & Veltkamp, 2013; Yeshurun et al., 2021). Maryanne Wolf (2018) describes the phenomenon of how stories emotionally transport readers as *cognitive patience* acquired when they immerse themselves in the world of characters who become their friends. She explains, "The act of taking on the perspective and feelings of others is one of the most profound, insufficiently heralded contributions of the deep-reading processes" (p. 42). She explains how when we read we leave ourselves momentarily. We become characters, and when we return to our own lives beyond the pages of a book, we are often changed emotionally thanks to the "conscious-changing dimension of the act of reading" (p. 45).

In her work as a scholar of literature-based instruction and loss, Dunn (2022) calls for reframing care in our literature-based instruction to address the range of human emotions students experience. If emotionally transporting texts have the potential to deepen care, expanding what counts in literature response will "reposition school as a place where human beings relate and connect with one another" (p. 1062). In this way, selecting and using emotionally transporting texts is an act of moral courage with the potential to not only enhance students' capacity for care but to also foster equity and inclusivity by leveraging, rather than limiting, students' identities, experiences, and emotions.

One fictional picture book we turn to again and again to address the range of human emotions is *The Rabbit Listened* by Cori Doerrfeld (2018). Written in response to witnessing several of her friends experience difficult times, Doerrfeld has crafted a deeply poignant, unforgettable tale rooted in a childhood scenario that both children and adults can draw meaning from. When Taylor's block tower is suddenly destroyed by several swooping crows, his animal friends all have ideas about what to do about the fallen blocks from talking about it to pretending nothing happened. When hope starts to fade for Taylor, a rabbit does what many of us need when something traumatic happens—he simply listens—and when Taylor is ready, the rabbit offers a hug. Named as a Notable Children's Book of 2018 by *The New York Times* and a Huck Award recommended title, *The Rabbit Listened* emotionally transports readers into Taylor's world offering us a blueprint for how to help others in our lives who are experiencing loss, disappointment, and grief from the seemingly simple to the profound.

Another selection that emotionally transports readers is *The Year We Learned to Fly* by Jacqueline Woodson (2022), which honors the feelings of boredom all children experience at some point. Written with Woodson's signature lyrical language, this book tells a moving story about a brother and sister who learn to follow their grandmother's advice in moments of challenge to "Use those beautiful and brilliant minds of yours. Lift your arms, close your eyes, take a deep breath, and believe in a thing" (n.p.). In a story told across four seasons, we witness the siblings encounter a range of childhood predicaments: rainy spring days suffused with boredom; hot summer days filled with bickering; the darker days in autumn giving rise to loneliness; and a sudden move in winter causing newfound isolation. With trust in the truth-seeking capabilities of children, Woodson includes a four-page sequence where the grandmother explains how she learned to fly from enslaved ancestors who came before them: "They were aunts and uncles and cousins who were brought here on huge ships, their wrists and ankles cuffed in iron, but . . . nobody can ever cuff your beautiful and brilliant mind" (n.p.) As explained in the Author's Note, *The Year We Learned to Fly* is a loving tribute to Virginia Hamilton's *The People Could Fly: American Black Folktales*. Bright, vibrant artwork by Rafael López complements the emotional landscape the children experience and the limitlessness of their imaginations. A brilliant companion to their earlier picture book, *The Day You Begin*, Woodson's and Lopez's latest collaboration will remind children that they have the courage and capacity to "fly" past their most difficult times.

What makes books like *The Rabbit Listened* and *The Year We Learned to Fly* impactful is that while readers may not have encountered the same situations in life, they have experienced the same feelings: joy-sadness, anger-fear, trust-distrust, surprise-anticipation. These basic emotions serve as building blocks to more complex emotions like love, serenity, awe, boredom, annoyance, and optimism that allow readers to emotionally transport into the world of the characters to better understand themselves and others. As you take another look at the books in your classroom bookshelf, we recommend purposefully selecting books where readers feel something strong in response to the situations of the characters—moments that are hard and moments that are hopeful—across texts that represent diverse society.

The Importance of Realistic Characters

A growing body of research shows that children more readily apply what they have learned from narratives that are realistic (Larsen et al., 2018) and that children's literature can be used to support a dynamic learning frame that instills in students a sense of agency (Enriquez et al., 2017). Data from the Cooperative Children's Book Center (2021), though, show us that "despite slow progress, the number of books with BIPOC creators and protagonists lags far behind the number of books with white main characters—or even those with animal or other main characters" (Tyner, 2021, para. 12). In 2019, nearly 30% of books written for children had an animal as the primary character, while only 11.9% of books had primary characters who were Black, 8.7% who were Asian or Asian American, 5.3% who were Latinx, only 1% who were Indigenous, and less than 1% who were Arabic. While children's literature with anthropomorphized animals remain tools for thought and can spark the imaginations of children, our text selection should offer students opportunities to grow in their capacity for care with characters that represent a more diverse, inclusive, and equitable world.

Does this mean we abandon books where the main characters are animals or anthropomorphized animals? Of course not. We see the power of anthropomorphized animals in how Ted's students responded to *The One and Only Ivan* (Applegate, 2012) in the opening vignette. The first-person narration emotionally transports readers by giving us inside knowledge on what Ivan may have been thinking and feeling while held in captivity. Children have learned from and engaged with stories with anthropomorphized animals for thousands of years through oral storytelling traditions across the globe. Anthropomorphized animals often display character traits like agency as seen in Humpty Dumpty in Dan Santat's (2017) *After the Fall: How Humpty Dumpty Got Back Up Again*. They also demonstrate compassion and social responsibility as seen in Jerry Pinkney's (2009) largely wordless retelling of *The Lion and the Mouse*. While anthropomorphized characters have the potential to expand students' capacity for care, there are also pitfalls to be mindful of when selecting and using texts that center animals rather than humans, including the perpetuation of stereotypes through words and images (Nel, 2014), the normalization of whiteness, and the normalization of dominant cultures of gender, family structure, disability, religion, sexuality, and socioeconomic class (Cunningham et al., 2021).

To honor the increasingly diverse classrooms and world our students live in, we recommend that you take stock of your classroom bookshelf and seek books with characters that are realistic, dynamic, and multidimensional. But, do not stop there. Get to know the multiple identities and interests of your students without typecasting them as readers for particular texts. Include students in selecting texts for read-alouds and invite them to make suggestions for characters they would like to meet and cultures they would like to explore in the classroom bookshelf. Rethink the perspectives and positions you privilege through the texts you select for reading and writing instruction. Refresh your text selections by ensuring contemporary representations of communities and cultures are centered. Support students to engage with texts by building upon their strengths. These actions can support students to dive deeper into texts, expanding their care for themselves and one another in the process.

Two books with compelling, realistic characters that we often turn to include *New Kid* by Jerry Craft (2019) and *Maybe Maybe Marisol Rainey* by Erin Entrada Kelly (2021b). In *New Kid*, which was mentioned in Chapter 1, Jerry Craft has taken the daily dramas of middle school life (cafeteria hierarchy, social anxieties, and tween hallway banter) to an arresting and devastatingly accurate new level. At Riverdale Academy, Jordan finds himself one of a few token students of color, where White teachers mistakenly mix up the names of African American students, and where being on financial aid becomes a social stigma. Balancing serious and lighthearted moments, Craft portrays the two worlds Jordan feels caught between: home in his predominantly Latinx and African American Washington Heights neighborhood in northern Manhattan and at school, where buildings are named after his friend's philanthropic grandfather, where salmon-colored shorts signify status, and where winter break means trips to Vail, Aspen, or Jackson Hole . . . not the local Chinese restaurant. Thoughtfully inclusive, Jordan's friendships at Riverdale are from a diverse cast of characters despite the overwhelming whiteness of the school's population and school culture. Episodic in nature, *New Kid* portrays Jordan's school year from beginning to end. The graphic novel format deepens the experience for middle-grade readers to interpret the words, actions, and facial expressions of the characters, providing an additional layer of context for complex race and class dynamics. Including Jordan's notebook sketches offers further insight into him as a character and adds to the narrative in poignant ways.

In *Maybe Maybe Marisol Rainy*, Newbery Award–winning author Erin Entrada Kelly (2021b) portrays the inner life of Marisol with both grace and humor. Short chapters with hand-drawn, black-and-white illustrations by Kelly invite early chapter-book readers into the story of a quirky, endearing 8-year-old girl who wonders if *this* summer she will know what it is like to be brave. Maybe. Or if she should give swimming another try. Maybe. Or whether she will climb the tree in her backyard that she named Peppina. Maybe tomorrow. As in Erin Entrada Kelly's previous novels, the cast of characters represent a mosaic of ethnic and racial diversity. We meet Marisol's mother, born in the Philippines, who speaks four languages and is the smartest person Marisol knows. We meet Marisol's best friend, Jada, who makes silent films with her. And we long to meet Marisol's father, working on an oil rig in the Gulf of Mexico. *Maybe Maybe Marisol Rainey* is a tale of the everyday experiences of a young girl making her way through the world. This is a story primed for early elementary grade readers for read-alouds, book club conversations, and to join the series bin of your classroom library.

As you refresh your classroom libraries and consider texts for instruction, we recommend purposefully selecting books with realistic, multidimensional characters who represent diverse society and who navigate life's complexities, such as overcoming self-doubt and repairing harm with friends.

Compassion as an Alternative to Empathy

We have found in our work with educators that helping students become more empathic is often an implicit, if not explicit, goal in their literature-based instruction and is often synonymous with care. Empathy, a concept with cognitive and affective dimensions, has been described as "the spark of human concern for others, the glue that makes social life possible. It may be fragile but it has, arguably, endured throughout evolutionary times and may continue as long as humans exist" (Hoffman, 2000, p. 3). It is commonly argued that empathy is important because of its positive association with creativity, better learning outcomes, better health outcomes, and prosocial and cooperative behaviors (Konrath & Grynberg, 2013; Xiao et. al., 2021). Research has also found that empathy can be cultivated (Kirby et al., 2017; Teding van Berkhout & Malouff, 2016), particularly through the power of emotionally charged stories. Yet, we acknowledge there are also limitations to the promotion of empathy as a laudable trait. Educator Aeriale Johnson (2020) urges educators to move beyond empathy to help children become compassionate. She explains that

> Empathy can easily become a form of erasure. Now, I teach children to embody compassion. Compassion was derived from the Latin word *compati*—to suffer with.

Empathy sees injustice and thinks, "How sad! I'd be so broken-hearted if that happened to me." Compassion shows up in the middle of the storm, remains long after it has passed, and centers the individuals having the experience, giving them space to identify their own feelings and solve their own dilemmas, be their own heroes. (para. 9)

While an empathic lens assumes one can step into a character's shoes, a compassionate lens supports students to see beyond their experiences, interpretations, and positionality to walk alongside those who are suffering—a more nuanced and justice-oriented approach to care. This distinction between empathy and compassion is aligned with culturally relevant pedagogies (Ladson-Billings, 2009), culturally sustaining practices (Paris, 2012; Paris & Alim, 2014), and the ethical and moral commitment to critical love and racial literacy development (hooks, 2001; Jackson et al., 2014; Watson et al., 2014). It is also aligned with Boler's (2006) work on the risks of passive empathy, which she explains "falls far short of assuring any basis for social change, and reinscribes a 'consumptive' mode of identification with the other" (p. 253). Boler argues that teachers should embrace "testimonial reading," which places the reader in a position of responsibility not only for their own thoughts, feelings, and actions but for the world outside themselves.

Throughout this book and throughout our decade-long work as the creators of The Classroom Bookshelf, we have sought to model how purposeful text selection and intentional teaching practices can support children to become more compassionate while also becoming more critically conscious (more on this in Chapter 5). To do so, we have focused our examples on works of children's literature that we have found to be emotionally transporting while being mindful of texts that represent our diverse world and honor the intersectionality of children's identities (Jiménez, 2021). We hope that you find our suggestions offer entry points for the important work of deepening students' capacity for self-compassion and supporting them to become more compassionate, critically minded global citizens of the world.

In this chapter's opening vignette, teacher Olivia introduces a book we turn to again and again to model self-compassion—*I Am Every Good Thing* by Derrick Barnes (2020). In it Barnes writes, "I am every good thing that makes the world go round. You know—like gravity, or the glow of moonbeams over a field of brand-new snow. I am good to the core, like the center of a cinnamon roll. Yeah, that good" (n.p.). In a series of dynamic, present tense "I am" statements, Barnes emphasizes the joy of everyday small moments while also resolutely affirming for Black boys: "I am not what they call me . . . I am what I say I am." Oil paintings by Gordon C. James invite readers to linger on each page and take notice of the smiles, gazes, and pride in the faces of Black boys and girls in a series of richly textured single- and double-page spreads. Readers will find faces they recognize, including President Barack Obama and Kid President (Robby Novak). *I Am Every Good Thing* affirms for Black boys and readers everywhere—you matter. You belong. You are worthy of love. And, yes—you are every good thing. Figures 2.2 and 2.3 demonstrate how

Figures 2.2. and 2.3. *Third-Grade Affirmation Writing Based on Mentor Sentences in* I Am Every Good Thing *(Barnes, 2020)*

I am two eyes widely open, reading an interesting book about my culture, filled with curiosity and determined to find out what my ancestors did. I read as my brain is filled with a big bundle of questions.

"Who were they?"
"What did they do?"
"What caused their death?"
"Would they be proud for who I am now?"

I AM proud, I am curious everywhere, always I can ask and learn I am… grateful for these books so I could know my past, after all, I love my country.

I AM A CULTURE girl when I am reading about it, I read everywhere when I feel like it so I don't feel forced, I want to be free.

I am reading as I feel as I'm IN the book itself, its majestic, and non believable. I wake up and finally realize it was a dream.

I am me Wherever I am.

—By Ninjin Nyambat

I am the sun bulging with energy shining to my core, bringing sunshine to the world.

I am the universe like I am growing and growing.

I am wielding a screwdriver turning and turning, hammering nails on and on, adding parts to other parts, making something that will change the world.

I am an inventor constructing things and if it fails I still keep on going.

I am energetic allllll days every where I can have fun and never being slacky, so I can get my heart pumping and and to feel accomplished.

I am a son, a brother, a cousin, a nephew and a friend always helping them in need, and loyal to them as a soldier is to there king.

But I am not always what I say. Sometimes I might try and try but give up or I will not be able to help a friend in need.

I am confident not being afraid of the future and rather looking forward to it.

I am a learner always trying to learn and expand my mindset.

I am resilient.

—By Arnav Gupta

Olivia's 3rd-grade students used *I Am Every Good Thing* as a mentor text for their own affirmational writing.

Another book we introduced earlier in this chapter to help foster compassion is *Bear Island* by Matthew Cordell (2021). In *Bear Island*, Caldecott-winning author and illustrator Matthew Cordell affirms for children that they can find resilience and hope in the midst of grief. In it, Cordell writes, "'It's not fair,' thought Louise, 'when the things we love must end'" (n.p.). With deep respect for the child as a reader, Cordell gently invites readers in the opening pages to infer that Louise's beloved dog, Charlie, has passed away. In the pages that follow, Louise ventures out to an island thinking about Charlie. There, we witness the range of emotions Louise experiences as she processes her grief. She thwacks a tree and declares "I'm leaving." She stares in wonder at a kaleidoscope of butterflies and delights in the sudden appearance of deer. Just when she is feeling "something new and good was happening" both on the island and within her, comes a disgruntled bear who confronts Louise with a raging ROAR only to be roared at even more ferociously by Louise. With the bear defeated and dejected, Louise ventures away only to look back at the bear to notice "a familiar feeling, a familiar sadness." From that moment of shared recognition, the bear and Louise forge a bond in their journey toward healing. Cordell's loose pen, ink, and watercolor illustrations complement and extend the print, inviting children to lean into the emotional tone of each page. With rare subtlety and without a trace of didacticism, Cordell's *Bear Island* offers a timely and timeless text for centering compassion by helping readers come to understand the feelings of a dynamic character without assuming we have experienced the same thing she has or that we would react in the same way.

As you select and use books for the purpose of care, we recommend reconsidering empathy in favor of compassion. Look for books that support students to develop self-compassion as an essential cornerstone of self-care. Also, look for books that allow students to become the kinds of humans who show up in the middle of the storm and remain long after it has passed, especially when it is hard to do so.

SELECTING BOOKS THAT CENTER CARE TO TEACH AND REACH THE WHOLE CHILD

We believe books are a powerful portal for students to love themselves more, to treat one another with greater compassion, and to expand their understanding and appreciation of our increasingly diverse world. Think about the books you routinely use that evoke a strong emotion in students or the books you read in your own life that evoke strong emotions in you. Usually the responses of student readers to these books include the following:

- **Caring about the characters.** They usually struggle with things that readers struggle with in real life: friendship woes, the pursuit of self-

acceptance, loss of loved ones or beloved objects, and injustice that stems from prejudice. But readers also root for characters' success and admire their resilience, support of others, and hard-earned pride.
- **Finding connection to readers' own lives.** While one book can be a mirror to one student and a window to another, some books foster in many a sense of connection at some point in the story because they have experienced the same feelings. Basic emotions that humans universally experience and can identify in others' facial expressions, regardless of language or culture, are: joy-sadness, anger-fear, trust-distrust, surprise-anticipation. These basic emotions serve as building blocks to more complex emotions like love, serenity, awe, boredom, annoyance, and optimism. Some of the greatest moments of connection with characters are because readers can identify how the character feels, how they would feel in the same situation, and times when they had similar feelings.
- **Wondering about lives different from readers' own.** Some characters remind readers of themselves, and others have different life experiences. Students grow in compassion for others when they encounter stories that allow them to imagine a different life and how they might respond in such situations.
- **Wanting to linger on the page.** Illustrators and book designers are using a variety of techniques, including mixed media and use of white space, to give readers visual reasons to closely attend to each page and to return to pages to see the text with fresh eyes.

One way to make decisions about books to recommend for classrooms is by using these reader-response characteristics to assess whether a book positions students to care for themselves and others. Once you know you have a book or several that can support teaching for care, we recommend you turn to Chapter 6 in Part II for invitations to instructional practices focused on teaching and learning for the purpose of centering care. For a list of guiding questions about how to select books for the purpose of care for ourselves and one another, see our online material under the download tab at https://www.tcpress.com/reading-with-purpose-9780807768501.

CHAPTER 3

Connect to the Past to Understand the Present

"To know the past is to know the present. To know the present is to know yourself."

—Ibram X. Kendi, *Stamped: Racism, Antiracism, and You*

CLASSROOM STORY: THE VALUE OF KNOWING THE PAST

It's early November in Salem, Massachusetts, and Natalie's 3rd-graders gather on the rug to listen to a read-aloud of Cherokee author Traci Sorell's (2021) *We are Still Here! Native American Truths Everyone Should Know*. In Natalie's classroom, multilingual students whose families have recently arrived from Central and South America and the Caribbean learn side-by-side with monolingual English-speaking students whose families have lived in the community for generations. As Natalie turns the pages that outline the ways in which Native American tribes and nations have resisted the broken treaties and punishing policies of the United States over the last 150 years, the children have questions.

Some do not know that Native Americans *are* actually still here. None have ever heard of discrimination against Native Americans. Sometimes interrupting Natalie's reading, they question why the U.S. government would prevent people from speaking their language and practicing their religion. They question why some tribes and nations were forced off their land, some to relocate to big cities.

Some students remember what they learned in primary-grade picture book read-alouds about the experiences of Black Americans during the 20th-century Civil Rights Movement. Leveraging their knowledge of school segregation, the 3rd-graders make connections between the U.S. government-run Indian boarding schools that separated children from their families and forced them to assimilate to White European cultural norms and the segregated schools of the U.S. South.

Connect to the Past to Understand the Present 41

When Natalie agreed to cocreate a revised first history unit covering Indigenous and colonial history in Massachusetts in the midst of the COVID-19 pandemic, she wanted to make it as relevant as possible to her 3rd-graders, to use high-quality children's literature about the present and the past combined with artifacts, primary sources, and pictures of the community to position students to make connections across time and place, within and outside of their community.

Just a few miles away from their school lies the 1692 Salem Witch Trials Memorial. Their city is known for that atrocity. Growing up in the "Witch City," Natalie's students are used to the thousands of people who show up each fall in elaborate costumes or simple witch hats ready to party. How do adults make sense of this dichotomy, the carnivalesque amidst a historic backdrop of Puritan terror, let alone 8-year-olds? In Massachusetts, like many other states, 3rd-graders dig into history for the first time, and the social studies standards include the witch trials. Given these weighty expectations, Natalie knew she wanted to build bridges between the past and present, immerse her students in narratives that helped them to make sense of the complexities of their community and nation, and offer pathways to advocacy to create change.

To accomplish this, we positioned children's fiction and nonfiction in conversation with one another. As beginning 3rd-graders, students did not have a sense of historical linearity or cause and effect. By moving away from presenting this Indigenous and colonial history unit in a fixed chronology, space was created for students to make connections and identify patterns of power and privilege. Through read-alouds of carefully curated texts and structured conversations, Natalie saw students' understanding build. She noted, "When you read narratives of historic figures as children, when students talk to older community members, when they hear immigration stories, they make a connection." Across time periods, students recognized how different groups facing discrimination fought for their rights, as marginalized and oppressed peoples continue to do today. They began to piece together a mosaic of central concepts that shape the human experience, past and present: migration, immigration, colonialism, injustice, disinformation. But they also explored the past in ways that are more joyful, drawing on evidence from historic photographs and paintings to imagine what Salem looked like in the past, wondering what might be found underneath their school building if they did an architectural dig.

Throughout, Natalie reinforced connections to the present. For example, the morning after Natalie and her class examined *We Are Still Here*, she read aloud *We Are Water Protectors,* written by Carole Lindstrom (2020), an enrolled member of the Turtle Mountain Band of Ojibwe, and illustrated by Caldecott Award–winning Michaela Goode, enrolled with the Central Council of Tlingit and Haida Indian Tribes of Alaska. She also shared video clips about the Dakota Access Pipeline protests, fictionalized in the picture book, showing contemporary Standing Rock Sioux and their allies fighting for the right to clean water. Natalie pivoted to sharing videos of contemporary Wampanoag teenagers in Massachusetts participating in the Wampanoag Language Reclamation project, before pivoting back to the past and the arrival of corporation employees and Puritans in the 17th century. Natalie knew the power of expository and narrative texts, read in conversation with one another, to shape and frame students' emerging understandings of contemporary and historic Native American Peoples.

As Natalie watched her students' learning unfold, she became even more determined to make social studies relevant, sharing, "There is no point in teaching history if kids are not making connections to their lived experiences. What's the point of teaching history if we're not going to use it as an avenue to make a better world today?"

WHY CONNECT TO THE PAST?

History Shapes Our Present

Children's lives are shaped by the histories of their families, their communities, and their cultures—the stories told by their abuelas; the commemorations of important moments in their community's past; the local tensions and injustices regarding school funding, redlining, and access to public transportation; and the larger national and international political and economic systems. Because the past continues to shape our students' lives, they deserve opportunities to explore it in their classrooms, to learn the tools of historical inquiry, and to consider the ways in which they can make the world a better place. As Terrie Epstein (1993) reminds us

> History speaks to our individual and collective humanity. It keeps us connected to our ancestors and enables us to understand and appreciate the minds, mores, and experiences of others. History provides a sense of common heritage at the same time that it presents the origins and development of our diversity. History promotes a consciousness and critical sense of citizenship in national and global communities. And in its lessons about the ordinary, the extraordinary, and the extreme, history divulges the depth and breadth of human experience. (p. 5)

History connects us. The "Seventh Generation Principle" of the Haudenosaunee Confederacy, sometimes known as the Iroquois Confederacy, operates with the notion that the present is the past for future generations. The nations that comprise the confederacy "are taught to respect the world in which they live as they are borrowing it from future generations" (Haudenosaunee Confederacy, 2023, para. 2). When our contemporary actions are viewed as someone else's past, we live with a sense of stewardship. "Each of us develops the plot twists with which future generations will have to cope. . . . history forces us to consider what it means to be a participant in this human drama" (Levstik & Barton, 2001, p. 1). We are all products of the past and conduits of the future.

There is no single narrative of history, no matter how small the event. There are always multitudes. Knowing this, we always strive to share texts in conversations with one another in the classroom. No single text can do the job. By exploring the ways in which people's lives have intermingled with one another—sometimes by choice, sometimes not; sometimes because of terrible conflicts, sometimes because of new opportunities—young people can better understand their own intersectional identities (Crenshaw, 1991; Jiménez, 2021). Learning about the challenges faced within communities of the past allows young people to understand that they are not alone in their own challenges.

Historical Knowledge Is a Tool for Change

Exploring the past is necessary work for our present. Literacy scholar Gholdy Muhammad (2020) uses historical inquiry into 19th-century Black Literary Societies to build the Historically Responsive Literacy Framework as a means of pedagogical liberation in 21st-century classrooms. In the best-selling *Stamped From the Beginning: A History of Racist Ideas in America*, Ibram X. Kendi (2016) traces the life stories of public figures over a several-hundred-year period to develop an antiracist framework to apply to the present. When young people examine the events and stories of one specific time and place in relation to another specific time and place, within the comfort and safety of their classroom community, they can better understand the stories and perspectives of our present, which shapes their decision-making, critical thinking, and moral compass.

WHY NOW? BARRIERS AND BRIDGES

Barriers to Access

One is never too young to begin thinking about our connections to the past and our impact on the future. But there is a long history of denying children in elementary school the opportunity to do so, from misunderstandings about children's developmental readiness to the narrowing of the curriculum due to expanded standardized testing.

For decades, it was a common belief that elementary children "are first concrete thinkers, who need things spelled out in systematic steps tied to objects they can touch and manipulate" (VanSledright, 2002). The work of doing history, of considering multiple perspectives and evidence, of grappling with abstract concepts, was thought to be beyond them. As a result, many elementary-grade social studies units focus on holidays more than histories, and on students' local communities at the exclusion of global. However, research has shown that children have the capacity to "do history," to employ critical thinking, consider evidence, and draw conclusions (Brophy & VanSledright, 1997; Levstik & Barton, 2001; National Council for the Social Studies, 2017, 2019; VanSledright, 2002; Zarnowski,

2003). This research is not new, but implementing change continues to be a challenge (Anderson, 2014; Martell, 2013).

Another barrier to children learning about the past is the diminished role of social studies in the elementary school day in the aftermath of the No Child Left Behind legislation of 2002. In the two decades since, elementary teachers have spent less time on untested subjects generally, and social studies specifically (Au, 2009; Fitchett et al., 2014; Heafner & Fitchett, 2012). In states where social studies is a tested subject, more space is carved out for social studies instruction (Fitchett et al., 2014).

Yet another barrier is the recent concerted effort across the United States to ban books from school and public libraries and restrict teachers' ability to discuss challenging topics in the context of history and contemporary life. "More than 17.7 million public school students enrolled in almost 900 districts across the country could have their learning restricted by local action and the recent slate of laws and policies aimed to ban teaching concepts related to race, racism, and gender" (Pendharkar, 2022). These "Divisive Concepts laws," passed in over 14 states at the time this book was written, threaten children's access to our complex historical past. As Sam Wineburg (2021) has noted

> The goal of historical study is to cultivate neither love nor hate . . . History that impels us to look at the past, unflinchingly and clear-eyed, does not diminish us or make us less patriotic . . . Understanding who we were allows us to understand who we are now. Only then can we commit to doing something about it. That should be the goal of history education. Our children deserve nothing less. (p.11)

In the face of these challenges—from policy to prejudice—now, more than ever, we are called on to carve out classroom time for exploring the past. It is not a luxury only some schools can afford, but a necessity for all.

Bridges to the Past: Children's Literature in the Classroom

Exploring the past is deeply personal. Students' responses to historical books and primary sources will be filtered and interpreted through their identities and sociocultural contexts (Epstein, 1998, 2000, as cited in VanSledright, 2002, p. 20). It is important that young people are given texts from or about the past that reveal a wide range of human experiences, cultures, and perspectives. If not, "students who do not see themselves as members of groups who had agency in the past or power in the present, who are invisible in history, lack viable models for the future" (Levstik & Barton, 2001, p. 2). To "do history," students benefit from opportunities to explore its interpretive nature, hear from a range of people and perspectives, grapple with important questions, and situate themselves within controversial moments.

Books of all genres can do what textbooks, oversimplifications written within rigid formats, by multiple authors, cannot. "Personal narratives, historical fiction, and other literary forms bring history to life. Such sources invite an engaged reader to enter into other times and places by creating images of and feelings for the historical experiences of others" (Epstein, 1993, p. 5). High-quality trade books reveal the past and the present in ways that are personalized and deeply contextualized, making them valuable teaching tools in language arts and social studies curricula.

CONNECTING TO THE PAST

Through imagined and lived narratives, young people can experience the past vicariously. With the additional support of carefully curated photographs, art, and artifacts, or beautifully rendered illustrations informed by research, young people can begin to imagine the past. Using developmentally appropriate fiction, nonfiction, and biography to learn more about a specific historic event or a particular moment in time is nothing new. There are topics and time periods within social studies state standards well-documented in a range of picture books and chapter books for young people—for example, the mid-20th-century Civil Rights Era in the United States. But beyond coverage of content, we have other goals for using books about the past, goals that surfaced across our Classroom Bookshelf entries over the years.

In the sections that follow, we will advocate for the use of children's books to connect with the past with three different purposes in mind. First, we will explore the ways in which well-written nonfiction books model the disciplinary practices of history. Next, we will examine the ways in which nonfiction and historical fiction provide students with opportunities to visualize the past in their imaginations through specific attention to setting. Finally, we will look at the ways in which children's literature can allow students to see patterns over time, the continuity between past and present.

"Doing History": Disciplinary Literacy Through Inquiry

Over the last 2 decades, history education researchers have advocated for teachers to support young people to "do history" (Levstik & Barton, 2001; VanSledright, 2002; Wineburg, 2010), by providing K–12 students with opportunities to explore primary source documents, to corroborate evidence, and to compare and contrast perspectives across multiple sources. Primary sources can include documents, photographs, paintings, newspapers, and more.

When the National Council for the Social Studies adopted the College, Career, and Civil Life (C3) Framework (2023), it asserted that "inquiry is at the heart of social studies," and that "social studies involves interdisciplinary applications and welcomes integration of the arts and humanities." What's more, the framework "changes the conversation about literacy instruction in social studies by creating a context that is meaningful and purposeful. Reading, writing, speaking and listening and language skills are critically important for building disciplinary literacy and the skills needed for college, career, and civic life." This embedded literacy is visible in recently published articles centered on using children's literature in social studies (An, 2022; Baytas & Schroeder, 2021; Groce & Gregor, 2020; Patterson & Shuttleworth, 2020; Spencer, 2022).

High-quality nonfiction can serve as both an important model *of* and a catalyst *for* this work. Considered "the literature of fact" (Moss, 2003) and the "literature of questions" (Sanders, 2018), nonfiction books can reveal the process of historical inquiry and research. With passion for their subjects and topics, book creators take their research seriously, striving to be as accurate as possible. In that way, nonfiction is indeed fact-based. Authors weigh competing evidence, and attempt to corroborate information, and often share this research journey within the primary or peritext. As Sanders (2018) has observed, there are also moments within nonfiction books that are ripe for critical engagement and investigation, moments when authors reveal conflicting sources or historical gaps, share their tentative understanding, or model when their historical inquiry leaves them with some conclusions but also unanswered questions. As such, nonfiction is indeed also question-based.

Next, we will discuss the ways in which nonfiction books can be used in the classroom to support students' development of disciplinary practices in history. We will discuss how book creators "do history" by exploring the role of backmatter and examining language use in nonfiction.

Leveraging Backmatter. Have you ever been surprised to discover so many additional pages at the end of a new nonfiction picture book? Backmatter in nonfiction books continues to expand. *Who* is the backmatter for? Is it for the child reader or the adult who reads with them? What does it *do*? At its most basic, backmatter confirms for readers of all ages the sources used by the author or the illustrator to create the primary text.

When we look at backmatter to leverage disciplinary practices, we look for more than just the sources used by the author and illustrator, though those sources are essential. We also are looking for a discussion of those sources, ways in which the book creators might discuss a historical silence on the topic, or the way that a newly discovered source has changed historians' understanding of a topic (Cappiello & Hadjioannou, 2022).

One nonfiction book whose backmatter is ripe for supporting students' developing understandings of the disciplinary practices of history is Beth Anderson's *Cloaked in Courage: Uncovering Deborah Sampson, Patriot Soldier* (2022). Sampson disguised herself as a man in order to fight with fellow colonists against the British crown during the American Revolution. Anderson's picture book biography highlights Sampson's independence and agency in her early life. When she first enlisted as Timothy Thayer, Sampson was discovered. Undeterred, she ran away and enlisted again as Robert Shurtliff, performing admirably, and after a musket ball injury, volunteering for new noncombat responsibilities and earning the respect of superiors.

The verb "uncovering" in the title is apt, for in the backmatter, Anderson delineates her research process, from the challenges of nonstandardized 18th-century spelling to the arbitrary nature of available primary source evidence related to Sampson. Anderson then follows with information about the secondary sources that she used to learn about everyday life in the 18th century. Toward the end of her backmatter, Anderson identifies the dead ends in her research, the questions without answers. Finally, she puts Sampson in a contemporary context for her young readers, connecting to their lives, informing them that "on January 5, 2021, the Deborah Sampson Act was signed into law. This legislation protects female soldiers and veterans against gender-based harassment, improves medical care, and provides other needed programs and benefits. More than two hundred years after Deborah fought for her pension, the law bearing her name will bring equity for nearly two million women veterans." Anderson's backmatter ends with questions for her readers. Positioning herself alongside them, she asks, "What would we have done in her time and place?"

Backmatter anchors readers in the disciplinary practices used by historians and book creators, and is ripe for classroom explorations.

Looking at Language: *Visible Authors and Hedges.* Another way that educators can mentor students into the disciplinary practices of the historian is by doing a close examination of how nonfiction books are written, the language that authors use to explain gaps in sources or competing interpretations. This is in contrast to textbooks, which often take on a tone of unfailing authoritative truth; history is presented as a finished product rather than a process of evolving understanding. Nonfiction books offer young readers the opportunity to understand the process more deeply through the writing styles adopted by authors.

Myra Zarnowski has written extensively about the knowledge-building processes used by nonfiction authors and the ways in which those authors make their thinking visible within their writing (Zarnowski, 2013, 2014, 2019; Zarnowski & Turkel, 2011, 2012, 2017). Some authors reveal their process of knowledge construction by inserting themselves within the text as "visible authors" (Paxton, 1997, cited by Zarnowski & Turkel, 2012). According to Paxton (1997), the presence of an author within a text creates "a rhetorical atmosphere of empathy and collaboration with the reading audience" (p. 244, as cited by Zarnowski & Turkel, 2012). One way to do that is by presenting history "as mystery," introducing "students to the thought processes that historians use as they evaluate evidence and construct historical accounts" (Zarnowski & Turkel, 2017, p. 235).

When Natalie chose to read aloud Traci Sorell's (2021) *We Are Still Here! Native American Truths Everyone Should Know*, she was reading a book with a visible author. A fictionalized classroom provides an overall context for that book, in which each student is assigned 1 of 12 concepts to explore in preparation for an Indigenous People's Day presentation. These concepts offer a framework for exploring federal policy and Native advocacy, including topics such as assimilation, termination, relocation, tribal activism, self-determination, religious freedom, and more. Providing just the right calibration of information to situate the reader, Sorell presents complex ideas and histories in manageable doses, and offers extensive additional information in the backmatter. The author adopts the use of "our" and "we" within the first two sentences: "Our Native Nations have always been here. We are indigenous to the continent now called North America" (Sorell, 2021, p. 4). Throughout the book, Sorrel uses "our" and "we" to communicate the history between Native tribes and nations and the U.S. government since 1871. Her first-person narration is essential to the text's authenticity.

Sanders (2018) has noted that nonfiction authors for young people also make their decision-making visible in specific moments within the text through "hedging," when authors use qualifiers such as "perhaps, might, to a certain extent, and it is possible that" (Crismore & Vande Kopple, 1988, as cited in Sanders, 2018). Hedges are cues to the reader that the author is uncertain, that the specific information is not yet known.

Historian and professor Erica Armstrong Dunbar and middle-grade author Kathleen Van Cleve collaborated on the 2019 adaptation of Dunbar's 2017 National Book Award Finalist, *Never Caught: The Washingtons' Relentless Pursuit of Their Runaway Slave, Ona Judge*. After an engaging author's note from Dunbar that invites middle-grade readers and teachers into Judge's story, an action-packed introduction details the moment of her escape the evening of May 21, 1796. A chronological narrative of Judge's life continues, one that weaves in details about the everyday lives of enslaved men, women, and children on Washington's Mt. Vernon estate, 18th-century Philadelphia, the Washingtons' efforts to prevent the enslaved men and women in their household from taking advantage of Pennsylvania's Act of the Gradual Abolition of Slavery, and the intricate and intimate ways in which the personal lives of George and Martha Washington and the enslaved men and women they owned were tangled together.

Dunbar and Van Cleve (2019) make specific stylistic choices, including the use of hedges, as they focus on Judge's perspective throughout the narrative. For example, on page 49, they consider her thoughts before relocating to Philadelphia with the Washingtons in May of 1789:

> On her journey north Ona was also probably full of questions when she finally pushed back the wall of fear in her heart. Where would she sleep? What would the house be like? How different would the work be? Ona had only lived at Mt. Vernon, where there were three times as many black people as white people, even though all of them were enslaved. William Lee, George Washington's valet, had already told them that in the North there were more white people living side by side, and it was all supposed to be very crowded. What about looking at expanses of fields? What about the joy Ona may have felt when she was running errands and paused for just a second to look at a flower or a particularly beautiful tree? What about all the people whom she knew and who knew her?

As you read this passage, how do the authors use language to let you know that they do not know exactly what Judge thought? What are the clues? Students can track this perspective-taking throughout the book. When does it bring Ona Judge to life? When might it lean toward fictionalization? What is the line between literary nonfiction and historical fiction? Students can experiment with this literary technique in their own writing of someone's biography or in short vignettes.

When we look for nonfiction books that include the kind of language that signals the presence of the author or historical uncertainties or complexities within their research, we look at all aspects of the book, from global writing styles to specific instances—those hedges—within the primary text and the backmatter.

Visualizing the Past: Building a Sense of Place Through Setting

Books for young people can provide them with a portal into the past by supporting their ability to visualize it. We often talk about visualization as an important reading skill (Shanahan et al., 2010). Can a reader have whatever they are reading "up and running" in their mind? Of course, visualizations will look and feel different depending on the text that you are reading. Picture books or graphic books of historical fiction or nonfiction focused on the past do the visualizing for the reader—the photographs or illustrations show readers a version of the lived past. But the reader still has to hold a mental picture in their mind as they turn the page. These visualizations offer readers an imaginative foundation for all the future books, primary sources, and art and artifacts with which they may engage.

Picture Book Visualizations. Illustrators of nonfiction picture books pay a great deal of attention to historical accuracy. They draw upon the author's research and expand into their own research. Many have discussed the revisions they have made to paintings and drawings to construct a more accurate visual representation of the past for their young readers. But accuracy is not their only aim. They also try to build a connection with their intended audience with each and every page turn. As Matt Tavares (2011) has shared, "My goal was to show this moment in history in a way that felt more immediate than the old photos, so the reader could imagine being right there" (p. 50). We recommend giving students multiple opportunities to explore the illustrations in historical picture books of all genres, and to double-check what they see within the illustrations and what, if anything, the illustrator has discussed in the backmatter about the process. For example, in the backmatter of *Unspeakable: The Tulsa Race Massacre* (Weatherford, 2021), illustrator Floyd Cooper reveals his personal connections to Tulsa, having grown up there. His approach to illustration was shaped by his deep experiences of the city and its sense of place. In preparation for illustrating *Dave the Potter: Artist, Poet, Slave* (Hill, 2010), illustrator Bryan Collier traveled to Edgecomb, South Carolina, to photograph the landscape and to clasp the clay that David Drake used to create his famous pottery.

When we are considering picture books to help students visualize the past, we seek out books with illustrations that transport us, that immerse us in the time period in unique ways. But we also seek out books that have backmatter confirming the kind of research that Tavares and Collier have done, or the personal connections, such as Cooper's. We want to know that the book creators have been vigilant about accuracy and authenticity, recognizing that there are still gaps that must be filled in by the illustrator's imagination.

But chapter-length works of historical fiction or nonfiction also can bring the past to life for readers in lasting ways, through their written descriptions of setting.

Setting in Middle-Grade Historical Fiction. *The Great Trouble* (Hopkinson, 2013) immerses readers in London's 1854 cholera outbreak. Eel, the earnest and honest protagonist, is a "mudlark," a boy who dives into the filthy Thames River to retrieve things he can sell or trade in order to survive. As a narrator, Eel is a participant in all the action, demonstrating a powerful sense of agency that feels authentic given the brutal reality of 19th-century urban life. Hopkinson brings to life a vivid cast of characters, a snapshot of the "haves" and "have nots" of Victorian London, and draws particular attention to the dire circumstances faced by orphans and children of the working poor. This historical mystery reveals the origins of the public health system, a staple of modern culture that we have come to rely on during the COVID-19 pandemic. How does Hopkinson establish the setting? Consider these paragraphs, in which the protagonist, Eel, describes London:

> Seemed like we all should have been laid low by now from inhaling that filthy, smelly air that rose off the Thames. Especially since so much of London's garbage and human and animal waste got dumped into it. . . . The whole city reeked of fish, rotten fruit, horse droppings, and worse. The thick, foul air stung our eyes. Each morning the sky turned a murky yellow. That was day. It stayed that way till, hours later, the sickly yellow sky faded away to a hot, muddy gray. That was night. (pp. 19–20)

In these passages, Hopkinson focuses on three senses: smell, touch, and sight. One has to wonder, what smells worse than fish, rotten fruit, and horse poop? Just thinking about the foul smell stings our eyes as we read. Readers might at first be confused when Hopkinson transitions into a description of the sky. Why is it murky yellow? One has to infer that the daylight never gets very strong because of all of the smoke and smog from chimneys, factories, and open fires across the city of London.

Middle-grade students love juicy details. Rich descriptions of settings can hook them as readers, and offer models of descriptive writing that can be applied to different writing contexts.

Setting in Middle-Grade Nonfiction. Candy Fleming mined archives and treasure troves of materials unavailable to researchers for most of the 20th century to write *The Family Romanov: Murder, Rebellion & the Fall of Imperial Russia* (2014), an intimate portrait of the Romanov family. Fleming weaves the personal and the political life of the Romanov family together so adolescent readers

Connect to the Past to Understand the Present

can understand the private family dramas and delights as well as the concurrent political missteps, misunderstandings, self-centeredness, and naiveté of Tsar Nicholas. Additionally, she includes in this tapestry the voices of everyday citizens struggling to survive in the "real" Russia, in sections called "Beyond the Palace Gates" that punctuate the text. This is a masterful piece of research and a compelling in-depth examination of the Romanov family, income inequality, and oppression at the dawn of the 21st century. How does Fleming use setting as a way to introduce these contrasts? Consider the book's opening paragraphs, which bring the reader into the opulence of the tzar's palace:

> On the night of February 12, 1903, a long line of carriages made its way through the Imperial Gates of St. Petersburg's Winter Palace. The great mansion, which stretched for three miles along the now-frozen Veva River, blazed with light, its massive crystal and gold chandeliers reflected a hundred times in the mirrored walls of its cathedral-size reception rooms. The light cast a welcoming glow that contrasted sharply with the snow and ice outside. Bundled in sable, ermine, or mink wraps, the passengers alighted. Bracing themselves against the icy wind howling off the Gulf of Finland, they hurried through the arched doorway.
>
> Inside, the strains of the court orchestra greeted them. Masses of fresh roses, lilacs, and mimosas imported just for the night from the South of France perfumed the air. Handing their furs to the waiting footmen, guests paused in front of the pier glass to straighten silk skirts and pat pomaded hair into place before ascending the wide marble staircase to the second floor. (p. 1)

Within this introduction, four of the five senses are activated. We see the long line of carriages, the blazing lights. We feel the icy wind howling against our cheeks. Once inside, we hear the orchestra playing as our noses take in the scent of fresh flowers. Through this rich description of the setting, the author has revealed so much about the over-the-top decadence for which the Romanovs were famous. The reader experiences their decadence *through* Fleming's writing. In contrast, just a few pages later, Fleming introduces the squalor of the Russian peasantry with equal attention to sensory detail.

Either of these two chapter books are ideal for showing the vivid ways in which young people can visualize the past by drawing upon the words on the page. Both books are ideal mentor texts for descriptive writing, particularly of setting. Setting is an important element of fiction and nonfiction, and both texts can support readers' ability to read like writers, and write like readers.

When we are considering longer books, we look for writing that has rich descriptions of settings, with lots of sensory details that makes us feel as if we are there. With longer nonfiction, we want that same level of description of setting, but we also want to see illustrations, photographs, maps, and more that bring the time and place to life more fully.

Continuity and Change: Understanding Concepts and Patterns Over Time

Children's literature also offers teachers and their students opportunities to explore continuity and change over time, an important theme in social studies education according to the NCSS (2010). When Natalie launched her revised history unit in Salem, she positioned contemporary works about immigration and migration, such as the Caldecott Award–winning memoir *Dreamers* (Morales, 2018) and the fictional *Islandborn* (Diaz, 2018) against historical texts, to offer students the opportunity to talk about issues of immigration in the present before diving into the successive waves of immigrants in Salem, from initial encounters between British colonial settlers and the Naumkeag Nation to the forced migration of enslaved Africans, to the French Canadians who came to work in mills, followed by Polish and Irish families immigrants, and the Latinx diaspora of today.

By the time Natalie and her students began to talk about the first encounters between the Naumkeag and Wampanoag and Puritan colonial settlers, the students were already comfortable exploring multiple perspectives (see Figure 3.1).

Figure 3.1. *Third-Grade Exit Ticket Reflections on First Contact Between Native Americans and Puritan Settlers in the 17th Century*

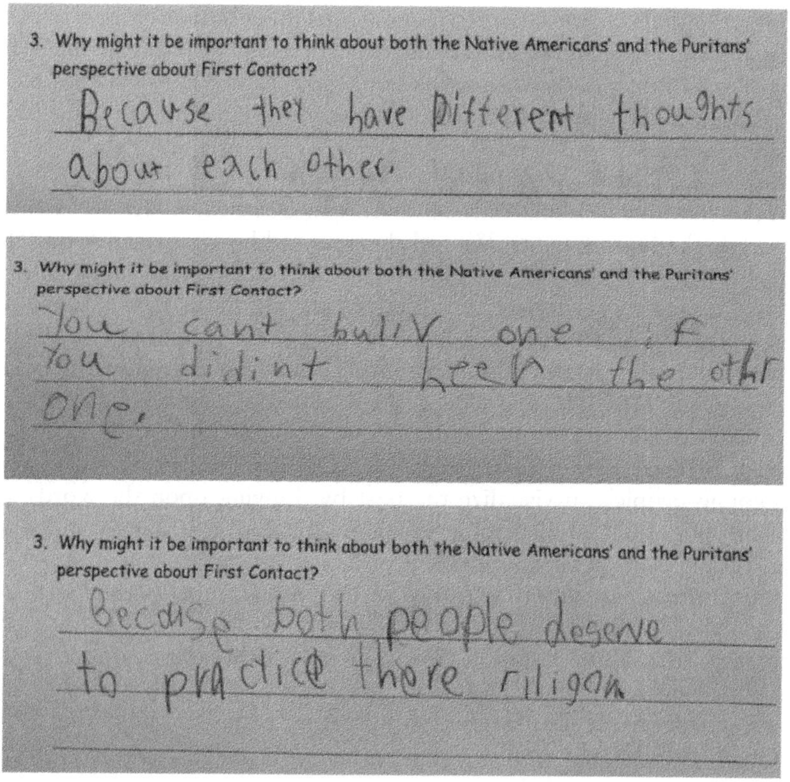

3. Why might it be important to think about both the Native Americans' and the Puritans' perspective about First Contact?

Because they have Different thoughts about each other.

3. Why might it be important to think about both the Native Americans' and the Puritans' perspective about First Contact?

You cant buliv one if you didint heen the othr one.

3. Why might it be important to think about both the Native Americans' and the Puritans' perspective about First Contact?

Because both people doserve to pradice there riligan.

Natalie's students' first introduction to this history was not presented solely from the Puritan colonizer perspective, which gave them the opportunity to consider multiple perspectives, but particularly those of Native Americans, throughout. They recognized the pattern of migration, drawing upon their prior conversations about community, immigration, and migration—through books, and with one another and community members—and the importance of considering perspectives of all involved.

Being able to identify patterns is also a valuable skill for reading historical fiction and fiction in literature circles in language arts. As students compare and contrast within and across their groups, they see the ways in which people have faced similar challenges across different time periods as well as in the students' present lives.

Migration. A text set focused on migration patterns can illuminate continuity and change. In 2020, there were more migrants globally than at any other point in history. According to The Pew Center, drawing on statistics in the U.N. Migration Report of 2022, there were 89.4 million displaced people globally in 2020, despite a global lockdown due to the COVID-19 pandemic (Natarjan et al., 2022). While students may be aware somewhat of prior global migration patterns, due to industrialization and urbanization in the 19th century or the events of World War II, they could be unaware of all that is happening now due to climate change, political instability, and more, despite a 24/7 news cycle. And, of course, *Homo sapiens* and their ancestors have been migrating throughout the world from Africa since their origins.

By offering students a range of perspectives on migration, chosen or forced, in various time periods, they can understand more deeply the *concept* that shapes so much of the past, present, and, likely, future. There are many books we can draw upon to explore this topic. Here are two examples. *Islandborn*, written by Junot Diaz (2018) and illustrated by Leo Espinosa, offers readers a deep respect for young people's intuitive ways of understanding complexity. This contemporary fictional picture book reveals a young girl's quest to find out more about her home country, the Dominican Republic, which she left as a baby. With the guidance of her older cousin, Lola gathers the memories of neighborhood adults who *do* remember their first home in the Dominican Republic: bats as big as blankets; music everywhere; mangoes so sweet they make you cry; rainbow people in "every shade ever made"; and beaches as beautiful as poetry. Not all island memories are happy ones; hurricanes arrive, and monsters lurk, specifically during the violent mid-20th century dictatorship of Rafael Trujillo. Espinosa's mixed media illustrations merge memory and imagination in joyful portraits. At the turning point, they also represent unspeakable horror, and honor human fortitude and resilience.

Veera Hiranandani's (2018) gorgeous historical novel *The Night Diary* offers readers a window on the Partition of India and Pakistan, the largest human migration in history, and an event that American students, and perhaps teachers, are likely to know little about. The novel unfolds in the form of a diary kept by protagonist Nisha from July 14, 1947, to November 10, 1947. When Britain relinquished colonial rule over India on August 14, 1947, India was partitioned into two countries: Muslim Pakistan and Hindu India. In the novel, Nisha and her Hindu family leave their home, now in Pakistan, and their Muslim friends, and head to safety in Jodhpur, India, facing armed refugees, deprivation, sadness, and uncertainty. Hiranandani's writing reads like poetry—sparse, lyrical, and descriptive all at once. This is a story of family and identity; of religious differences and the ways that humans overcome them again and again; and of an important historical moment whose effects endure to this day. Loosely based on the author's father's childhood experiences during the Partition, it is ultimately a story of love.

When looking for high-quality fiction and nonfiction picture books and chapter books to provide young people with an entryway into an enduring concept, we look for strong, developmentally appropriate narratives that can serve as an emotional and historical framework that will allow them to consider more deeply information they explore in other sources. We also strive to find authors and illustrators whose own identities and histories are reflected in their subjects. We look for books that show agency, strength, and resilience on the part of the children and adults, and collaborative action rather than casting advocacy as something that happens at the individual level. Change is rarely accomplished by a single person.

Friendship as a Theme in Historical Fiction. Of course, we do not want to offer readers historical fiction and nonfiction that only focus on painful episodes of history. Pain is always mixed with joy, and the human experience is complex. Even in wartime, people go about their daily lives. Children go to school. Friendships are made. All the developmental milestones that our students experience are the same developmental milestones that children of the past experienced, despite different contexts, cultures, and expectations.

Students connect with the past when they explore a literary theme in historical fiction and nonfiction. As Levstik (1998) notes, such explorations should focus on "how learners use literary texts to build historical understanding, how texts themselves structure history, and how teachers mediate among children, texts, and history" (p. 67). Levstik goes on to note that "a well-written narrative that is historically sound also supports informed and disciplined imaginative entry into events" (p 71). Historical fiction as a genre can vary greatly. Some novels for children and young adults provide their readers with a window into a particular time and place. Some may include actual events or real people. But the very best historical novels for young people transport them into a past that is not merely a static backdrop, but the very fabric of the conflict, tension, and mood of the story.

Friendship is a central theme—though not the only theme—in the following middle-grade novels: *Towers Falling* (Rhodes, 2016); *The Inquisitor's Tale: Or, the Three Magical Children and Their Holy Dog* (Gidwitz, 2016); *The Beatryce Prophecy* (DiCamillo, 2021); *A Bandit's Tale: The Muddled Misadventures of a*

Pickpocket (Hopkinson, 2016); and *The Long Ride* (Budhos, 2019). Each book grounds readers in time and place, though to varying levels of specificity. For example, *The Beatryce Prophecy* is fairy tale–like and historical fiction–like—both but neither. *Towers Falling* centers on a 5th-grade class in Brooklyn learning about September 11th in 2016. While not historical fiction, protagonist Dèja ultimately pieces together that her father's struggles with mental health are rooted in his post-September 11th PTSD. Readers learn about the historic event, now a generation ago, along with Dèja. The books grapple with issues related to religion, class, educational access, and gender in the times in which they are set. But the novels also invite readers to think about the role of friendships in their own lives as well as in the lives of the characters with whom they, too, share a friendship.

When looking for novels that allow students to connect with the past, we find ourselves looking first and foremost at characters that will resonate with readers. Who are the protagonists? In what ways are their struggles mirrored in contemporary life, something students can leverage as a connection between past and present? What enduring human conflicts are at work? Additionally, we look for culturally specific conflicts and norms and settings that allow readers to visualize themselves within the novel. Finally, as we are considering books for literature circles, we look for the connective tissue across the texts, the themes that will reflect themes in students' lives.

SELECTING BOOKS THAT CONNECT TO THE PAST TO BETTER UNDERSTAND THE PRESENT

We believe that books can inspire students to explore the past more deeply, and that such explorations of the past can help students to better understand and make sense of their present. When we make deliberate choices to include books about the past as read-alouds, text set explorations, book club choices, or as part of our classroom library, we know that we build students' capacities to live with an awareness of the people who came before us, and to act on behalf of those who may come after us. The responses of student readers to books that build their skills to investigate the past include the following:

- **Visualizing the past.** The illustrations in a picture book offer readers imaginative and informed representations of past places. The artfully crafted passages from authors also stitch together a vision of a past time and place, supported by the inclusion of art, artifacts, primary source documents, and historic photographs.
- **Developing an insider view of the processes that historians use to make sense of the past.** Books can reveal the ways that historians collect evidence, develop ideas, and share their evolving understandings. Readers can come to see themselves as historians who collect art and artifacts from their community in order to document its history. Care should

be taken to select books with broad representation of the sociocultural diversity of our societies, past and present.
- **Learning about the lives of changemakers in the past.** Biographies offer insight into the life stories of people who served as agents of change, who took brave stands, who worked on behalf of others, and who created the kind of change whose ripples continue to make an impact. Biographies with broad representation of the sociocultural diversity of past societies, cultures, and communities allow readers to understand more about our world.
- **Understanding continuity and change.** The world changes dramatically, and different cultures change in different ways. But there are also throughlines from "then" to "now," the ways in which conflicts, such as the migration of peoples and Indigenous activism and advocacy, can be better understood over time rather than just one single time period.
- **Engaging fully with the present.** By giving young people deeper roots in the past, they have more tools with which to make sense of the present. By reading about America's history of racial injustice and segregation, for example, young people can better recognize it in the present.
- **Recognizing empowerment to act as stewards of equity for the next generation.** It is empowering to know history and to have a sense of why the world is the way it is, the patterns and cycles of action that have churned for generations. With their understanding of the past and present, young people can become aware of future generations to come, and act with their best interests at heart.

One way to make decisions about books to recommend for classrooms is by using these reader-response characteristics to assess whether a book positions students to become aware of and engage with the world of the past. Once you know you have a book or several that can support teaching for connecting with the past, we recommend that you turn to Chapter 7 in Part II for invitations to instructional practices that are purposeful and engaging. For a list of guiding questions about how to select books for the purpose of connecting to the past to understand the present see our online material under the download tab at https://www.tcpress.com/reading-with-purpose-9780807768501.

CHAPTER 4

Closely Observe the World Around Us

"She painted how she felt on the inside/ when she experienced nature outside. / The wind. / The sunshine. / The flowers. / How nature made her heart sing and dance, even when life could be hard and unjust."

—Jeanne Walker Harvey, *Ablaze with Color: A Story of Painter Alma Thomas*

CLASSROOM STORY: IDEA MAKING AND LEARNING TO LOOK CLOSELY

In a prekindergarten class lead by Eliza and Madeline, teachers and students coconstruct an emergent curriculum, merging student ideas and wonderings, responding to seasonal and current events, and focusing on student voice and choices in their learning. A thread throughout this year's discussions and activities has been idea making and what it means to be an "Idea Maker." In January, the students were reading *Harlem Grown: How One Big Idea Transformed a Neighborhood* (Hillery, 2020), growing herbs in containers in their classroom, and thinking about what is required to create a food-producing garden in a city. In their view, Tony Hillery was an Idea Maker because he brought fresh food to an urban environment. Because their teacher provided them with the opportunity to grow plants in their own classroom, these 4- and 5-year-old learners were afforded a close look at the growing process and the life cycle of plants. They sketched their herbs as they grew, cooked with them, and engaged in important discussions about access to fresh food.

When coteachers Eliza and Madeline subsequently read aloud *Ablaze With Color: A Story of Painter Alma Thomas* (Harvey, 2022), a picture book biography of the first Black woman artist to have a solo show at the Whitney Museum in New York City, the prekindergartners identified Alma as an Idea Maker, too, because of the ways that she brought children of different backgrounds together to make art during a time of segregation. While the children engaged in responses to the book that harnessed all four purposes of our framework, most of all, they were supported to observe the art that Alma made as an inspiration for them to look closely—at Alma's art, at their own artwork, and at nature in their classroom and beyond. Throughout this chapter we will share examples of the ways that these two picture books sparked close observation (see Figure 4.1).

Figure 4.1. *Emulating the Expressionist Style of Painter Alma Thomas, a Prekindergarten Student Paints the Lavender Plant the Class Is Growing After Reading* Harlem Grown

WHY CLOSELY OBSERVE?

Young children are naturally close observers of the world around them. Sights, sounds, smells, touch, and taste sensations all provide opportunities for learning. Researchers have described this disposition as a learning advantage; by attending broadly to their surroundings, young people tend to adapt and adjust more quickly than their adult counterparts, who tend to be more selectively attentive (Blanco & Sloutsky, 2019). It can be easy to forget in our screen-saturated world that we are sensory creatures. To be a close observer is to notice all that is going on around us, including human and animal behavior; the phenomena of growth and change; and the patterns and cycles of our daily lives on planet Earth. As Eliza described: "Close observation is also an invitation to slow down, to look, to consider, and to see what might not be seen before. In a world that abundantly honors speed, through close observation we engage in a different way of thinking that brings about our best work, and our most intimate noticings of the world around us" (personal communication, February 14, 2023). We observe in order to learn, to understand, and to truly experience what it means to be human in the world.

In Pre-K–12 education literature, the practice of observation is most frequently associated with science pedagogies. While the Next Generation Science Standards focus strongly on observation and pattern finding as key skills and habits of mind in the practices of science, these skills also serve broader purposes. Project Zero researcher Shari Tishman (2018), who details close observation as a comprehensive pedagogical approach, notes: "whatever sensory form that it takes, slow looking is a way of gaining knowledge about the world. It helps us discern complexities that can't be grasped quickly, and it involves a distinctive set of skills and dispositions that have a different center of gravity than those involved in other modes of learning" (p. 2). Observation of phenomena and human behavior through all of the senses leads children to wonder and imagine, and to inquire and develop hypotheses and theories. This in turn, leads to ideas that improve and beautify our world.

Looking closely also inspires the creation of art in all forms, supporting us to see our world from new perspectives. Additionally, observation helps us to practice mindfulness, to live more fully, and to experience and appreciate the world around us more intensely. As teachers seek to develop students' abilities to observe and interact with the world, books can serve as provocation. This chapter will guide you to select and use books that launch close observation with the goals of fostering the disciplinary literacies of science; appreciation of beauty and artistic expression; and mindfulness.

WHY NOW? THE CLIMATE CRISIS AND DISCONNECT WITH THE NATURAL WORLD

Browse any news source, print or digital, and you will find headlines expressing concern over climate change, rising temperatures, extreme weather, and loss of biodiversity. Important conversations are taking place about sustainability, conservation, and environmental stewardship. We see examples of young people, like Autumn Peltier, an Anishinaabe Indigenous rights advocate from the Wiikwemkoong First Nation, and Greta Thunberg, Swedish climate justice activist, taking leadership roles in these conversations. Clearly, the scope and impact of these issues call for collective responsibility. At the same time, concern abounds around the current state of children's and young adults' mental health and many experts agree that anxiety over climate change is a contributing factor (Akpan, 2019; Holson, 2019). Engagement with literature can harness the idea-making capabilities of students to address these pressing global challenges.

Fostering Wonder and Environmental Stewardship

As an alternative to sharing worries and dire scenarios with children, teachers and caregivers can foster a sense of appreciation for and wonder about our world (ACEE, 2017; Wells & Zeece, 2007). Children who are more connected to nature experience many benefits, including cognitive, physical, and social–emotional growth (Ardoin & Bowers, 2020). The hope behind this approach for our youngest learners is that great experiences with nature will lead to greater care for nature and a disposition toward environmental stewardship (Wells & Lekies, 2006). Our older elementary students will benefit from this approach also, but they likely will want to engage in more direct conversation about actions we can take to benefit our environment. While getting out into nature is arguably the best way to deepen appreciation, books can serve as a complement, revealing aspects of the natural world from new perspectives and offering views of places and phenomena beyond our immediate surroundings.

The potential of books to foster positive views of nature and environmental stewardship has been recognized by researchers' efforts to identify award-winning books that feature outdoor experiences and outdoor play. Williams et al. (2012) reviewed Caldecott Award–winning titles beginning in 1938 to examine representation of the natural world over time. They wondered whether growing concern for the environment and biodiversity would lead to increased representations in these books or whether the "increasing isolation of people from the natural world" would lead to less prevalence (p. 146). Their analysis found the latter was true for this particular grouping of books. In a more recent analysis of award-winning titles, Shimek (2021) examined Caldecott and Ezra Jack Keats winners and honors from 1995 to 2020, seeking books that included examples of outdoor play. Using the lenses of ecocriticism and multicultural education, she looked at *who* was depicted playing outdoors. She found surprisingly few representations of outdoor play, but more important, Shimek noted inequity in representation. Shimek calls on children's book "creators and publishers to include outdoor spaces and diverse, intersectional characters living and playing in outdoor spaces" (p. 59). Her call becomes a lens for us to evaluate the books we choose to share with our young readers for the representations they convey.

Arguing that we are in a New Nature study movement, op de Beeck (2018) outlines the roles that contemporary picture books may play in engendering a deeper relationship with nature. Listing many recent titles as evidence, op de Beeck notes: "An opportunity exists in which the books we study might lead us into a natural world as close as a backyard or local park, or familiarize us with locales as distant as the Arctic" (p. 60). We share a stance of optimism that books with a focus on nature engagement and environmental stewardship will grow in numbers and will increase their representations of diverse life experiences. Recently established awards, such as the Green Earth Book Award and the AAAS/Subaru SB&F Prize for Excellence in Science Books, as well as newly founded imprints that focus on nature, such as Greystone Books and Blue Dot Kids Press, demonstrate a current focus on such titles.

Reconnecting With the Natural World

The world around us is endlessly fascinating, yet at the same time, the digital world holds great appeal for young people. Take a ride on the subway, go to a shopping mall, or even take a walk in the park and you will notice many people around you with their heads bent down, staring at the screen of a smartphone or tablet. You might even notice young children in strollers engaged with devices. While we sometimes can exhibit the same behaviors, we are concerned by recent statistics that indicate an average screen time of 246 minutes per day for youth, a 52% increase since the COVID-19 pandemic (Madigan et al., 2022). When combined with the time that children spend daily in school buildings, it is hard to imagine that students have much time to explore outside.

In 2005, Louv coined the term "Nature Deficit Disorder" to call attention to the disconnect between children and nature and to advocate for specific efforts to increase children's experiences outdoors. Children's literature that centers nature can be an antidote to children's increased engagement with technology. Drawing on theories of embodiment, posthumanism, and Sipe's (2002) categories of reader response, Harju and Rouse (2018) sought to examine how children's literature and play can foster greater connection between humans and nature. They observed that the play students engaged in after reading picture books representing "wildness" demonstrated children's connectedness to the outdoors, even when the play occurred in indoor spaces.

Some authors of nonfiction books for children write with the clear intention that their books will bring children closer to our natural world. In an interview for *Publishers Weekly*, late author April Pulley Sayre, when asked what she hoped she would spark in readers, responded: "It's more important than ever for us to share our love of nature with the kids in our lives . . . I hope that readers will feel a connection to the world of a frog or some other creature, large or small, and that they will open themselves to that experience in their everyday walks and wanders" (Kantor, 2020, para. 9). Sayre's books merge nonfiction poetry with vivid and immersive photography and serve as a clear invitation to readers to share her awe for nature and her regular practice of observation.

CLOSE OBSERVATION: STRENGTHENING OUR CONNECTION TO OUR WORLD

Books can be vehicles to spark students' natural curiosity and invitations to look closely. In the sections that follow, we will advocate for the use of children's books to inspire close observation with three goals in mind. We begin by discussing the skill of observing as a key disposition in the study of science and consider the ways that children's books can develop disciplinary literacies. Next we note the role of observation in fostering awareness and appreciation of beauty in our world, considering how picture books can prompt children to find beauty in their surroundings and how the lives of artists can inspire them to create their own art. Finally, we will discuss how the practice of close observation is connected to the practice of mindfulness and to well-being.

Observation and the Disciplinary Literacies of Science

Inspired by Tony Hillery's urban garden *(Harlem Grown*, 2020), Eliza, her coteacher Madeline, and the prekindergartners were growing food in their classroom.

As they watched the herbs they planted develop over time, they made sketches in their Observations Journals, and had lots of opportunities to describe and discuss the processes they were witnessing. Eliza asked the group: "We have been talking about plants, and growing, and we even have a little farm growing in our classroom. I'm wondering, what do you know about planting? You are experts about this. What's your idea?" The students responded:

> *So, you have to dig a deep hole and then you have to put a seed in it and dump a little water in it and then you have to put sand back in it. Oh wait! No, it's dirt. You have to put dirt to cover it up.*
>
> *Sometimes it takes years and years and years and sometimes it takes a day or two. Because sometimes it takes years for a tree to grow because it has to grow so tall but for plants it can take a few days.*
>
> *Wait, wait, wait. You has to mix it. It's a sun, and a water, and a seed, and a dirt. You got to mix it. It's a recipe.*
>
> *So like ivy sometimes grows down and up, down and up.*
>
> *You have to make it stay up so it doesn't go down so it can grow up like beautiful flowers so we can have a good good big farm in the school*
>
> *When it's dying, that means it's going down. Going down is dying.*

We can see the understandings these young learners are forming about the plant life cycle, understandings that were likely shaped both by their reading of *Harlem Grown* (Hillery, 2020) and by their classroom experiences of planting. We see the ability to describe the sequence of seed planting; the required elements for growth; differences in growing times; and what a healthy plant looks like compared to a plant that is dying. They are practicing thinking and talking like scientists, sharing what they have observed and think they know. Eliza and Madeline also guided the students in close observation and documentation of the plant growth in their classroom in a regular classroom sketching practice they call "Looking Like Scientists" (see Figures 4.2–4.3). The details included in these sketches are evidence of close study—these prekindergarten learners have represented the shapes of the leaves of these herbs and the structures of the plant stems.

The Next Generation Science Standards (NGSS Lead States, 2013) highlight the role that observation plays in the construction of scientific knowledge. This document forefronts the intersections of science and literacy practices, describing how scientists use inquiry methods to observe and document evidence, to communicate their findings to other scientists, to construct an evolving body of models, laws, and theories to explain the phenomena of our world. While inquiry and hands-on learning are primary in science education, well-crafted science texts can play a role in student learning by inspiring close observation, pattern recognition, and inquiry. Science texts can include nonfiction picture books, informational fiction books, and chapter books that explore concepts and phenomena

Figures 4.2–4.3. Two Prekindergartners' Observational Drawings of the Herbs They Have Grown

in our world and "convey ideas about the central activities of science" (National Academies of Sciences, Engineering, and Medicine. 2014, n.p.).

Literature and Science Learning, Tensions, and Possibilities. For children's science books to contribute to science learning, they must model the processes and dispositions of doing science. Science educators have traditionally expressed some cautions regarding the use of children's literature for science teaching. Mayer (1995) offered a checklist to evaluate a book's science teaching potential, emphasizing accuracy and realistic illustration. Royce and Wiley (1996), responding to the movement to integrate literacy and science, named cautions and possibilities, including the importance of selecting books directly related to the science concepts being taught, as well as using activities to highlight the scientific information, such as graphic organizers.

Shifting the conversation, Pearson et al. (2010) placed inquiry at the heart of the debate over science and literacy integration. They warned against text-centric methodologies and decried the poor quality of texts available for science instruction, but saw potential in a combined focus on texts and inquiry. Citing several successful curriculum initiatives, they suggested "when science literacy is conceptualized as a form of inquiry, reading and writing activities can be used to advance scientific inquiry rather than substitute for it" (p. 459). Mantzicopoulos and Patrick (2011) offered evidence that informational texts could improve kindergarten students' vocabulary, support them to connect science to their lives, and promote understanding of the practices of science. Varelas et al. (2014) conducted research from an inquiry-based stance, investigating the impact of combining science read-alouds with hands-on explorations in an urban school with a multilingual population, concluding that these Latinx 3rd-graders expressed scientific ideas with deeper meanings.

Researching the potential of teaching with multimodal, multigenre text sets, coauthors Mary Ann and Erika collaborated with children's book author Melissa Stewart and 3rd-grade teachers in a suburban district to explore how children's literature and experiential learning could be integrated in comprehending the abstract concepts of adaptation and evolution (Cappiello & Dawes, 2021). Students read a series of nonfiction titles arranged in text sets to learn more about life cycles, parent–offspring relationships, adaptations, change in one location over time, the dinosaur–bird connection, and evolution. At the same time, they observed and documented local bird activity; conducted hands-on explorations of different feathers, beak shapes, and bird feet; talked to local scientists; and wrote about the unique adaptations of a local bird species. Student work demonstrated that their conceptual understandings of adaptations and evolution grew over the course of this integrated science and literacy unit.

Over the last decade, the children's book world has changed significantly, particularly in the area of children's nonfiction books (Graff & Shimek, 2020). Today's classroom teachers have access to a broad range of high-quality engaging nonfiction books, as well as to resources that review the quality and accuracy of these books (for example, the National Science Teachers Association's annual listing of Outstanding Science Trade Books, K–12). While we advocate for the use of high-quality, engaging nonfiction texts that model the disciplinary literacies of science, we want to echo our science educator colleagues' reminders that you learn science by doing science, not just by reading about it. Books can inspire wondering, launch inquiry, and model science processes and disciplinary literacies, but they cannot stand alone; experiential learning is an essential element of science education (Cervetti & Pearson, 2012; Welsh et al., 2020; Worth et al., 2009; Wright & Gotwals, 2017).

When we select books to inspire close observation of our world, we seek books that encourage active exploration of the natural world, highlight fascinating features of the natural world that make children want to learn more, reveal patterns and cycles, and emphasize interdependence.

Processes and Doing Science. We seek books that explicitly model the processes used by scientists, naturalists, and conservationists to study our world. Books that feature scientists in action, such as the Houghton Mifflin Harcourt's *Scientists in the Field,* invite readers to follow the day-by-day activities of conducting scientific research and are especially engaging (Wooten & Clabough, 2014; Zarnowski, 2013).

Titles of this type also include biographies, such as Evan Griffith and Joanie Stone's (2021) picture book biography *Secrets of the Sea: The Story of Jeanne Power, Revolutionary Marine Scientist*. Griffith describes how Jeanne Villepreux-Power, as a young woman in Sicily in the early 1800s, developed inventions that helped to change the way scientists studied animal life. She also fiercely defended her research in the face of male skepticism. Fascinated by ocean creatures, Jeanne devised a way to observe live ocean animals at a time when most marine biologists were studying dead specimens. She invented a holding tank that was placed in the ocean and a large aquarium to bring animals into her home for observation. A close reading of *Secrets of the Sea* reveals many disciplinary literacies of science, including Jeanne's observation boxes and aquariums, her journaling, and her evidence and reports.

Wonder and Inquiry. Situating ourselves within inquiry-oriented practices, we are always on the lookout for books that inspire questions. These might be books that immerse readers in particular environments, books that model ways of watching and questioning, or books that present information about the natural world that is so fascinating, readers cannot help but want to know more. *Wonder Walkers* (Archer, 2021) and *Being Frog* (Sayre, 2020) are two books that fit these descriptors.

Students are invited to go outside, wander, explore, and wonder after reading Micha Archer's *Wonder Walkers* (2021). "Is the sun the world's light bulb? / Is fog the river's blanket?" (n.p.) are first in a series of questions posed by a young pair on their wonder walk. The two children featured in this Caldecott Honor–winning picture book embark on a journey through the wonders of the world around them, taking a ramble through fields, forests, valleys, and shoreline. Readers are invited along, immersed in Archer's stunning collages that span the page spreads. Richly textured, the images incorporate a variety of perspectives and viscerally convey the sheer joy these two children find in their natural surroundings. The text is playful, incorporating metaphor and personification. The children often compare Earth's features to those of the human body, emphasizing the interconnectedness of humans and nature: "Are rivers the earth's veins? / Is the wind the world breathing?" (n.p.). The final image in the book depicts the two children back in their home at the end of the day and a bird's-eye view of the home incorporates all the places they visited on their wonder walk. *Wonder Walkers* is a clarion call to get outside, to wander, and to wonder.

Books such as April Pulley Sayre's photo essay *Being Frog* (2020) propel students to spend time observing the animals they encounter in their neighborhoods and at local parks. Sayre's stunning photographs depict the frogs she and her husband observed weekly in a local pond. The rhyming text is spare but deep, conveying information about frog behavior and life cycles (being a frog), while also prompting more existential consideration of the frog as a being in our world. The author's note at the conclusion of the book is a wonderful invitation to discuss what it means to do science and to be a scientist. Sayre creates a bridge from the informal observations she did to the work of scientists, noting that "wondering and imagining are a part of science" and "a scientist would go beyond pondering and design an experiment to find the truth." Watching the frogs in her pond over time, Sayre had gotten to know these frogs as individual beings with individual behaviors and habits, and her observations will inspire backyard scientists of all ages.

Understanding Patterns, Cycles, and Interdependence. Close observation can lead to an understanding of the patterns, cycles, and interdependency that characterize the ecosystems of our natural world. Books can help provide context and content information as children make connections between their observations and their scientific understandings, bridging the space between what can be observed and what cannot.

Lita Judge's *The Wisdom of Trees: How Trees Work Together to Form a Natural Kingdom* (2021) provokes awe and questioning as students ponder the concept that trees communicate with each other through their network of roots. Judge deepens readers' understanding of and respect for the interconnectedness of trees by presenting current research on tree communication, framing forests as communities. Drawing on the groundbreaking findings of forest ecologist Suzanne Simard, Judge offers a series of poems in the voice of a variety of tree species that highlight how trees can share resources, alert other trees to danger, provide for their offspring, and make our environment cleaner and healthier. For example, a poem reads, "We clean the air / and seed the clouds, / we drench the thirsty land / with rain. / We are like / wizards" (n.p.). One of the many amazing aspects featured in the book is the Wood Wide Web, a network of mycorrhizal fungi that allows trees to convey electrical and chemical signals to their neighboring trees. Each poem appears on a double-page spread accompanied by engaging expository text that offers further explanation and watercolor paintings that immerse the reader in different forest ecosystems.

The Wisdom of Trees can inspire work with your local conservation department or a local arborist to learn more about the trees in your community. Students could take photographs of or draw or paint the notable trees in your community and create a class book sharing what they have learned. In Figure 4.4, we see a sketch that 6th-grader Carla created of a tree in her neighborhood that she likes to climb. Reading *The Wisdom of Trees* led her to view this tree in new ways. Under her sketch, Carla included a list of questions inspired by the ideas of interconnectedness that are explored in this book. She views the familiar tree with new lenses and new questions, including: How old is it? How many branches does it have? What creatures reside in its branches? How many other trees does it communicate with?

Books like the ones described above invite readers into the processes of scientific inquiry and inspire wonder and close observation. The world of children's nonfiction continues to evolve; we expect that we will be adding to our book selection strategies for modeling inquiry as book creators "remix" and reinvent the genre (for examples, see Graff & Shimek, 2020). As we have described in this section, close observation is a key skill in science learning, but it is also a disposition that serves us more broadly in our everyday interactions with our world. In

Figure 4.4. *Carla's Tree Sketch and List of Wonderings*

What creatures reside in its branches? How did is it? How many branches does it have? What other types of trees does it communicate with? How many other trees does it communicate with?

the next section, we consider how books can prompt a closer look and deeper appreciation of the beauty that abounds around us.

Observation, Appreciation, and Engagement: Finding Beauty in Our World

In the Caldecott and Newbery awards–winning title *Last Stop on Market Street*, author Matt de la Peña and illustrator Christian Robinson (2015) take readers on a city bus ride with C. J. and his Nana as they travel from church to the soup kitchen where Nana volunteers. Along the way they encounter a diverse array of people from all walks of life, with different physical abilities, skin tones, and socioeconomic backgrounds. As they travel, C. J.'s Nana invites him to use all his senses to see the beauty in the city around them and in their fellow travelers: "[C. J.] wondered how his Nana always found beauty where he never even thought to look" (n.p.). *Last Stop on Market Street* pays homage to the beauty of everyday life and the powerful relationship between a grandmother and her grandson. Picture books like *Last Stop on Market Street* model close observation and invite young readers to appreciate the beauty of their surroundings.

A unique medium, the picture book conveys meaning equally in image and in text. We hold in reverence the picture book as an art form; a picture book is an opportunity for a child to hold a work of fine art in their hands, an opportunity to view, process, and appreciate that art at their own pace and as often as they wish. We know that picture books help develop young people's visual literacies and aesthetic appreciation (Arzipe, 2021; Keifer, 1991, 1994; Nodelman et al., 2017; Wolfenbarger & Sipe, 2007). They also can serve as a catalyst for developing students' observational skills and their abilities to express what they are noticing. Connecting the experience of reading picture books with learning "the habit of mind of careful observation," Pantaleo (2018, 2020, p. 40) draws on Tishman's (2018) concept of "slow looking" when engaging children with picture books and teaching the elements of artistic design. Merging the models of visual competencies (Müller, 2008), Studio Habits of Mind (Hetland et al., 2013), Visual Thinking Strategies (Yenawine, 2013), and reader response theories, Pantaleo's studies offer evidence that when students are given language to express the elements of design, time to look, and opportunity to share what they notice, they become more practiced at expressing the meanings they make when they experience art. Picture book experiences that focus young readers' attention on images and their responses help to develop observational skills.

The Caldecott Medal is awarded annually to the artist of the most distinguished American picture book for children (American Library Association, n.d). In Chapter 3, we introduced the 2021 Caldecott winner, *We Are Water Protectors* (Lindstrom, 2020), which invites young readers to closely observe the natural world and features environmental activism. An essential understanding of our interconnectedness—each of our actions impacts someone else—is at the heart of this picture book written in verse by Carole Lindstrom and illustrated by Michaela Goade. Lindstrom begins the book by grounding readers in the Ojibwe (her tribal affiliation) cultural beliefs about water, and then introduces the Anishinaabe prophecy about a black snake that brings "destruction and harm" to the natural world. Readers bear witness to Indigenous activists of all ages and from a range of tribes and nations coming together as one to protect the water at the Standing Rock Sioux Reservation threatened by the Dakota Access Pipeline. Detailed backmatter provides readers with more information about the environmental justice activism as well as the ways in which the author's and illustrator's Indigenous identities inform the book's creation. Goade's stunning, immersive illustrations in a palette of blues and greens shape the reader's emotional experiences with the text and emphasize interconnectedness and diversity throughout. Readers will notice repeated motifs in the page spreads that create a sense of flow and honor the patterns, cycles, and textures of the natural world.

In her Caldecott acceptance speech, Michaela Goade describes the deep sense of responsibility she felt while illustrating *We Are Water Protectors* (Lindstrom, 2020): "I contemplated how sorrow, frustration, and anger wove together with courage, resiliency, and hope, and how the art might speak to this gravity. I would need to create a visual narrative grounded in tradition and history yet respect different living, thriving cultures" (Goade, 2021, para. 13). After listening to her acceptance speech, students can be invited to choose a special location in their lives, their communities. How would they choose to represent that place through art? What colors, shapes, lines, and spaces would they use? How might they infuse a sense of history, culture, community, and connection into their artwork?

Young readers also can be inspired to make art by reading about the lives and commitments of artists. Working with a class of 3rd-graders, Erika and Mary Ann (Dawes et al., 2019) researched a genre study of picture book biographies featuring the collaborations of Jen Bryant and Melissa Sweet, including *A Splash of Red: The Life and Art of Horace Pippin* (2013). The 3rd-graders, after studying a range of picture book biographies as mentor texts, interviewed community members and composed their own biographies featuring the lives of their interviewees. They drew inspiration from Sweet's artwork, including careful detail and artistic motifs well-matched to the lives of their subjects. Close observation of their subjects led to thoughtful artistic expression as these students shared the life stories of their community members.

Now we invite you to recall this chapter's opening story, in which coteachers Eliza and Madeline read aloud *Ablaze with Color: A Story of Painter Alma Thomas* (Harvey, 2022), to their prekindergartners, who made observations about Alma's artistic style and her passion for creating art based on her experiences with nature. This picture book biography is as vivid and color saturated as the art it celebrates. Alma Thomas (1891–1978), as pointed out earlier, was the first Black woman to have a solo art exhibition at the Whitney Museum of Art, and she created the first artwork by a Black woman to be displayed as part of the White House's permanent collection. While highlighting her accomplishments, Harvey emphasizes Alma's early appreciation of the beauty of nature, the joy she found in making art, and her commitment to providing art education to underserved children in Washington, DC. Harvey's text is poetic, drawing readers into the sensory experiences that inspired Alma: "She fell back on the grass beneath poplar trees and gazed at quivering yellow leaves that whistled in the wind." Loveis Wise's illustrations vibrate with color and provide readers with a gallery walk of images that emulate Alma's distinctive style.

Throughout her life, Alma Woodsey Thomas found solace and beauty in the natural world. Her abstract art reflects the colors and patterns she saw in nature and imagined in the galaxy above. As the prekindergartners read and reread *Ablaze with Color*, Eliza and Madeline invited them to look closely at Alma's art. They were fully engaged as they explored Alma's expressionist art, in particular *Resurrection*, which hangs in the dining room of the White House, and they had observations to share:

> *I noticed the circles are on a square.*
> *It kind of looks like she painted really big squares and then circles . . . really big squares to MAKE a circle!*
> *I notice that the circles aren't just one color. It's like a big circle, a bit smaller, a bit smaller, a bit smaller and a bit smaller again.*

When asked how Alma got ideas for her art, the young readers noted that she drew inspiration from nature:

That's where she got her painting colors—outside.
So she was learning about colors with her flowers but then it inspired her to paint.
There's like, this painting may look just like the flowers. If you look at the flowers very closely they're just like the painting.
I think that's where she got inspired. From those big flowers. Because they also have an outside and circle, circle, circle.

Eliza asked: "Can you see nature in this painting? What kind of nature?"

Green, like grass.
It makes me feel warm like the sun.
It looks like the flowers that were in the painting on the second page of the book.
Some red that looks just like the red on rose.

With their responses, the students were demonstrating that they were looking closely and making connections, considering both Alma's painting and Wise's illustrations in *Ablaze with Color,* multiple layers of representations.

The prekindergartners also had the opportunity to paint like Alma, to emulate her style. Eliza described how they wanted to be sure their colors were as vivid as Alma's; this required some experimentation and learning how to clean the brush in between color changes. The children were more used to painting in watercolors and they were intrigued by the techniques and textures that were possible with tempera paint. Eliza noted that some of the students copied Alma's paintings directly, reproducing the shapes and colors that they saw, talking all the while. Others focused more on experimenting with colors, textures, exploring what was possible with this medium (refer back to Figure 4.1).

Ablaze With Color holds appeal and inspiration across the grade span. Isis, a 7th-grader, spent time engaged in close observation of an outdoor location she identified as special to her. She recorded elements she hoped to capture in her subsequent painting on a graphic organizer that focused on the sensory experiences in the space: "I see tannish gray cut wood, with darker brown knotholes. I see brown bark with white speckles. This wood has a wavy striped pattern. I see yellow sunbeams on greenish brown grass" (see Figure 4.5).

Art and observation are inseparable. Writing about the intersections of art and science, Bensusen (2020) noted, "Observation is a concentrated study requiring attention to the characteristics of an object, a scene, or a situation: light, shape, texture, pattern, color, detail, and changes of these over time and under varying conditions" (p. 60). The art in picture books can inspire students to engage in close study of their environment and to express their observations by creating their own works of art.

Closely Observe the World Around Us   71

Figure 4.5. *Using Alma Thomas's Style, 7th-Grader Isis Paints Her Favorite Outdoor Location*

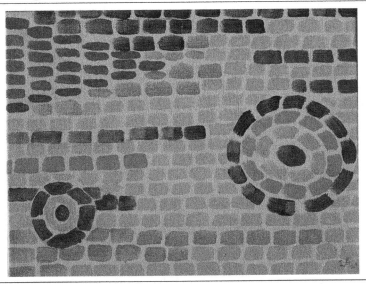

Mindfulness and Awe: The Role of Close Observation

Slowing down, focusing on our immediate surroundings, immersing oneself in the sensory details that envelop us—these are all aspects of mindfulness. Mindfulness, defined by Kabat-Zinn (2017) as "the awareness that arises from paying attention, on purpose, in the present moment, and non-judgmentally" (p. 1127), is having a moment in education and for good reason; there is strong evidence of the health benefits of practicing mindfulness (Dalal et al., 2022; Kabat-Zinn, 2017). Fostering students' abilities to be centered in the moment, that is, focusing their mind and bodies on presence, is a key component of trauma-sensitive instruction, has cognitive benefits, and develops important life skills, such as stress reduction. Mindfulness in education has been interpreted from different approaches: meditative mindfulness draws from Buddhist traditions (Kabat-Zinn, 2017), but mindfulness has also been explored from a sociocognitive approach (Langer, 2016) with a focus on noticing, inquiring, and engaging (Deringer, 2017).

When looking for books that foster mindfulness, we adopt a fairly broad definition of the term, holding respectful awareness of the spiritual and philosophical origins of the term (Kabat-Zinn, 2017; McCaw, 2020). While there have been an abundance of recent titles that explicitly focus on breath, the body, and mindfulness, we seek titles that focus on deliberate explorations of our surroundings, or have deep focus on an element of nature, and books that encourage immersion in nature.

Both *Harlem Grown* (Hillery, 2020) and *Ablaze With Color* (Harvey, 2022) proved to be titles that fostered mindfulness for the prekindergartners in Eliza and Madeline's classroom. Continuing their exploration of nature and growing, noticing, and representing in art, the coteachers crafted a morning message that invited the students to consider: "Alma was inspired by nature. How can you make art from nature? How does nature make you feel?" To make the question more concrete for these young learners, the teachers made connections to their classroom, bringing their lavender plant to the middle of the morning meeting. They asked "How does this part of nature make us feel?"

> *It makes me feel happy because like that everything is growing on the outside of you and it's also growing on the inside.*
> *It feels like it's getting bigger every day and it also makes me feel happy because if it was this big then it would grow this big!*
> *I like one side of it here, because it's so big and soft-green, and I'm sad about one side because two of it are wilty.*
> *Plants look like trees. It looks nice but when it gets bigger and bigger and bigger it looks like a tree.*
> *It makes me feel like I'm a plant. Like I'm growing too, like our plants.*

The prekindergartners' responses indicate deep engagement with their lavender plant. They sense the power of growth and change over time; the lavender is growing just like they are! They care about their plant and its health. They see how this plant in their classroom is part of the nature they observe beyond their classroom, noting similarities in the patterns of growth of smaller plants, like lavender, and larger plants, like trees. Their detailed observations and consideration of how the lavender "makes them feel" resonate with the principles of mindfulness, deep presence, and connectedness to nature (Kabat-Zinn, 2017). Next, it was time to paint their lavender plant (see Figure 4.1). Inspired by Thomas, their abstract works demonstrated intriguing variety in their representations of the plant they had grown.

Another example of a title that fosters mindfulness is *Tiny, Perfect Things*, written by M. H. Clark (2018) and illustrated by Madeline Kloepper. Brimming with double-page, intricate illustrations, this picture book features simple prose that invites young readers to pay attention to the beauty and mystery of the world around us. The opening page shows a young child holding hands with her grandfather as he tells her that "Today we will keep our eyes open for tiny, perfect things." Subsequent pages offer readers one tiny, perfect thing to focus on per page as the child's grandfather points out nature's delights like "a yellow leaf that the wind blew down" and "a snail that climbed the fence last night." When they arrive home, the child's voice emerges as they tell her racially diverse parents about the things they found today. The book ends with two fold-out pages that give a facade view of the neighborhood with seemingly countless tiny, perfect things for readers to find.

Tiny, Perfect Things is a book that invites readers to walk in their neighborhood, finding tiny, perfect things. Axel, a kindergartner, did just that, creating his own version of tiny, perfect things in mixed media (see Figure 4.6).

Figure 4.6. *A Kindergartner Creates a Collage About the Tiny Perfect Things Noticed on a Walk*

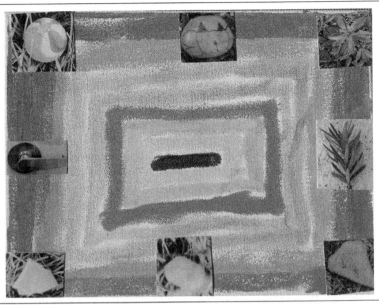

Books that promote mindful engagement with our environments are a powerful invitation to slow down, to be present, and to notice detail. Observation creates greater attunement with the people around us, with nature, and with the rhythms and patterns of our daily lives.

SELECTING BOOKS THAT INSPIRE CLOSE OBSERVATION TO SEE THE WORLD IN NEW WAYS

We believe that books can inspire students to observe and interact with the world around them more deeply and with a greater sense of wonder and awe for the beauty of nature, as well as develop as caretakers for the environment. The responses of student readers to books that build their skills as careful observers include the following:

- **Wondering and inquiring about.** Our world with its unique animals, plants, places, and phenomena is fascinating. Reading about the intricacies and endless varieties of life on our planet can inspire readers to have more questions about ecology.
- **Developing an insider view of the processes that scientists use to study our world.** Books can reveal the ways that scientists collect evidence, develop ideas, and share their evolving understandings. Readers can

come to see themselves as citizen scientists, able to observe and collect data about their environment. Care should be taken to select books with broad representation of the sociocultural diversity of our societies.
- **Learning about the lives of scientists, conservationists, and artists.** Biographies offer insight into the life stories of close observers of our world, featuring scientists, conservationists, and artists. Biographies reveal early influences and interests, challenges, and accomplishments, and what it means to devote oneself to careful study, thought, and communication about the world around us.
- **Understanding connections and interdependence of the natural world.** The concept of interdependency is critical to an understanding of our world and to the preservation of human, animal, and plant life on Earth. Book creators find unique and engaging ways to reveal interdependence to child readers, focusing on topics such as life cycles, food webs, and habitats. Books also can help readers understand how human actions impact the world around them and the importance of conservation efforts to keep balance in the natural world.
- **Realizing the uniqueness and beauty of our world and considering different perspectives, new ways of viewing our world.** The illustrations in a book can offer different lenses on our surroundings. Artists can include close-ups, panoramic views, or unique perspectives such as bird's-eye, worm's-eye, or fishbowl views.
- **Slowing down and experiencing the world around us more deeply.** Book creators can invite readers to practice mindfulness through the modeling of a book character or through a series of prompts to readers.
- **Interacting with our natural world more fully and acting as environmental stewards.** By taking an active stance toward involvement and change-making, children's books can model activism for conservation and climate justice, especially in local communities.

One way to make decisions about books to recommend for classrooms is by using these reader responses to assess whether a book positions students to become keenly aware of and closely attuned to the world around them. Once you know you have a book or several that can support teaching for close observation, we recommend that you turn to Chapter 8 in Part II for invitations to instructional practices that are purposeful and engaging. For a list of guiding questions about how to select books for the purpose of inspiring close observation, see our online material under the download tab at https://www.tcpress.com/reading-with-purpose-9780807768501.

CHAPTER 5

Cultivate Critical Consciousness

"If ever there was a need for critical literacies, for a universal, free education that includes an ongoing dialogue and conversation about how the worlds that we live in are selectively represented and portrayed, by whom, in whose interests, and to what ends, it is now."

—Luke, 2018, preface

CLASSROOM STORY: RAISING CRITICAL CONSCIOUSNESS ACROSS THE CURRICULUM

"Hello everyone. The adults and kids in K217 are working on being mindful (being present in the moment). Sometimes we get distracted when we are focused and people interrupt us. Please stop and think . . . Is it something that will help us be mindful or can it wait? If it can wait, please leave us a note and we will get back to you" (see Figure 5.1).

This letter, written collectively by the students in Jessica's combined junior kindergarten and kindergarten class, is their idea. It is April, and the class has been reading books since the beginning of the school year around the guiding question "What makes someone powerful?" During the last few weeks, they have been exploring a subquestion of this inquiry—"Where does power come from?" In fact, this subquestion is a result of the students' wondering about fairy tales—one of the required reading units in the primary grades—and why the villain is often a "big, bad wolf." Capitalizing on their authentic engagement with this topic, Jessica read aloud Jon Scieszka's (1996) *The True Story of the Three Little Pigs* and Emily Gravett's (2012) *Wolf Won't Bite* to show wolves positioned differently from the "big bad" trope and to consider how authors use words and illustrations in books to present a specific way of thinking about things. "Authors," Jessica told them, "make choices about what they write about and how they write about it."

It is a lesson she has repeated and reinforced on a regular basis throughout the year and with each book she has shared with them. With these two books, she has shown students how words and illustrations could shift a reader's perspective about the topic. Reflecting on this work, Jessica expounds, "I just think it's hilarious when authors flip the perspective, and then it's like, 'Well, what is true?' I like

Figure 5.1. Combined Junior Kindergarten and Kindergarten Letter to Their School Community

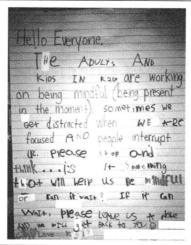

the idea of having kids figure out what is true for themselves. I think 5-year-olds can do that and then figure out how they can be powerful with that."

The idea of using words to shift perspective and highlight the power an author has in doing that caught on immediately. Her students began listening to read-alouds more critically, honing in on specific words an author used or specific artistic techniques an illustrator used to make readers think and feel certain ways. In November, they wrote opinion pieces, agreeing or disagreeing with Andrew Clements (1997) about whether the main character in his picture book *Big Al* should be described as "scary" when the character was actually really kind and helpful to others. In December, they read the nonfiction picture book *Animals Nobody Loves*, by Seymour Simon (2002), and debated the bold claim that "nobody loves" any of the animals included. In March, they discussed the specific words in *Each Kindness* that author Jacqueline Woodson (2012) used to describe the new girl Maya, whose "coat was open and the clothes beneath it looked old and ragged," from the perspective of the main character, Chloe, who "moved my chair, myself, and my books a little farther away from her." This read-aloud was followed by Kevin Henkes's *Chrysanthemum* (1991), and a discussion about how other kids made fun of Chrysanthemum's name. Then, students wrote reader response entries about what they would do if someone used words to point out their differences in a harmful way—"I would tell her to stop. Don't do that. That's mean to do" and "I would say it's okay to be different" (see Figure 5.2).

Jessica believes, though, that to really teach students how words can shift perspective and harness power, they need to use what they learned from reading and analyzing these books to cultivate a critical consciousness about the world. She mused, "What could we do to take all of this reading and learning to the next level? That is the goal." After witnessing how the youngest students in the school

Figure 5.2. *Junior Kindergarten and Kindergarten Responses about Harmful Words*

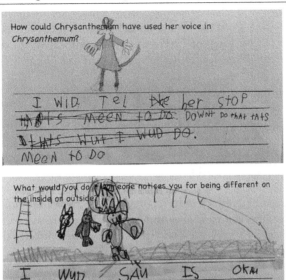

were able to develop the higher-order skills needed to think deeply and critically about how words can be used to influence others' thinking and make the world more equitable and just, she decided to get the students' input and asked them how they want to use words to make their immediate world a better place. They landed on an issue they had been dealing with lately—the daily disruption of their lessons by other adults in the building who just needed to ask Jessica a quick question, make an impromptu announcement, or borrow a book or other items. So, they wrote the letter that opens this chapter through a shared-writing activity and posted it outside their classroom door with the hope that their words can enact a powerful change in the world around them.

WHY CULTIVATE CRITICAL CONSCIOUSNESS?

What does it mean to be literate? As we shared in Chapter 1, almost 4 decades ago, educators Paulo Freire and Donaldo Macedo (1987) proposed a remarkable answer—that being literate, *truly* literate, means not just being able to read words on a sign or a page, but also being able to read the world. Reducing literacy to the functional process of decoding letters and literal comprehension, they argue, also reduces its purpose to basic personal service and economic utility. Freire and Macedo keenly understood that literacy offers many more benefits beyond the individual, such as social acceptance, cultural wisdom, and political promise.

Literacy, they proposed, is "'the language of possibility,' enabling learners to recognize and understand their voices within a multitude of discourses in which they must deal" (p. 54). At the turn of the 21st century, educators Peter Freebody and Allan Luke (1990; Luke & Freebody, 1999) reiterated this definition, positing that we actually draw upon four resources while reading:

1. Decoding the text to determine sound-letter relationships
2. Making meaning of the text to build comprehension
3. Understanding the text's organization and genre structure to figure out how to use a particular text
4. Analyzing the text to discern how its words and content position readers to think about the world

In other words, reading allows us to recognize the power and potential that words have to influence how we view and understand the world around us. To be truly literate, then, means to have the savvy to contemplate critically the voices, viewpoints, and representations within the texts we read (Leland et al., 2017; Thomas, 2016).

When we teach our students to read the world along with the word, we work to cultivate their critical consciousness of the social, cultural, and power dynamics of our world. This cultivation also involves reflecting deeply and honestly about our own lived experiences and cultural values to perceive how they have shaped our understanding of texts. Jones et al. (2010) added another layer to Freebody and Luke's (1990; Luke & Freebody, 1999) Four-Resources Model of Reading, asserting that our identities as readers influence how we approach decoding, meaning making, text using, and text analyzing. When we teach our students how words can help us rethink worlds, we help them fuse "the political and the personal, the public and the private, the global and the local, the economic and the pedagogical, for rethinking our lives and for promoting justice in place of inequity" (Shor, 1999, p. 2). When we use books to teach students how to center care (Chapter 2), to connect the past (Chapter 3), or to closely observe the world around us (Chapter 4), we help them reflect on their lives and the world around them. Books, then, are tools that help us develop our social, cultural, and political awareness and help us work toward building a more equitable world for all.

Generating action toward social equity and justice is ultimately the goal of critical conscious raising, or what Freire (1970) called *conscientização*. When we read aloud books like *The Little Red Hen* (Pinkney, 2006) or *Room on Our Rock* (Temple & Temple, 2019) to help students grapple with the concepts of fairness and equity, or books like *Oliver Button Is a Sissy* (dePaola, 1979) or *Counting on Katherine: How Katherine Johnson Saved Apollo 13* (Becker, 2018) to examine gender assumptions and discrimination, we engage in *conscientização*. When we share books like *Julián Is a Mermaid* (Love, 2018), *Beauty Woke* (Ramos, 2022), *Eyes That Kiss in the Corners* (Ho, 2021), or *Crown: An Ode to the Fresh Cut* (Barnes, 2017) to affirm the value of students' identities, we cultivate critical consciousness. When we share books like *Brave Girl: Clara and the Shirtwaist Makers' Strike of 1909* (Markel, 2013), *The Undefeated* (Alexander, 2019c), *Stonewall: A Building. An Uprising. A Revolution* (Sanders, 2019), or *Unspeakable: The Tulsa Race Massacre* (Weatherford, 2021), we teach them how to analyze books through the lenses of power and equity. And when we share books like *Change Sings: A Children's Anthem* (Gorman, 2021a), *No Voice Too Small* (Metcalf et al., 2020), or *Dictionary for a Better World* (Latham & Waters, 2020), we also give our students the words and tools they need to turn their goals into reality through social action.

WHY NOW? AGENCY, EQUITY, AND JUSTICE IN AN EVER-CHANGING WORLD

The 21st century has shone a spotlight on literacy in new ways. This attention is not just a matter of educational concern, but also of economic, technological, political, and social debate. Federal policies and state guidelines have emphasized standardized reading and writing benchmarks as measures of academic and professional success. Global competition and economic sustenance, particularly in the aftermath of the COVID-19 pandemic, have fomented fears about some children "falling behind" other students. Advancements in digital technology have generated global access to numerous tools for creating and sharing text, and shifts in social demographics and dynamics have emphasized the need to rethink how we communicate with one another. Across all of these arenas, our approaches to literacy and literacy education need to consider what we communicate with one another, how, and why.

Reading to cultivate critical consciousness is a responsive and flexible way to address these shifts with an eye toward equity and justice. When words and images are used to propagate divisive rhetoric via social media and channels, we need to strengthen students' literacy skills by supporting them to discern the bias and fearmongering underlying those texts. When scientific facts and well-documented histories are disputed and dismissed as "fake news," or unfounded claims are presented under the guise of journalistic objectivity, reading to cultivate critical consciousness can help students distinguish between the two. And when historically marginalized communities are disenfranchised and denied fundamental rights to education, healthcare, or even a life free from violence, reading to cultivate critical consciousness can help students determine not just the underlying causes of such oppression but ways to combat it. We cannot stop the world from changing, or even artificial intelligence tools from impacting how literacy gets taught, but we can work to ensure that these changes do not harm or perpetuate discrimination, oppression, and injustice for the children we teach. Using children's literature to cultivate *conscientização* and embrace Freire and Macedo's (1987) definition of literacy as reading the word and the world helps us do this.

Critical Literacies

To begin developing the skills involved in critical consciousness, we must first take an honest look at ourselves. Our individual intersectional identities are shaped by the multiple discourses we experience throughout life. In turn, those identities "reveal the subjective positions from which we make sense of the world and act in it" (Shor, 1999, p. 3). Likewise, authors bring their own identities to the texts they create, conveying certain understandings of the world as well. Critical literacies, then, ask readers to examine the perspective, privilege, positioning, and power active in the social forces and texts they encounter (Comber, 2015; Jones, 2006). *Perspective* encompasses one's point of view on a matter. Our perspectives are rooted in our sociocultural identities, experiences, values, assumptions, and ways of learning. To help readers identify perspective in a text, we might ask the following questions:

- Who is the author/illustrator of this text? What does the author's/illustrator's identity tell you about their point of view on the topic?
- Who is the audience supposed to be? What makes you think so?

Privilege deals with the perspective that an author or illustrator wants to center as "normal," "right," or "true." Privilege also considers how different perspectives are represented, communicated, or silenced (Janks, 2000). To help students discern which perspectives are privileged in a text, we might ask the following questions:

- What perspective(s) is given the most attention in this text?
- What perspective(s) does the author/illustrator seem to value?

Positionality asks us to reflect on our relationship with the text. Doing so requires us to consider how a text might have bearing on our identities (Luke, 2012). To help students discern the ways a text positions them, we can ask the following questions:

- Does this text make you feel like an insider or an outsider in relation to its content? Why?
- Who else might this text position as an insider or an outsider? Why?

Finally, we must consider *power*—the lens that undergirds all the others. Since power deals with issues of dominance and control, exploring a text to determine its perspectives, what it privileges, and how it positions readers ultimately means inquiring how a text uses words and images to attribute power. To help students analyze the way power works within a text, we might ask the following questions:

- Who benefits from the words and messages in this text? How?
- How do the representations in this text work to uphold or challenge stereotypes?

- How does this text work to uphold or challenge the status quo? For whose and what goals?

Renowned literacy scholars Vivian Vasquez, Hilary Janks, and Barbara Comber (2019) speak of critical literacy as a way of being and doing that one applies to everyday life. Vasquez (in Miller & Kissler, 2019) explains:

> To make this powerful work possible, critical literacies need to unfold in the everyday as we incorporate a critical stance in our everyday lives. When this happens, it becomes much easier to support children in taking up, understanding, and analyzing the social and political issues around them. (p. 75)

Put differently, critical literacy nurtures a critical consciousness by asking what the ideological and social functions of a text are.

The Power of Words

Across history, literacy has been framed as a tool of power. For centuries, the development of literacy was used to support systemic forms of governance for elite management and religion (Gallego & Hollingsworth, 2000). Although today, literacy is understood as a fundamental human right that "drives sustainable development, enables greater participation in the labour market, improves child and family health and nutrition, and reduces poverty and expands life opportunities" (UNESCO, 2023), the use of literacy education to perpetuate power structures continues today. The relationship between literacy and power stems from the understanding that words influence thoughts, beliefs, and action. As we share children's literature with our students, questioning the way words are used to influence readers is an important concept in cultivating their critical consciousness to make the world a better place for all.

Such was the objective for the five 7th-graders whom literacy specialists Tory and Kate cotaught. They met with this small group of students of diverse cultural identities once a week to offer them additional support in reading. To Tory and Kate, helping these students strengthen their reading abilities did not mean just working more on their decoding and comprehension skills; it also meant helping them perceive the potential of words to impact their individual lives, as well as the lives of entire communities.

This small group has been reading the first few chapters of *Breaking Stalin's Nose* (Yelchin, 2011). In this Newbery Honor–winning historical fiction novel, 10-year-old Sasha Zaichik has just witnessed his father's arrest by the Soviet State Security in Joseph Stalin's Communist regime. A neighbor proudly took credit for reporting Sasha's father and has been rewarded by moving into the roomy apartment where Sasha and his father now no longer live. Sasha believes the arrest of his father, a loyal and high-ranking government official, is a mistake, but he readily accepts that until he can convince Stalin otherwise, the neighbor rightly deserves the apartment.

"It's important to question what's true and what you're told," Tory muses, then jokes that doesn't mean you should question your mother when she tells you to put away the laundry. "So why doesn't Sasha question this?"

"It's the propaganda," Nicholas responds. When Tory asks him to explain to his peers what *propaganda* is, he replies, "A small message, like something catchy. Like 'I want you to join the U.S. Army.' It grabs your attention."

"Is it always good? Is it always true?" Tory asks.

"I thought it was," another student, Steven, admits.

Propaganda can be based either in truth or lies, but its main purpose is to evoke a strong emotional response in readers and audiences. She and Kate offer more current examples of propaganda: posters urging people to wear a mask to stop the spread of COVID-19 and posters proclaiming "Stop the Steal!" in attempts to discredit the 2020 U.S. presidential election. Several times throughout the group's discussion, Tory returns to the message about not assuming something is true just because someone says or writes it. "Sasha's old enough now to question what he's told," Tory reflects.

Kate flips through a few slides projected on the screen of various posters from Stalin's era, asking students what they notice about the words and images, but more important, how those details make them feel. Although they cannot understand the Russian words on the posters, the students point out the glowing light shining on Stalin, the presence of children, and the smiles and sense of pride on many of the faces. Kate then directs them to reread a line from the novel: "The Kremlin is where Comrade Stalin's office is. Everybody knows his window—it's lit all night long. Our leader works hard" (Yelchin, 2011, p. 35).

"Why might this information be spread? What does it help people believe?" Tory asks, then directs students to juxtapose those statements with the author's note at the end of the novel, which describes Yelchin's harrowing childhood growing up in Stalinist Russia. She distributes a worksheet with discussion questions that encourage students to think further about the power of words that asks, "Why might the government have spread this question? What sort of feelings does it create?" and "What is the message in these lyrics and how is it used to be convincing?"

Like Jessica's young students from this chapter's opening vignette, Tory and Kate's 7th-graders knew that becoming truly literate meant becoming attuned to the power of words. As education scholar and activist bell hooks (1994) observed, "Words impose themselves, take root in our memory against our will" (p. 167). Words—and the meanings they carry—seep into our being, both consciously and subconsciously, conveying messages about the world we live in. In doing so, words foster possibilities for better or worse. There is both danger and hope in that possibility, in the influence that words can have. This theme is reflected throughout popular culture as well, in film, music, drama, and literature. More important, it is the way words are used that matter. Are they being used to uplift and inspire? Are they used to insult and bully? Are they used to provide insight and compassion? Or are they used to divide us by perpetuating stereotypes, fear, and misinformation? hooks (1994) clarifies this point: "I know that it is not

Cultivate Critical Consciousness

Figure 5.3. Seventh- and Eighth-Grade Reader Response Propaganda Posters

the English language that hurts me, but what the oppressors do with it, how they shape it to become a territory that limits and defines, how they make it a weapon that can shame, humiliate, colonize" (p. 168). Reading children's literature to cultivate critical consciousness helps students not just perceive the power of words and images, but also determine for what purpose that power is being used.

With that understanding, of course, comes agency. Once students perceive the influential power of words, they can learn to channel it for their own use as well. That's what Jessica's junior kindergartner and kindergartner students did when they harnessed that power to write the letter to their community. Tory and Kate's students created their own propaganda to show their understanding of the power in words and images (see Figure 5.3). Later, Tory's 8th-grade students created propaganda posters using Canva, an online design tool, in response to their reading of *Animal Farm* (Orwell, 1946) (see Figure 5.3). What can your students do with words and images to influence others' thinking and make the world a better place for all?

Equity and Justice

Issues of equity and justice are central to reading for critical consciousness. In particular, it is important to help students distinguish between equality and equity. *Equality* assumes that everyone is given the same resources and opportunities in the exact same way; *equity* acknowledges that people come from different starting circumstances, so for everyone to have a fair chance at succeeding, they may need different resources and opportunities to help them. *Justice* aims to create and maintain equity by attending to the resources and opportunities at both the individual and the systemic level.

Educational research has shown over and over again that addressing issues of equity and justice in all aspects of teaching—from instructional methods to assessment tools—is fundamental to ensuring all students succeed as learners (Chang & Cochran-Smith, 2022). But equity and justice are concepts that also work to ensure all our students continue to succeed in the world beyond school. These concepts ask us to honestly reflect on the ways different people are privileged and marginalized in their daily lives because of their individual resources and the systemic structures surrounding them. We live in a time when politicians rather than doctors get to make decisions about women's bodies and healthcare, Black and Brown children are denied the right to learn about their own histories in school, and immigrants and refugees seeking to escape violence and poverty are passed around like playthings and refused safe haven. Literacy educator Gholdy Muhammad (as interviewed by Ferlazzo, 2020) explains that such critical consciousness work:

> means helping students understand content from marginalized perspectives. As long as oppression is present, students need spaces to name, interrogate, resist, agitate, and work toward social change. This will support students toward being critical consumers and producers of information. It will also help to build a better humanity for all. (n.p.)

Cultivating critical consciousness requires us to investigate the values, assumptions, and worldviews underlying existing social structures and experiences and work toward determining actions and solutions to address inequities and injustices.

It's important to recognize, however, that cultivating critical consciousness does not just mean identifying what is "unfair," "wrong," or "broken." It also means helping students view themselves as agents who can reframe what gets valued and accepted as truth (Luke, 2012; Souto-Manning & Yoon, 2018). It means supporting students "to take a moral stand on the kind of just society and democratic education we want" (Shor, 1999, p. 24). In other words, equity and justice do not always require conflict or strife; in essence, they require us to open our hearts and minds to consider ways we can provide opportunities and resources for those who do not have the same footing as others. Keeping these goals in mind can help us choose children's literature to cultivate critical consciousness toward equity and justice.

CULTIVATING CRITICAL CONSCIOUSNESS: CREATING A BETTER WORLD FOR ALL

In purposefully selecting children's literature that cultivates critical consciousness, we can guide readers to books that harness the power of words, inspire agency, and underscore the importance of equity and justice for all. In the sections that follow, we offer five considerations when selecting books for cultivating students' critical consciousness: (1) integration of authentic texts; (2) integration of diverse texts; (3) text deconstruction for perspective, positioning, privilege, and power;

(4) text reconstruction or counterstorytelling to hear marginalized voices; and (5) use of texts to inspire social action.

Integration of Authentic Texts

To help our students realize the power of words and determine how perspective, privilege, positioning, and power work in the world around them, we must provide them with frequent opportunities to work with authentic texts. Freire (1970) defines authentic thinking as "thinking that is concerned about reality, [and] does not take place in ivory tower isolation, but only in communication" (p. 77). It makes good sense, then, that students should practice reading texts that are authentically used in the world—children's literature, author and illustrator interviews, the news articles, websites, and podcasts that authors and illustrators use to research the content for their books. In these authentic texts, readers see and hear examples of language and images used in real life, so they are able to determine how texts convey different perspectives, privilege and position readers in different ways, and use power differently to uphold or challenge the status quo.

The notion of authenticity extends perhaps most significantly to the identity and expertise of the author/illustrator. Multiple award-winning author Jacqueline Woodson (1998), who identifies as a Black, gay woman with a multiracial family, explains that "the myriad cultures once absent from mainstream literature ... want the chance to tell our own stories, to tell them honestly and openly" (para. 14). Using authentic texts means scrutinizing whether a book does that or whether it is "a book that did not speak the truth about us but rather told someone on the outside's idea of who we are" (para. 14). In doing so, we make sure we are not reinforcing inequities and injustice by communicating those stories.

Cultivating critical consciousness, however, can only go so far if we only share authentic texts sporadically. One way we can avoid this is by juxtaposing texts of various genres with one another in text sets to see how different words and images are used to communicate information about the same topic (Cappiello & Dawes, 2021). Another is by making sure authentic texts are part of all our curricular units for all our students, whether we use them as whole-class read-alouds, for small group support, or independent work. Integrating authentic texts into our purposeful teaching with children's literature means making such texts an ongoing part of students' work with language throughout the year.

Integration of Diverse Text

Reading to cultivate critical consciousness means asking whose lives we encounter through books and how those lives are portrayed. Do we see the same kinds of characters, settings, events, and achievements depicted over and over again? Or do we get to learn about diverse people, places, and plots? And whose voices get to tell the stories? These were the kinds of questions that young adult literature authors Ellen Oh and Miranda Lo asked on social media almost a decade ago, confirming that they weren't the only ones having this conversation and laying the groundwork for the #WENEEDDIVERSEBOOKS movement (We Need Diverse Books, 2023).

In considering diverse books for our teaching, we must take care around what counts as diverse. One book alone does not qualify as "diversity," as it only continues to perpetuate binary thinking about one group of people as the standard and another as the deviant. *Diverse* means various, multiple, and many. In using diverse books in our classrooms, we need to consider the diversity of voices across the collection of texts we use for teaching to ensure we include various, multiple, and many of them.

Additionally, providing students with diverse books is not enough. As we introduced in Chapter 1, Rudine Sims Bishop (1990) asserts that books can be mirrors that reflect our own lives, windows that allow us to learn about the lives of others, and sliding glass doors we can step through to take part in that experience. At times, we as teachers may have unintentionally created *foggy mirrors*, *tiny windows*, and *heavy doors* for children to walk through, leaving them with inaccurate approximations of themselves or limited experiences with single books or single units that are supposed to represent entire cultures (Enriquez, 2021).

Students' identities are never just one characteristic; they are a complex web of intersecting backgrounds, traits, experiences, interests, and abilities. When we approach our students' identities with books that superficially essentialize or overgeneralize who they are, we give them foggy mirrors that do not truly reflect their experiences. Novels like *When You Trap a Tiger* (Keller, 2020) and *Hello, Universe* (Kelly, 2017), and picture books like *Beauty Woke* (Ramos, 2022) and *A Different Pond* (Phi, 2017) show characters grappling with the assumptions made about their identities, exploring how they are more than just the color of their skin or economic class.

Likewise, we need to be careful not to set up "us–other" paradigms when teaching about cultures different from those of our students. When we treat different cultures as something that can be simply studied in one book or unit, the windows into those cultures that we offer through books are tiny ones that limit what can be learned. Instead, we can design text sets, juxtaposing several texts about the same topic for comparison and contrast to deepen student learning (Cappiello & Dawes, 2021). For example, picture books about refugee experiences, such as *Marwan's Journey* (De Arias, 2018) and *The Day War Came* (Davies, 2018), can be shared alongside a novel like *Boy, Everywhere* (Dassu, 2021) to complicate assumptions about refugees. In the two picture books, the authors show a familiar, but nonetheless harrowing, tale of the loss, loneliness, and danger children experience as refugees. We also understand the poverty involved. But *Boy, Everywhere* chronicles the sudden fleeing of Sami's family from their comfortable middle-class life in Damascus. In her Author's Note, A. M. Dassu explains that she wanted to shatter stereotypes about refugees as the "other" and to show that many of them had led lives and enjoyed material privileges just like children in any other country.

We can also check to see if the titles we share to teach about certain cultures and communities repeatedly focus on oppression and tragedies or if we also include titles that celebrate what it means to belong to those groups. Books that chronicle the injustices faced by certain groups of people are plenty, but books like *Crown: Ode to the Fresh Cut* (Barnes, 2017), *Eyes That Kiss in the Corners* (Ho, 2021), and *Laxmi's Mooch* (Anand, 2021) focus on celebrating the identities and joys that come from being children in those communities.

We also need to remember that the most powerful learning happens when students are authentically engaged with and curious about a topic. When we consider students' interests into lives, experiences, and cultures they genuinely want to know more about, we owe it to them to help open the sliding glass door into the world of books that can support their learning.

In other words, as we aim to share books to cultivate students' critical consciousness about concepts of identity, inclusion, and representation, we must reframe our thinking about text selection "to clear the mirrors, enlarge the windows, and push open the sliding glass doors of children's literature, so the texts we share with students have lasting power beyond our classrooms" (Enriquez, 2021, p. 106). Without this kind of careful thinking about who students are and how we are using books to expand their understanding of others, diversifying our text selection can miss its overall purpose.

Text Deconstruction

We know the words we use reflect our identities, experiences, knowledge, values, and assumptions—in other words, language is socioculturally and ideologically constructed. Text deconstruction involves employing the lenses of perspective, positioning, privilege, and power to analyze the sociocultural and ideological roots of its language and images. Acknowledging again the potential of words to influence what we understand as knowledge and truth, deconstructing texts recognizes that "truth no longer exists. What matters is what story gets spun" (Lankshear & Knobel, 2006, p. 8). Viewing children's literature "as sociopolitical art calls us to re-envision ourselves as critical curators who nurture classroom conditions for literary experiences that welcome a vast and varied representation of life . . . , and curate discussions that interrogate deficit portrayals and resist racist tropes" (Zapata, 2022, p. 86). In other words, text deconstruction sharpens our literacy skills and critical consciousness by helping us discern whose knowledge and truth is being communicated. Jessica, Tory, and Kate engaged their students, 5-year-olds and 12-year-olds alike, in text deconstruction by asking questions about what is true and who says it is so around the books they chose to read with students.

Books that present the same information from different points of view are well-suited for cultivating students' text deconstruction skills. *Echo Echo: Reverso Poems about Greek Myths* (Singer, 2016) reviews the events of popular Greek myths through the eyes of the different characters who were involved. Author Marilyn Singer employs the Reverso poem, a form she invented, to show that the story told is a different one if you read it backwards from a different point of view. Singer does the same with fairy tales in *Mirror Mirror: A Book of Reverso Poems* (2010) and *Follow Follow: A Book of Reverso Poems* (2013). Novels that alternate chapters through the narration of different characters also are helpful for practicing text deconstruction, as are novels that employ literary devices like flashback and embedded storytelling to show another way of telling the story of an event. Newbery-winning author Rebecca Stead's middle-grade novel *Goodbye Stranger* (2015) uses the braided narrative device to ponder the question, "Who's the real you? The person who did something awful, or the one who's horrified by the awful thing you did?" (p. 257) from three different characters' perspectives. The Coretta Scott King honor book *The Parker Inheritance* (Johnson, 2018) addresses the complexities of racial discrimination and civil rights through the voices of different characters across generations, emphasizing that "truth" is not just a matter of perspective, but also time and space in history.

Text Reconstruction and Counterstorytelling

Reading to cultivate critical consciousness means considering issues of identity, inclusion, and representation in the books we share. Text reconstruction and counterstorytelling, therefore, involve retelling the story from another set of identities, experiences, knowledge, values, and assumptions (Jones, 2006; Souto-Manning & Yoon, 2018). The books described above involve reconstructing events in different ways, redistributing the power in texts to get at some more accurate version of what's true. Children's authors also have engaged in text reconstruction and counterstorytelling by approaching well-known histories from marginalized or silenced viewpoints. For example, *Ada Lovelace, Poet of Science: The First Computer Programmer* (Stanley, 2016) and *Nothing Stopped Sophie: The Story of Unshakable Mathematician Sophie Germain* (Bardoe, 2018) introduce readers to two women who made invaluable and field-changing contributions to science, technology, engineering, and mathematics. Their biographies challenge the popular histories that privilege the contributions of men. Even *After the Fall* (Santat, 2017) extends the story of Humpty Dumpty beyond the abrupt nursery rhyme to show the trauma he faced after tumbling from the wall—a counterstory that forces readers to question what they knew and assumed about the events.

Social Action

The ultimate goal of cultivating critical consciousness, of course, is to use that awareness of power, equity, justice, and agency to make the world a better place for all. This call to action is why Freire (1970) referred to literacy education as *praxis*, or "theory-based action/action-based theorizing" (Shor, 1999, p. 16). For him, literacy is not just a personal endeavor, but one that ties us to our communities and surroundings. Reading the word means reading the world and determining how to use what we have learned about both to make the world a better place for all.

Cultivate Critical Consciousness

Several noteworthy fiction and nonfiction books can help students hear that call to action. As described earlier in this chapter, a number of high-quality picture books can help raise awareness about the plight of refugees and displaced people. To support students in helping those communities, we can share nonfiction informational titles like *Finding Home: The Journey of Immigrants and Refugees* (Lee, 2021) and *Making It Home: Real-Life Stories from Children Forced to Flee* (Naidoo, 2004). In both books, students gain a broader understanding of the history of human migration and immigration policies, as well as the many complex reasons why people leave their homes and why others make it harder for them to resettle in another land. To contextualize the current crisis, authors Jen Sookfong Lee and Beverly Naidoo, respectively, also provide photos and transcripts of interviews with immigrant and refugee children and adolescents to humanize their stories and ground them in the reality of today, as well as resources in the backmatter to launch students on their way to providing aid.

Peaceful protest is another way people have collectively worked to challenge injustice throughout history. Some protests have challenged inequitable working conditions. *Si, se puede! Yes, we can! Janitor Strike in L.A.* (Cohn, 2005), relates the experiences of a young boy who supports his mother in advocating for better pay for the custodians who work hard to clean Los Angeles's skyscrapers, and *Brave Girl: Clara and the Shirtwaist Makers' Strike of 1909* (Markel, 2013) tells the story of a young immigrant girl who organized thousands of other girls working in the New York garment industry to protest their unsafe and untenable working conditions. *Sit-In: How Four Friends Stood Up by Sitting Down* (Pinkney, 2010), covers the 1960 peaceful protest of four college students against the "Whites Only" policy at a Woolworth's lunch counter, and *Boycott Blues: How Rosa Parks Inspired a Nation* (Pinkney, 2008) chronicles the 382 days of the Montgomery bus boycott.

Other books directly address the capacity and efficacy of young children and educators to engage in social change. *Let the Children March* (Clark-Robinson, 2018) describes how thousands of Black children marched in opposition to racial segregation policies in 1963, and *No Voice Too Small: Fourteen Young Americans Making History* (Metcalf et al., 2020) uses poetry to introduce readers to young activists who are making a positive difference in today's world. *Can We Help? Kids Volunteering to Help Their Communities* (Ancona, 2015) covers a range of ways children can make the world immediately around them better for all, such as tutoring, training assistance pets, and volunteering at community farms that provide food for soup kitchens and food pantries for food-insecure families. Each of these books shows students that no matter what age they are, they can do something to challenge oppression and enact change for the better.

The kindergartners in Paige's class were just learning about the possibilities for helping others in need. On a cold, wet, gray mid-January day in New England, Paige's class gathers on the rug for read-aloud time. "What is privilege?" she asks and tells students to touch their hands to their heads if they have heard the word before. A few do, and when Paige asks what the word means, she gets a variety of answers that circle notions of helping others and being responsible. Knowing that privilege can be a complex concept for 5- and 6-year-olds to grasp, she acknowledges their attempts and use of big words, then projects a definition for them on the front board:

Privilege means . . . You don't have to worry about some things because of
- Where you live
- What you look like
- How much money you have
- Your gender

She provides some examples and contrasts the notion of privilege with that of rights—"Privileges can be taken away, but rights can't (or if they are, they shouldn't be!)"—and then shows photographs of their school's recently renovated facilities, contrasting them with photos of the dilapidated and unsafe buildings in which students attend school in other parts of the country. "It is a privilege that we get to go to a school as nice as [ours]," she reflects.

As the children wonder aloud about why other schools have less than theirs, Paige introduces the picture book biography *One Wish: Fatima al-Fihri and the World's Oldest University* (Yuksel, 2022), explaining, "We are going to a read a true story about a child named Fatima who lived long ago when girls did not have many privileges, and they did not even have the RIGHT to go to school. In this story, you will see that Fatima worked really hard to learn and help others who were less privileged than she." The book tells the true story of how Fatima al-Fihri, a Muslim woman in the 9th century, grew up and turned into reality her childhood wish of establishing a school where anyone could study and become anything they wanted. After reading aloud *One Wish*, students reflected on what they would miss if they could not go to school (Figure 5.4); some responded by identifying teachers, people, and science. To push them further and connect these reflections to the idea of social action and praxis, Paige asked students to think back to the photos she showed them earlier of poorly resourced schools: "What are some things that we could do to help some of those schools?"

Helena: Some teachers at our school could help at their school.
Bella: Maybe some of those kids could come here.
Carlos: Give things from our school to their school.
David: We could ask them to build a nicer school.
Frances: We could give them some of our money.

As the lesson ended, the seeds for critical consciousness had been sown. Reining in the students' ideas to something perhaps more viable for their age and stage in critical consciousness development, Paige suggested, "Maybe we could even put together a box of things we have extra of and give it to them," and was met with lots of enthusiastic nods. Later, after the class had gone to the cafeteria for lunch, Paige mused, "I think some of these kids will take this seriously. I could

Cultivate Critical Consciousness

Figure 5.4. Kindergarten Students' Responses to *One Wish*

see Frances, for example, really going home and asking her parents for money to give to these schools." Her class was on its way to taking action steps that would make their world better. Whether those steps manifest into using their literacy skills, like Jessica's class (refer to Figure 5.1), or using their other abilities, Paige's class was learning that books could show them that they, too, could directly address the social issues they want to change.

SELECTING BOOKS THAT CULTIVATE CRITICAL CONSCIOUSNESS TOWARD CREATING A BETTER WORLD FOR ALL

We believe books can expand students' awareness of their existence, relationships with others, and impact in the world. Being purposeful and thoughtful about the books you share with students can communicate that you are conscious of the power, inequities, injustices, and agency in their lives and the world. The responses of student readers to books that cultivate critical consciousness include the following:

- **Learning about the intersections of identity and the complexity of social issues.** Individuals are different, even when they look like one another or speak the same language. Books that showcase, with honesty and authenticity, the intersections and complexities of identities, experiences, and relationships can help students make better sense of their world.
- **Being inspired by the power of the book's words and images.** Words can change minds, offer hope, and provide healing. We deliberately search for

books written with language that illuminates, influences, and inspires us to create a better world for all.
- **Identifying their assumptions and rethinking what they know.** Students cultivate their critical consciousness with books that challenge them to question what they know by highlighting the assumptions and possible misconceptions underlying that knowledge.
- **Engaging in the stories of people whose voices and experiences have been neglected often throughout history.** History is often written by those in power; thus, those who have been oppressed have had their histories relegated to the margins. To honor their contributions to the world, we look for books that provide a forum for stories that have been overlooked or disregarded throughout history.
- **Discerning the power of individuals versus social systems and institutions.** We recognize that individual potential is often bound by the systems and institutions at work in society. Books that demonstrate to students this power differential portray the challenges faced in effecting social change with more honesty, yet they also provide valuable insight into the ways individuals can work collectively to mobilize action in powerful ways.
- **Being motivated to make a positive difference in the world and lives of others.** Simply put, books that inspire students to take action against oppression and injustice help move their critical consciousness toward those steps. Thus, we search for books that underscore agency and power to make the world a better place for all.

One way to make decisions about books to recommend for classrooms is by using these reader responses to assess how a book positions students to cultivate critical consciousness of themselves and the world around them. Once you know you have a book or several that can support your teaching to cultivate critical consciousness among students, we recommend that you turn to Chapter 9 in Part II for invitations to instructional practices that are purposeful and engaging. For a list of guiding questions about how to select books for the purpose of cultivating critical consciousness, see our online material under the download tab at https://www.tcpress.com/reading-with-purpose-9780807768501.

Part II

AN INVITATIONS APPROACH TO ENCOURAGE PURPOSEFUL READING

In the chapters in Part II of this book, as well as at The Classroom Bookshelf, we take an "invitations" approach. That is, we believe students should be supported to be agentive in their decision-making as readers, writers, communicators, and creators. Teachers can invite students into new learning with an implicit trust in students' decision-making capacities. In the chapters in Part I, we laid out a framework for selecting books to foster care, connection to the past, close observation, and critical consciousness. We have provided book examples and described the characteristics of books that are well-suited to teaching for these purposes. But we believe teachers should be empowered to make instructional decisions based on knowledge of the field coupled with knowledge of the students in their care.

In this second part of the book, we offer a range of teaching invitations for you to consider for the books you have selected to use within the framework of purposes for reading that we have shared. Each chapter in Part II is focused on one of four purposes and relates to the corresponding chapter in Part I. Within the Part II chapters, the teaching invitations are organized by instructional-practice categories meant to construct a bridge between the purposes we emphasize and the everyday practices of schools. You may notice that we have not identified age ranges for these activities. We invite you to use your knowledge of your students to adapt the invitation to match their strengths and needs. At the end of each teaching invitation, we list a few titles well-matched to the activity to get you started, but these invitations can work well with a wide range of titles. As you review these teaching invitations, consider the ways they could shape the read-aloud and independent-reading responses your students make throughout the year and across texts. We hope you and your students enjoy these opportunities to engage, inquire, and create!

CHAPTER 6

Invitations to Use Books to Center Care for Ourselves and One Another

In Chapter 2, we described the many ways that books can support students to care for themselves and others. This learning can be deepened through teaching invitations that encourage students to affirm who they are and where they are from and respond to their emotions and the world around them, including experiences of loss. In this chapter, we offer a collection of such invitations to facilitate student responses, to inspire self-reflection, to create joy, to build compassion, and to interrogate inequity as a part of your literacy program using the children's literature selections we include or other books you have available. For a complete list of teaching invitations across purposes and practices, see our online materials under the download tab at https://www.tcpress.com/reading-with-purpose-9780807768501.

TEXT SETS

Message Books

In her review of *The Rabbit Listened* (Doerrfeld, 2018), Elizabeth Bird (2018) writes about "message books"—books where the message of the story gives us some instruction for how to live our lives. Some authors allow us to infer messages and how they apply to our own lives rather than using more didactic approaches. Classic children's book authors like Arnold Lobel of *Frog and Toad* and Leo Leonni of *Frederick* and *Matthew's Dream* remain some of the most poignant examples of message books as well as the more recent works suggested below. Gather together a "message books" text set and explore with students their responses to the characters and their situations. What are the messages these authors and illustrators offer us for how to live our lives with meaning, purpose, spontaneity, and joy?

Extra Yarn (Barnett, 2012)
The Rabbit Listened (Doerrfeld, 2018)

After the Fall (Santat, 2017)
The Antlered Ship (Slater, 2017)

Enduring Friendship

Books can help provide a roadmap for students to think of others and navigate the problems that can arise naturally in any friendship. Support students to describe the traits that make characters worthy friends using words like *compassionate, amiable, considerate, gracious, good-natured,* and *generous*. Invite students to notice the ways characters help one another in small ways by using text evidence to support their thinking. Also, draw students' attention to the various moments of conflict between characters who are friends that may mirror conflict in their own lives. Extend this conversation by supporting students to detect when conflicts seem to be fueled by social, racial, economic, or cultural differences and how those conflicts are resolved. Invite students to consider their own enduring friendships. Challenge students to surprise one of their friends by helping them in an unexpected way. Then, have students share what they did and what happened.

Maybe Maybe Marisol Rainey (Kelly, 2021b)
Rescue and Jessica (Kensky & Downes, 2018)
Fox + Chick (Ruzzier, 2018)
The Adventures of Beekle: The Unimaginary Friend (Santat, 2014)
A Sick Day for Amos McGee (Stead, 2010)

CONTENT CONNECTIONS AND DISCIPLINARY LITERACIES

Noticing Our Emotions When Learning About the Past

Learning about people and events of the past can often evoke strong emotions and inspire students to care about injustices today. Books like Kwame Alexander's *The Undefeated* (2019c) call on us to confront the historical underpinnings of racism to create a better world. Books like *Stonewall: A Building. An Uprising. A Revolution* (Sanders, 2019) inspire readers to feel strong emotions as they learn about the Gay Rights Movement and collective resistance. We recommend gathering a variety of books all year long that blend the purposes of care and connection to the past like those suggested below and encourage you to invite conversations about the strong emotions students may experience as they learn about historic injustices and how we live with the past today.

The Undefeated (Alexander, 2019c)
The Long Ride (Budhos, 2019)
Indian No More (McManis & Sorell, 2019)

Stonewall: A Building. An Uprising. A Revolution. (Sanders, 2019)
Paper Wishes (Sepahban, 2016)

Noticing Our Emotions When Learning About the Natural World

Learning about the natural world through children's literature can often inspire in students feelings of awe and wonder while also motivating them to take action as they learn about topics like climate change. Books like the Caldecott-winning picture book *Wonder Walkers* (Archer, 2021) pay tribute to the relationship between children's curiosity and nature, while the body of work by April Pulley Sayre inspires students to become backyard scientists who are called to watch, wonder, imagine, and inquire. Books such as *We Are Water Protectors* (Lindstrom, 2020) inspire students to question the injustices communities, particularly Indigenous communities, have faced regarding utilization of natural resources. We recommend gathering a variety of books all year long that blend the purposes of care and closely observe the world around us like those suggested below:

Wonder Walkers (Archer, 2021)
The Wisdom of Trees (Judge, 2021)
We Are Water Protectors (Lindstrom, 2020)
Raindrops Roll (Sayre, 2015)

CRITICAL LITERACIES

Juxtaposing Pain and Beauty

In her interview with CBS News about *The Year We Learned to Fly*, Jacqueline Woodson discusses the decision to include references to enslaved ancestors in the story. She explains the ways that artwork by Rafael López provides a juxtaposition to the pain of enslavement through his bright, luminous illustrations that give us a sense of hope without diminishing the pain of the past. Invite students to consider how authors and illustrators can work together to write about difficult and painful truths, particularly in history. Engage in a class conversation about how students could apply this juxtaposition in their own writing and artwork. Consider having students work in writing and illustrating partnerships to apply this juxtaposition as part of your social studies curriculum in response to learning about historical events or as a way of juxtaposing struggle and hope in their narrative writing.

Never Caught, The Story of Ona Judge (Dunbar & Van Cleve, 2019)
Drum Dream Girl: How One Girl's Courage Changed Music (Engle, 2015)
Heart and Soul: The Story of America and African Americans (Nelson, 2011)
The Year We Learned to Fly (Woodson, 2022)

READING PROCESS

Static and Dynamic Characters

Stories range in their power to elicit in readers strong feelings as well as quixotic questions about our life's purpose. Take, for example, the original Humpty Dumpty from the nursery rhyme who is a rather simple or static character, having no attributes or action other than falling off a wall. Dan Santat's *After the Fall* (2017) reconstructs Humpty Dumpty into a dynamic character, one with complexity and agency, who encourages us to consider our own falls and how to get back up again. Engage students in an inquiry about static and dynamic characters in traditional tales. What makes a character dynamic and gives a character complexity and depth? Have students do the same with characters in other genres (e.g., biography, contemporary realistic fiction, fantasy). After exploring qualities and examples of dynamic characters, challenge students to reconstruct traditional tales to make the main characters more dynamic. You might have them write and illustrate a fractured version of the tale (i.e., a traditional tale that has been modified with an unexpected twist), write and perform a dramatic enactment of the tale, or create a poem or song about the main character. Encourage them to employ the mode of representation in which they are strongest so that students can succeed in this activity and see a variety of ways their thinking can be represented.

> *Amari and the Night Brothers* (Alston, 2021)
> *The Last Cuentista* (Higuera, 2021)
> *The Night Diary* (Hiranandani, 2018)
> *When You Trap a Tiger* (Keller, 2020)
> *After the Fall: How Humpty Dumpty Got Back Up Again* (Santat, 2017)

Character Change

At the end of a powerful story, readers often marvel at how characters have changed from the beginning. Introduce your students to the concept of metamorphosis or character transformation. First, invite students to consider popular story characters, either in traditional tales or contemporary and popular ones, who undergo a metamorphosis (e.g., the ugly duckling, the little mermaid, even perhaps Cinderella). Are those changes for better or worse? Why? Then, have students identify the ways in which characters transform in the books you have read aloud in both fiction and nonfiction. What led to their personal transformations? What were the obstacles they encountered along the way? In what ways do the characters disrupt the status quo, thereby challenging unjust and inequitable structures? Have students explore the concept of metamorphosis in a number of ways, like creating character timelines, dramatizing turning points in a story, or creating collaborative murals.

Above the Rim (Bryant, 2020)
New Kid (Craft, 2019)
Dancing Hands (Engle, 2019)
A Boy and a Jaguar (Rabinowitz, 2014)

Predictions and Surprises

Many of the books we recommend invite students to make predictions and notice the ways that they are surprised by what happens next. When you read aloud, pause periodically to ask students what they think might happen next and to note the ways in which authors sometimes set us up to be surprised. Encourage students to say more about their predictions by using text evidence to support their thinking. Picture books, wordless picture books, and graphic novels support students to engage in the thinking strategies that apply to both words and pictures. Support students to build on this experience with predictions and surprises and apply this strategy to their own independent reading selections.

Wolf in the Snow (Cordell, 2017)
The Beatryce Prophecy (DiCamillo, 2021)
It Fell From the Sky (Fan & Fan, 2021)
The Floating Field (Riley, 2021)

VISUAL LITERACIES

Close Reading: Illustrations That Reveal Emotions

Draw students' attention to the ways illustrators create emotion through color, texture, white space, and the expressions on characters' faces. Support students to zoom in on select illustrations to consider how these artistic choices reveal the mood of the scene, how characters feel, their hopes, their dreams, their fears, and what their motivations might be. Support students to notice the relationship between the text and the illustrations. Then have students create their own illustrations, using a variety of materials such as graphite, colored pencils, watercolor, or digital techniques, to portray a scene from their own lives with the goal of revealing the emotions they were experiencing.

The Rabbit Listened (Doerrfeld, 2018)
The Tantrum That Saved the World (Herbert & Mann, 2022)
Tomatoes for Neela (Lakshmi, 2021)
Radiant Child: The Story of Young Artist Jean-Michel Basquiat (Steptoe, 2016)

WRITING DEVELOPMENT

Mentor Sentences

We can support students to notice how authors combine words into a variety of sentences to convey ideas that are often simple but profound. After reading books like *I Am Every Good Thing* (Barnes, 2020), invite students to find their favorite "I am" statements from the book and notice and name what Barnes does as a writer, including the use of sentences and fragments for effect and a variety of punctuation, sound words, repetition, and comparisons. Encourage students to write their own "I am ____." sentences. Display the statements in a classroom or hallway with student portraits (refer to Figure 2.1) or create a virtual slideshow of the statements with selfies taken by students that depict the emotions they want their sentences to convey. Share other books that play with repetition and other craft techniques and invite students to look for mentor sentences they can adapt in their own writing.

> *I Am Every Good Thing* (Barnes, 2020)
> *Going Down Home With Daddy* (Lyons, 2019)
> *When We Are Kind* (Smith, 2020)

Figurative Language

Books that enhance our capacity to care may also include examples of figurative language as authors seek to convey emotions and tap into sensory information such as on the first page of Jerry Craft's *New Kid* (2019) where the main character, Jordan, explains that he feels like he is falling without a parachute. Keep an eye out for examples of figurative language, such as similes, metaphors, and personification, and share these with students, perhaps documenting the examples on an anchor chart. Use the examples you collect as a class as an invitation for students to try out these techniques in the writing they are doing across the content areas.

> *How to Read a Book* (Alexander, 2019b)
> *Everything Comes Next* (Nye, 2020)
> *I Am the Storm* (Yolen & Stemple, 2021)

MULTIMODAL RESPONSE

Retelling Through Drama and Movement

Picture books and wordless (and nearly wordless) picture books are ripe with opportunities for storytelling. Enjoy the many ways of telling and retelling books by inviting your students to participate in the storytelling process. You may want to have students each take a page to share what they see happening using words like *first*, *next*, *then*, *after that*, and *finally*. Students may enjoy using choral reading, which offer opportunities to become the characters. Encourage students to go back to the book's illustrations to notice the facial expressions and body language of the characters to help them become the characters. Think about simple props and costumes to make those role-playing opportunities come to life. Using their bodies, students can think about how to portray the characters' struggles and compassion for one another. They can even imagine what the characters are thinking and feeling along the way. You also may want to incorporate new technologies into the storytelling process to capture your students' voices by using apps like Voice Memos, Shadow Puppet Edu, or ShowMe, which offer audio, and in some cases, visual possibilities. Following group performances, have students share what they noticed were similarities and differences in their interpretations of the story. Support students to reflect on the ways this experience can enhance their understanding of characters in future books they read.

The Rabbit Listened (Doerrfeld, 2018)
We Are Water Protectors (Lindstrom, 2020)
The Year We Learned to Fly (Woodson, 2022)

Composing Graphic Texts

Extend student understanding of how to convey emotion through words and images by having students create their own graphic texts. Have students first consider a story worthy of telling either from their own lives or from their imaginations or from a hybrid of both. Create a class list of must-haves and can-haves with student input to support their composing process. Encourage students to engage in a composing process that works for them whether they choose to storyboard the illustrations first, write a scene with dialogue, or partner with a classmate to plan the story together. When completed, have students present their stories to one another either by projecting them with a document camera, scanning them into a class blog, photocopying them for distribution, or by making them available in the classroom library for independent reading.

Grace for Gus (Bliss, 2018)
New Kid (Craft, 2019)
Flora and Ulysses (DiCamillo, 2013)
March: Book Three (Lewis & Aydin, 2016)
Snow White: A Graphic Novel (Phelan, 2016)
Fox + Chick: The Party and Other Stories (Ruzzier, 2018)

Mixing Media

Illustrators today use a variety of media to craft their illustrations, including various paints, colored pencils, scraps of paper, pages of books, photographs, and other found materials, to convey ideas and evoke emotion in readers. Gather a variety of books that use mixed media for students to explore such as those listed below. After closely studying the illustrations, have students create their own picture books using a variety of media.

How to Read a Book (Alexander, 2019b)
The Undefeated (Alexander, 2019c)
Firefly July: A Year of Very Short Poems (Janeczko, 2014)
Brave Girl: Clara and the Shirtwaist Makers' Strike of 1909 (Markel, 2013)
Some Writer! The Story of E. B. White (Sweet, 2016)

SOCIAL-EMOTIONAL LEARNING

Self-Discovery

Books can serve as touchstones for students and their evolving identities. Questions like "Who am I?" "Why am I me?" "What is important to me?" and "Who will I be?" are often unstated but can be inferred as characters navigate complex social relationships. Support students to identify moments in texts where characters seem to wrestle with philosophical questions and their evolving identities on the path to self-discovery. Invite students to make connections to characters and events in texts and to ask questions about the ways in which their own identities are evolving (refer to Figure 2.3).

Why Am I Me? (Britt, 2017)
Islandborn (Diaz, 2018)
Hello, Universe (Kelly, 2017)
Here I Am (Kim, 2014)
Merci Suárez Changes Gears (Medina, 2018)
Where Are You From? (Méndez, 2019)

Affirming Our Worthiness

The books that fill our classroom bookshelves can help students better understand themselves, their aspirations, and their contributions. Gather a variety of books that explicitly support children to love themselves exactly as they are from the shape of their eyes to the melody of their names. Bettina Love gives us language for how to help students know and love themselves in her foreword to *Cultivating Genius: An Equity Framework for Culturally and Historically Responsive Literacy* (Muhammad, 2020): "You must know who you are and why you are important to this world, and learn how to be you" (p. 6). Read aloud a variety of books that explicitly support students to reflect on their strengths and inherent worthiness. Invite them to record through writing and artwork who they are as a way to build classroom community and support students to have an affirmational inner voice (refer to Figures 2.2 and 2.3).

Crown: An Ode to the Fresh Cut (Barnes, 2017)
I Am Every Good Thing (Barnes, 2020)
Eyes That Kiss in the Corners (Ho, 2021)
Fish in a Tree (Hunt, 2015)
Flying Lessons & Other Stories (Oh, 2017)
Your Name Is a Song (Thompkins-Bigelow, 2020)

Noticing and Naming Our Emotions

Many books that expand our capacity to care invite us to feel strong emotions and help us build our own emotional agility to navigate the complex and sometimes unexpected challenges and losses we face in life. Share with students graphics like an Emotion Wheel that can broaden students' emotional vocabulary as well as everyday tools for naming their emotions like the Mood Meter created by the Yale Center for Emotional Intelligence. Support students to use more precise vocabulary to describe how characters in books feel, including words like *frustrated, content, optimistic, dismayed, rejected,* and *exuberant*. Use books like those listed below as a way to launch a yearlong focus on how characters can help us recognize and navigate our own strong emotions with more precise language.

Joy (Averiss, 2018)
Bear Island (Cordell, 2021)
Your Name Is a Song (Thompkins-Bigelow, 2020)
I Am the Storm (Yolen & Stemple, 2021)

Listening With Care

Learning to listen is hard, especially when something upsetting happens to someone we love. As we described in Chapter 2, characters like the rabbit in *The Rabbit Listened* (Doerrfeld, 2018) can model for students how to respond when unexpected challenges or losses arise for the people in our lives. Use books like *The Rabbit Listened* to encourage students to consider what it looks like and sounds like to listen with care. Extend this by having students consider others way to listen like listening to nature, listening for peace, and listening for silence. Gather a variety of books that explore different ways we can listen as a way to bring care to others and calm and stillness into our own lives.

Extra Yarn (Barnett, 2012)
Shelter (Claire, 2017)

The Rabbit Listened (Doerrfeld, 2018)
Becoming a Good Creature (Montgomery, 2020)
A Stone Sat Still (Wenzel, 2019)

Love Is All Around

What is love? How can we pay more attention to it? How can we show love to others? Books can help us celebrate what it means to love and be loved. Use a wide variety of books to show students how love is communicated through actions, nature, objects, gestures, expressions, and the sharing of memories. Read aloud books that help students better understand love in families, friendships, and communities. Invite students to respond in some way such as writing letters to loved ones to express their gratitude, creating a class mural that artistically expresses love, or having students go out into the community to document moments of love that they see or hear.

Joy (Averiss, 2018)
Love (de la Peña, 2018)
I Am Loved (Giovanni, 2018)
Eyes That Kiss in the Corners (Ho, 2021)
Tomatoes for Neela (Lakshmi, 2021)
Going Down Home With Daddy (Lyons, 2019)
Dad Bakes (Yamasaki, 2021)

Honoring the Loss of Loved Ones

"It's not fair," thought Louise, "when the things we love must end." As we described in Chapter 2, in *Bear Island* (2021), Caldecott-winning author and illustrator Matthew Cordell affirms for children that they can find resilience and hope in the midst of grief. With deep respect for the child as a reader, authors like Cordell and those who wrote the books listed below offer children a path forward for how to wander through grief to a place of reassurance. We recommend reading aloud books that address grief without forcing conversation about loss or trauma on children. Rather, stories themselves may invite students to share connections about losing someone special in their own lives. Before initiating a conversation about grief and loss with children, the National Institutes of Health Clinical Center (2015) encourages adults to develop their own awareness about such topics and to reflect on their own feelings and beliefs. When talking with children, NIH recommends demonstrating an openness that invites children to communicate, shows acceptance toward children's feelings, offers honest information, and answers questions in understandable and age-appropriate language. How we process grief is personal, yet one thing we may have in common is a range of feelings that we experience, including anger, despair, and acceptance. Support students to discuss how the authors and illustrators use various techniques to convey the emotions that characters feel over the course of a story and how they process loss and rekindle hope.

The Crossover (Alexander, 2014)
The One and Only Ivan (Applegate, 2012)
Bear Island (Cordell, 2021)
The Rabbit Listened (Doerrfeld, 2018)
Ocean Meets Sky (Fan & Fan, 2018)

Living With Uncertainty and Doubt

"Life begins when you get back up"—so says the blurb on the back cover of Caldecott Medal winner Dan Santat's (2017) *After the Fall: How Humpty Dumpty Got Back Up Again*. But how does one "get back up" again? Through the events that transpire, *After the Fall* conveys some of the key tenets of living with uncertainty by embracing flexible thinking and having a growth mindset. Use *After the Fall* to spark discussion about what these concepts mean and how they can apply to all aspects of students' lives. Push students to think beyond how those concepts apply to themselves to how they can help foster a more socially just and kind world, moving toward a dynamic learning frame, which is a growth mindset incorporated with civil engagement and social thinking and responsibility.

After the Fall: How Humpty Dumpty Got Back Up Again (Santat, 2017)
Bear Island (Cordell, 2021)
It Fell From the Sky (Fan & Fan, 2021)
What Do You Do With a Chance? (Yamada, 2018)

Paying Attention to What Brings Us Joy

"Joy is what makes your heart happy and your eyes twinkle." So explains Fern's mother when her daughter asks, "What's joy?" Books like *Joy* and those below invite young readers to consider the power each of us has to pay attention to joy in our own lives and bring joy to others. Through shared or interactive writing, start a class joy list that documents students' ideas about things in life that bring them joy. Extend this conversation to include when learning, reading, and writing feel joyful. Have students create their own joy lists in notebooks and periodically provide opportunities for students to reflect on new things in life that bring them joy and invite them to share those things with the class. Go on a field trip around the school or local neighborhood for students to notice and name things they see that are joyful. Have students record what they find through pictures, words, and/or photographs. You may want to extend this to families as an opportunity for home-school literacy connections, and have students engage in a joy hunt in their homes or neighborhoods to add to their initial joy findings.

Wonder Walkers (Archer, 2021)
Joy (Averiss, 2018)
Tiny, Perfect Things (Clark, 2018)
Most Days (Leannah, 2021)

Out of the Book and Into the World

Many of the books we feature invite students to leave their mark on the world in some way. One such book is *Wishtree* by Katherine Applegate (2017) told from the refreshing point of view of Red, a seasoned oak tree. Each year on May 1st, Red becomes a wishtree following the ancient tradition of people hanging scraps of paper and bits of fabric (and the occasional gym sock) with wishes written on them. Reading *Wishtree* would be incomplete without inviting students to leave their own wishes on a local tree for those passing by to contemplate. Books like *The Tantrum That Saved the World* (Herbert & Mann, 2022) and *No Voice Too Small: Fourteen Young Americans Making History* (Metcalf et al., 2020) model for students how to engage in cooperative action for the causes they care about by making signs, engaging in marches, and using their voices to enact change. Books like these, both fiction and nonfiction, invite us to get out of the book and into the world. Consider the books in your classroom collections that invite students to engage with the world in some way to enhance their reading experience.

Can We Help? Kids Volunteering to Help Their Communities (Ancona, 2015)
Wishtree (Applegate, 2017)
Change Sings (Gorman, 2021a)
Dictionary for a Better World (Latham & Waters, 2020)
No Voice Too Small: Fourteen Young Americans Making History (Metcalf et al., 2020)
One Plastic Bag: Isatou Ceesay and the Recycling Women of the Gambia (Paul, 2015a)
Wangari Maathai: The Woman Who Planted Millions of Trees (Prevot, 2015)

CHAPTER 7

Invitations to Use Books to Connect the Past to the Present

In Chapter 3, we described the many ways that books can prompt students to connect to the past and think more deeply about the ways in which it shapes our present. This engagement can be deepened through teaching invitations that encourage students to investigate, document, wonder about, and respond to the world of the past. In this chapter, we offer a collection of invitations to facilitate student responses. For a complete list of teaching invitations across purposes and practices, see our online materials under the download tab at https://www.tcpress.com/reading-with-purpose-9780807768501.

TEXT SETS

Exploring an Enduring Concept: Migration

Provide your students with a range of texts—fiction, nonfiction, and poetry—about human migration. Some of these migrations are forced, some are chosen. All are complicated. Leverage these stories to document new ones. First, have students work in small groups to note the similarities and differences they see across the books in their text set. What are some common experiences of human migration? Next, turn to the memories of migration shared by members of your community. Work with leaders in your community to invite into your classroom parents and grandparents, neighbors, shopkeepers and business owners, senior citizens, artists, and fellow educators who have their own migration and immigration stories. Together with your students, brainstorm a list of questions they can draw upon in their interviews. Match each student or pairs of students with a guest. Use tablets, laptops, or phones to document the stories they tell. Have students write—or write with your guests, depending on their own facility with shared documents—and illustrate those stories, using photographs or original illustrations. Publish this class book, have copies available to all via your school and local public library, and, ideally, hold a celebratory public reading.

Ira's Shakespeare Dream (Armand, 2015)
Marwan's Journey (de Arias, 2018)

Islandborn (Diaz, 2018)
Never Caught, the Story of Ona Judge: George and Martha Washington's Courageous Slave Who Dared to Run Away (Dunbar & Van Cleve, 2019)
The Night Diary (Hiranandani, 2018)
Indian No More (McManis & Sorell, 2019)
La Frontera: El Viaje con Papá/My Journey with Papa (Mills & Alva, 2018)
Dreamers (Morales, 2018)
The Journey (Sana, 2016)
Escape from Aleppo (Senzai, 2018)

Comparing Within a Time Period

Text sets are ideal for digging deeply into a single time period to explore from a range of perspectives, places, and experiences. Gather fiction and nonfiction books to serve as the core of your text set. Drawing on available online primary sources, also curate a selection of multimodal resources that your students can examine. Support students in making connections across the different texts. What are the similarities and differences in the books they are reading? What are some of the overriding trends they can observe across different events? What are the primary tensions of this era? Allow students a range of multimodal choices for showing what they have learned. For example, they can create "new" primary sources from the time period, or create their own secondary source on the time period, with each student contributing a short chapter. For example, you'll find some books focused on the 18th century in the list below.

Ashes (Anderson, 2017)
Forge (Anderson, 2010)
Fault Lines in the Constitution: The Framers, Their Fights, and the Laws That Affect Us Today (Levinson & Levinson, 2019)
Mesmerized: How Ben Franklin Solved a Mystery That Baffled All of France (Rockliff, 2015)
The Notorious Benedict Arnold: A True Story of Adventure, Heroism, and Treachery (Sheinkin, 2010)
Mumbet's Declaration of Independence (Woelfe, 2014)

CONTENT CONNECTIONS AND DISCIPLINARY LITERACIES

Leveraging Backmatter

The presence of backmatter, which we introduced in Chapter 3, has expanded in nonfiction and historical fiction for young people, providing readers with many opportunities to consider the information they have learned in the primary text and its relation to the larger body of work available on the topic. Authors and illustrators not only share their source material, but they often discuss their research journeys, the challenges of sourcing, and the decisions they had to make about interpreting primary sources and navigating historical gaps. Have students explore a range of texts on a particular historical topic, and compare and contrast the backmatter and the ways in which it deepens their understanding of not only the topic of the book, but the process of "doing history."

> *Grand Canyon* (Chin, 2017)
> *Dave the Potter* (Hill, 2010)
> *Courage Has No Color* (Stone, 2013)

Hedges

As we explained in Chapter 3, historians, anthropologists, archeologists, and other professionals who study the past often use language to signal to their readers what they know or do not know about a topic on which they are writing. Sometimes information that is available is inconclusive. Sometimes extant information presents conflicting results. Oftentimes gaps persist. How do authors share these uncertainties with their readers? Have students track this perspective-taking while reading nonfiction books about the past. Support students in connecting the primary text and the backmatter by looking for connections between the two. When does the backmatter explain gaps in information or competing/conflicting sources? When possible, have students try out this technique in their own writing.

> *Cloaked in Courage: Uncovering Deborah Sampson, Patriot Soldier.* (Anderson, 2022)
> *Searching for Sarah Rector: The Richest Black Girl in America* (Bolden, 2014)
> *Never Caught, the Ona Judge Story: George and Martha Washington's Courageous Slave Who Dared to Run Away* (Dunbar & Van Cleve, 2019)
> *The Family Romanov: Murder, Rebellion, and the Fall of Imperial Russia* (Fleming, 2014)

Doing Historical Research

Your School. What is the history of your school? Whom or what is it named after and why? Is your class in the original building? How has it changed over the years? First, have students walk around the school looking for plaques, markers, or architectural features that might give them clues about the school's history and its relative age. Work with your local library and historical society to obtain resources about the history of your school building and its founding. Who attended? Who did not? Why? When did that change? If students attend a newly built school, have them interview local leaders about the decision to build a new school site. Why and how was the physical location and school name selected? Invite community elders into the classroom, and have students record interviews with them to learn about their memories of the school in years past, or work with alums of the school who have milestone reunions to capture their varied memories and experiences. Invite students to compose their own illustrated history of the school. The following books can be a catalyst for exploration of your school.

The Long Ride (Budhos, 2019)
The First Step: How One Girl Put Segregation on Trial (Goodman, 2016)
Rain School (Rumford, 2010)
Separate Is Never Equal: Sylvia Mendez and Her Family's Fight for Desegregation (Tonatiuh, 2014)
One Wish: Fatima Al-Fihri and the World's Oldest University (Yuksel, 2022)

Indigenous History of Your Community. You may be teaching in a community in which there remains a large Indigenous population; you and your students may be members or citizens of one of those nations. But you may be teaching in a community where there are fewer federally recognized nations, and/or smaller Indigenous populations. If so, have students use the Native Land interactive map to obtain the names of the Indigenous peoples who originally lived on the land upon which your school sits. Use the links provided from Native Land, as well as the resources such as the National Museum of the American Indian, the National Congress of American Indians, *Indian Country Today*, and tribal/national websites, to support your students in researching this Indigenous nation. When possible, bring in local members of the nation or have them Zoom into your classroom to talk about their lives and the current and traditional cultural norms of their nation. If possible, have students interview these members of your community, and coauthor texts with them. Students and Indigenous community members may want to write about 20th- and 21st-century events and experiences, or about contemporary culture. Host a community reading and celebration of these coauthored texts.

An Indigenous People's History of the United States for Young People (Dunbar-Ortiz et al., 2019)
We Are Water Protectors (Lindstrom, 2020)
Fry Bread: A Native American Family Story (Maillard, 2019)
Indian No More (McManis & Sorell, 2019)
Ancestor Approved (Smith, 2021)
We Are Still Here! Native American Truths Everyone Should Know (Sorell, 2021)

A Decade in Your Community's History. What reminders of the past exist in your town? Have students brainstorm different time periods they are curious about and what artifacts from that time (buildings, monuments, etc.) are still present. Select a single decade to focus your exploration. Take students to the local library and/or your local historical society to conduct research, or have representatives come to your school. Encourage students to look at primary sources, such as newspaper articles, signs and posters, official letters, and records. Once they have gathered enough information, have students consider the various ways they could write about and illustrate the selected decade. For example, have them try out different ways of organizing information they have gathered to create a coherent presentation, or try writing from different points of view. Once they have settled on some direction, have them write and illustrate a nonfiction picture book or a series of books of different genres about that time period. Students can draw upon the list of books below—fiction and nonfiction texts that feature Harlem during the Harlem Renaissance, mostly in the 1920s—as models for how you write about different people and moments within a community within a single era. Share your student writing with the larger community beyond the school.

Legacy: Women Poets of the Harlem Renaissance (Grimes, 2021)
Augusta Savage: The Shape of a Sculptor's Life (Nelson, 2022)
The Book Itch: Freedom, Truth, and Harlem's Greatest Bookstore (Nelson, 2015)
Jazz Day: The Making of a Famous Photograph (Orgill, 2016)
Josephine: The Dazzling Life of Josephine Baker (Powell, 2014)
The Harlem Charade (Tarpley, 2017)
Sugar Hill: Harlem's Historic Neighborhood (Weatherford, 2014)

CRITICAL LITERACIES

Comparing Biographies

Comparing and contrasting biographies of the same historical figure makes visible the historical process and the work of researching and writing history. In *History Makers: A Questioning Approach to Reading & Writing Biographies*, Myra Zarnowski (2003) encourages exploration of multiple biographies of the same figure to move students from the concrete to the more abstract. Through comparison and contrast, students are able to see how different writers may focus on different aspects of a subject's life, or use different sources, or focus on a different theme. Some may offer conflicting information. More recent biographies may draw on more recently available source material. An active and questioning stance "draws children closer to the discipline of history because it taps the kinds of questions historians ask and requires the kind of sense making that historians practice" (p. 3). Gather a collection of biographies on a historical figure and invite your students to compare and contrast the ways in which that figure is represented. When students have the opportunity to read across biographies of the same subject, they can be more critical readers of future biographies, empowered to read against the text to consider how else the information could have been shared. Below you will find excellent biographies to serve as your starting point for biography text-set development; multiple biographies have been written about these pioneers.

> *Counting on Katherine: How Katherine Johnson Saved Apollo 13* (Becker, 2018)
> *I Dissent! Ruth Bader Ginsburg Makes Her Mark* (Levy, 2016)
> *Ada Lovelace, Poet of Science: The First Computer Programmer* (Stanley, 2016)

READING PROCESS

Navigating Graphic Books About the Past

One aspect of reading is understanding the different types of tools needed to navigate a text beyond genre knowledge. We read picture books, chapter books, and graphic books differently. Immerse your students in reading about the past within a graphic book format. Some of your students prefer to read graphic books and may exhibit expert reading skills that you do not always see with traditional picture books or chapter books. Others may find the format overwhelming, and need support with understanding the ways in which the different text features and panels work together to create meaning.

> *Drowned City: Hurricane Katrina and New Orleans* (Brown, 2015)
> *In the Shadow of the Fallen Towers: The Seconds, Minutes, Hours, Days, Weeks, Months, and Years After the September 11th Attacks* (Brown, 2021)
> *March: Book Three* (Lewis & Aydin, 2016)
> *Snow White: A Graphic Novel* (Phelan, 2016)

VISUAL LITERACIES

Nonfiction Picture Book Illustrator Study

Collect a range of nonfiction picture books of interest to your students; look for books with backmatter that includes information from the illustrators about their research and creative process. Provide students with time to read and explore these books, and to note the similarities and differences across the illustrations and the backmatter. Have students learn more about the illustrators by exploring their websites. Have students share what they have learned about the creative process, and perhaps identify criteria that they would use to verify the authenticity of illustrations based on what the illustrators share in the backmatter and online.

> *A Splash of Red: The Art of Horace Pippin* (Bryant, 2013)
> *Grand Canyon* (Chin, 2017)
> *Separate Is Never Equal: Sylvia Mendez and Her Family's Fight for Desegregation* (Tonatiuh, 2014)
> *The Teachers March! How Selma's Teachers Changed History* (Wallace & Wallace, 2020)

Illustrating Nonfiction Chapter Books

As we discussed in Chapter 3, nonfiction illustrators take a great deal of care to research their topic to create authentic illustrations reflective of another time and place. Authors of chapter-length nonfiction identify important primary sources, documents, and photographs they include as illustrations in their book, to help readers visualize what they are reading. But sometimes, books are not heavily illustrated. Gather a range of nonfiction chapter books. Have your students compare and contrast their formats, when the books include visuals, and why. Next, divide them into groups and have them read a complete chapter within one of the books. Have the group decide what visuals they think belong in that chapter. Support them in doing research to identify possible visuals. Some students may choose to draw their own visuals to accompany the chapter, building off of the descriptions and information within the text. Some students may also decide to create charts or graphs to help facilitate understanding of important concepts or sequences of events. Have each group report their findings to the whole class.

> *Fault Lines in the Constitution: The Framers, Their Fights, and the Laws That Affect Us Today* (Levinson & Levinson, 2019)
> *Bomb: The Race to Build—and Steal—the World's Most Dangerous Weapon* (Sheinkin, 2012)
> *Courage Has No Color* (Stone, 2013)

WRITING DEVELOPMENT

Paragraphing Possibilities

As educators, we always are looking for mentor texts to support students with different craft moves. Gather together a collection of well-written nonfiction books and ask your students to explore how paragraphs operate. Ask them to notice how paragraphs vary in length to help shape mood and tone and build tension. Assign students a page or two to reread in pairs. What do they notice about the paragraph lengths? Why do they vary? What emotional impact does that have on the reader? How do the paragraphs help the reader process information? Have students share their observations and responses, and develop a classwide "Nonfiction Style Guide" in which they offer tips on varying paragraph lengths in their writing for different authorial purposes.

> *The First Step: How One Girl Put Segregation on Trial* (Goodman, 2016)
> *Thirty Minutes Over Oregon: A Japanese Pilot's World War II Story* (Nobleman, 2018)
> *The Teachers March! How Selma's Teachers Changed History* (Wallace & Wallace, 2020)

Descriptive Setting

Establishing setting is an important element of historical writing. Readers benefit from being able to visualize the past, as discussed in Chapter 3. Provide your students with opportunities to practice their descriptive writing techniques. Gather several samples of strong descriptions of setting from historical fiction, nonfiction, or biography. Look closely at different descriptions of setting from the various books and have students identify what makes them successful at conjuring a visualization within the reader's mind. Next, provide students with historic photographs or paintings curated from museum websites, and have them do a series of quick writes using the different pictures. Students can select a favorite one to further focus on. As students finalize their paragraphs, provide them with opportunities to compare and contrast their written descriptions with one another and the original visuals.

> *Ashes* (Anderson, 2017)
> *The Family Romanov: Murder, Rebellion, and the Fall of Imperial Russia* (Fleming, 2014)
> *The Inquisitor's Tale: Or, the Three Magical Children and Their Holy Dog* (Gidwitz, 2016)
> *The Great Trouble: A Mystery of London, the Blue Death, and a Boy Called Eel* (Hopkinson, 2013)

MULTIMODAL RESPONSE

History Podcasts

Create a "history podcast" in your classroom as a way to foster a spirit of historical inquiry throughout the year. Working with your school or public librarian, have a rotating shelf of "new-to-the-classroom" historical fiction, nonfiction, or biography available for students to read. As students finish books, they can write up a book review and then record it on a tablet or laptop as an audio or video file. Pick a time during the week when you play a history podcast in class or, better yet, have the history podcast played over the loudspeaker during morning announcements.

> *Counting on Katherine: How Katherine Johnson Saved Apollo 13* (Becker, 2018)
> *Unspeakable: The Tulsa Race Massacre* (Weatherford, 2021)
> *One Wish: Fatima Al-Fihri and the World's Oldest University* (Yuksel, 2022)

SOCIAL-EMOTIONAL LEARNING

Community Healing and Reconciliation

Throughout time, terrible things have happened to good people. Communities tear apart. Nations fight. Civil rights are denied to people because of their identities. But human beings are resilient and, eventually, collective action can work toward healing and change. Spend time exploring difficult moments from history with your students, with an emphasis on the ways in which healing work has happened in the aftermath. Who or what was the catalyst for healing or reconciliation? How did people work together to effect change? What work remains to be done?

> *In the Shadow of the Fallen Towers: The Seconds, Minutes, Hours, Days, Weeks, Months, and Years after the September 11th Attacks* (Brown, 2021)
> *Thirty Minutes Over Oregon: A Japanese Pilot's World War II Story* (Nobleman, 2018)
> *We Are Still Here! Native American Truths Everyone Should Know* (Sorell, 2021)
> *Unspeakable: The Tulsa Race Massacre* (Weatherford, 2021)

CHAPTER 8

Invitations to Use Books to Closely Observe the World Around Us

In Chapter 4, we described the many ways that books can prompt students to become close observers of the world around them. This engagement can be deepened through teaching invitations that encourage students to notice, document, wonder about, and respond to their world. In this chapter, we offer a collection of such invitations to facilitate student responses. For a complete list of teaching invitations across purposes and practices, see our online materials under the download tab at https://www.tcpress.com/reading-with-purpose-9780807768501.

TEXT SETS

Interdependence

The interdependence of plants, animals, and humans within an ecosystem is an important understanding to be gleaned from careful observations of the world around us and a key element of science content standards. Create a text set of titles that demonstrate how elements of the natural world interact and are dependent on those interactions. Students can work in small groups, each group exploring a title and creating a visual representation of the interdependence featured in their book, which they report to the rest of the class. Support the students to connect their learning to observations in the world around them. What examples of interdependence occur in their environment every day?

> *Seeds Move!* (Page, 2019)
> *High Tide for Horseshoe Crabs* (Schnell, 2015)
> *Welcome to the Neighborwood* (Sheehy, 2015)
> *No Monkeys, No Chocolate* (Stewart, 2013)

Biographies of Naturalists

Work with your school or local public librarian to create a text set featuring naturalists, conservationists, and/or scientists who study the natural world. Invite students to compare and contrast the lives featured in these books. What obstacles did they face? What discoveries did they make? How was their scientific work received? What differences do you notice across time periods? Pay special attention to how the processes of science are reflected in these life stories. What can students learn about how science is carried out?

> *Rachel Carson and Her Book That Changed the World* (Lawlor, 2012)
> *Life in the Ocean: The Story of Oceanographer Sylvia Earle* (Nivola, 2012)
> *Wangari Maathai: The Woman Who Planted Millions of Trees* (Prevot, 2015)
> *The Watcher: Jane Goodall's Life With the Chimps* (Winter, 2011)

Nature as Inspiration for Artists

Many artists draw their inspiration from the beauty of the natural world. Gather a text set of picture book biographies of artists known for celebrating nature through their artwork. Notice the different media used by the artists and differences in their style. Be sure to include a broad representation of artists with different cultural backgrounds and life experiences and from different time periods. Use museum sites and other online resources to view these artists' works. Offer students time to compare, contrast, and ask questions about the art. Collaborate with your school's art specialist or a local artist to offer students an opportunity to create their own nature-inspired works.

> *A Splash of Red: The Life and Art of Horace Pippin* (Bryant, 2013)
> *Edward Hopper Paints His World* (Burleigh, 2014)
> *Ablaze With Color: A Story of Painter Alma Thomas* (Harvey, 2022)
> *Georgia in Hawaii: When Georgia O'Keefe Painted What She Pleased* (Novesky, 2012)

CONTENT CONNECTIONS AND DISCIPLINARY LITERACIES

Observing Our Surroundings: A Sensory Exploration

Give your students small journals, even if they are simply folded and stapled pieces of paper; have them decorate the cover. As students begin to draft their observations of the surroundings, have them focus on what is beautiful. Each day for a week, ask your students to stop for 10 minutes and look around them. As they look, they should list the people and things they see. Have them also consider their other senses as well, to make sure that all students, including those who are visually impaired, can participate. What do they smell and hear? What do they taste? Next, they must try to draw a picture of the view as a whole or one close-up image. The one rule is that students cannot stop at the same time every day. They have to pick different points during the day. You might include a picture of a clock on the inside cover of the journal, for students to check off time slots as they move through the week. By doing this, they can capture before, during, and after school life. When they are done with a week's worth of observations, have students select a single moment to write about in-depth.

> *Last Stop on Market Street* (de la Peña, 2015)
> *Here and Now* (Denos, 2019)
> *Windows* (Denos, 2017)

Observing Animal Behavior

Students can practice the skills of scientists by being observers of live animals. Launch this exploration by sharing with the whole class an interesting animal video connected to your topic of study or relevant to students' current interests. Invite students to share their noticings and record them on a large anchor chart. Next, divide students into small groups and provide them with time to observe different animal species on webcams multiple times during a week or two at different times of day, recording their observations in journals (for example, see Earth Cam: Animal Cams and New York Times: The Best Live Animal Feeds From Around the World). Ask students to look back through their observation journals, noting any patterns they observed in animal behavior over time. Each group can share their findings with the whole class. Students who show particular interest in this activity can be encouraged to conduct a longer observation of an animal in nature near their home. If students or their neighbors have a pet, suggest that students take notes and photos (or draw pictures) of the pet at different times during the day. If you have a class pet or a class bird feeder, students can make these observations in the classroom when/if they have in-person learning. Students also can go for walks in their neighborhoods or nearby parks, or make observations in their yards if they have them, at different times of day about different kinds of animals. If possible, invite someone who studies the behavior of animals to your classroom to talk about their observational techniques and documentation processes.

> *Look Up! Bird-Watching in Your Own Backyard* (Cate, 2013)
> *Secrets of the Sea: The Story of Jeanne Power, Revolutionary Marine Scientist* (Griffith, 2021)
> *Becoming a Good Creature* (Montgomery, 2020)
> *Being Frog* (Sayre, 2020)

Collecting Questions/Wonder Walls

Fascinating information about the world around us can be found in nonfiction for children, including the processes of scientists and naturalists who ask questions and seek answers, and the work of artists and poets. Such information can serve as inspiration for children to develop a sense of wonder and a spirit of inquiry. Develop a culture in your classroom of honoring, documenting, and pursuing the questions that students have about the world around them. Create structures in your classroom to collect students' questions. These might be repositories, such as wonder walls, wonder boxes, and anchor charts, or they might be routines, such as a student-led "question of the day" discussion or a time dedicated to writing in "wonder journals."

>*Wonder Walkers* (Archer, 2021)
>*Grand Canyon* (Chin, 2017)
>*Giant Squid* (Fleming, 2016)
>*Dr. Fauci: How a Boy From Brooklyn Became America's Doctor* (Messner, 2021)

Ask a Scientist

Extend your exploration of the topic or theme of a book that invites close observation by arranging for students to meet with local naturalists or environmental scientists in person or via Zoom. Students can prepare for the visit by crafting a list of questions to pose to the scientists. Depending on the age of your students, you may want to do some modeling of the use of question words and explore the difference between "what" and "why" questions. Following the visit, invite your students to think about and share an aspect of the natural world that interests them—working as a naturalist or a scientist, what would they study?

Pattern Finding

Close observers of the natural world are inclined to notice and name the patterns they discover. These patterns might be visual, like the stripes on a zebra, the swirls in a seashell, or the shapes of fern leaves. They might also be patterns of behaviors or occurrences, cycles in nature. Books that note the patterns in our natural world serve as invitations to notice, document, and inquire about the patterns that students encounter in their daily lives. Patterns and cycles can be explored through visual arts, movement experiences, journal entries, and text-based responses.

>*Mysterious Patterns: Finding Fractals in Nature* (Campbell, 2014)
>*Round* (Sidman, 2018)
>*Swirl by Swirl: Patterns in Nature* (Sidman, 2011)

CRITICAL LITERACIES

Perceptions and Portrayals of Animals

As students read about different animal species in our environment, draw their attention to how words are used to reinforce or counteract stereotypes or negative perceptions of particular species. Discuss why some animals are not given more attention in children's literature or nonfiction texts. What kinds of animals get popular attention? Why? Consider the usefulness of the animal to humans, as well as the attractiveness of the animal. What do the answers to those questions tell you about the "objectivity" of nonfiction? For example, share Isabel Thomas's *Moth: An Evolution Story* (2019). Despite their delicate frame, moths are some of the most feared and detested insects. The sympathetic text and wonderful word choice of Thomas help to combat those perceptions. In reality, moths are greatly misunderstood, are often as beautiful as butterflies, and serve a critical role as pollinators. How different are they from butterflies? Ask students to select an animal they think is maligned or misperceived and invite them to play with descriptive language to construct a positive portrait of this animal.

Lesser Spotted Animals (Brown, 2016)
Superlative Birds (Bulion, 2019)
Wolf in the Snow (Cordell, 2017)
Moth: An Evolution Story (Thomas, 2019)

Youth Activists for the Environment: Writing About Agency and Activism

Gather and read a collection of titles that feature youth activists for climate justice and environmental literacy. Engage students in a close reading to examine the language that is used to describe the stance and actions of the youth featured in the book, and any adult interactions. How are the young people described—what verbs and adjectives are used? How do these words position the young people? Do they have power? Hope? Agency? Next examine the language that is used to depict the challenges to the environment. What kinds of nouns, verbs, and adjectives are used to frame the problem? How does the author use language to create an image/sense of what the future may hold? Is the language hopeful, despairing, threatening? Engage students in a discussion of how language influences our perceptions, perspectives, and emotions.

The Tantrum That Saved the World (Herbert & Mann, 2022)
We Are Water Protectors (Lindstrom, 2020)
No Voice Too Small (Metcalf et al., 2020)

READING PROCESS

Nature Poetry

Carry out a genre study of nonfiction poetry that is nature-based. Begin with a duet model exploration of nonfiction poetry such as *The Wisdom of Trees* (Judge,

2021) and *Winter Bees and Other Poems of the Cold* (Sidman, 2014). Notice the structures of each book and how the poems are connected to expository text and related to material the author has provided in the backmatter. Note the role of the illustrations in the books created by Lita Judge and by Rick Allen. How do they enhance the sensory experience of the poems and the nonfiction information that is shared? What poetic techniques and tools are used in the poems—how do they convey information about the world? Next, share additional collections of nonfiction poetry with your students to explore more forms, formats, and author and illustrator choices. After extensive experiences exploring the language use, poetic forms, and the aesthetics and information of nonfiction poetry, students will be ready to write their own.

>   *Outside Your Window: A First Book of Nature* (Davies, 2012)
>   *A Place to Start a Family: Poems About Creatures That Build* (Harrison, 2018)
>   *The Wisdom of Trees* (Judge, 2021)
>   *Water Is Water: A Book About the Water Cycle* (Paul, 2015b)
>   *Winter Bees and Other Poems of the Cold* (Sidman, 2014)

Nature Author Studies

For a broader look at language use and artistry in books that encourage observations of the natural world, consider carrying out an author study. Select a book creator who is known for writing about the natural world, such as April Pulley Sayre, Steve Jenkins, Jason Chin, and Joyce Sidman, whose books have been featured on our blog. Gather a collection of their titles and immerse your students in their work. What patterns do students notice across the books in the text and the visuals? What commitments and values are evident in the body of work? How does the author use language to convey nonfiction information? How does the author create an immersive, emotional, or evocative experience for the reader? What can your students learn about word choice and content organization from these books? Augment your study by exploring the book creators' websites and available interviews. Document the lessons learned about writing through this author/illustrator study and invite students to apply what they have learned in their own writing.

VISUAL LITERACIES

Nature Sketchbooks

Sketching is a wonderful way for students to record their observations outside the classroom both in the moment and over time. Gather clipboards and various sketching materials like colored pencils as well as cameras for students to document what they see. Prepare students to use all of their senses as they look, listen, jot, and sketch the world around them. When students return, create a class list through shared or interactive writing that documents the things students noticed, wondered, and imagined. Extend the activity by inviting students to keep observation journals over time in which they document the changes in a particular location or of a particular creature or structure. Encourage students to revisit their observations as they add to them, looking for and noting any patterns that emerge.

Look Up! Bird-Watching in Your Own Backyard (Cate, 2013)
The Watcher (Winter, 2011)

Exploring Perspectives

Illustrators of children's books can prompt us to see the world in new ways when they provide varying and unusual perspectives in their picture books. Gather a collection of Caldecott-winning titles—be sure to include Micha Archer's *Wonder Walkers* (2021)—and invite students to review several titles in small groups, using Post-it flags to mark pages that incorporate different perspectives such as close-ups, bird's-eye views, ground-level views, and multiple angles on the same scene. Groups can select several images to share with the whole class, ideally projected on a document camera. Use Visual Thinking Strategies (see www.vtshome.org) to discuss what students notice in the images they have selected. How do varying perspectives help us see the world around us in new ways? As an extension, invite students to play with perspective in their own artwork, connecting their images with the content, topic, or theme you are exploring in your curriculum.

Wonder Walkers (Archer, 2021)
It Fell From the Sky (Fan & Fan, 2021)
The Night Gardener (Fan & Fan, 2016)
Giant Squid (Fleming, 2016)

WRITING DEVELOPMENT

Figurative Language

Books that prompt close observation and appreciation of the world around us may also include examples of figurative language as authors seek to conjure imagery, sensory information, and emotional response for readers. Keep an eye out for examples of figurative language, such as similes, metaphors, and personification, and share these with students, perhaps documenting the examples on an anchor chart. Use the examples you collect as a class as an invitation for students to try out these techniques in the writing they are doing across the content areas.

Wait, Rest, Pause: Dormancy in Nature (Atkins, 2020)
Here Come the Humpbacks (Sayre, 2013)
I Am the Storm (Yolen & Stemple, 2021)

Onomatopoeia

To conjure up the sounds of nature, authors can use onomatopoeia, words that express sounds. The words might represent animal sounds or other sounds of nature like those created by wind, water, and movement. Take a listening walk with note-making materials and invite students to jot down any sounds they hear along the way. Or use animal cams to watch animals in their habitats, using letters and sounds to represent the noises you hear through virtual observation. As you read books that model and inspire close observation, notice any example of onomatopoeia—how does this literary technique enhance the reader's experience? Invite students to play with onomatopoeia in their own writing.

Bird Talk: What Birds Are Saying and Why (Judge, 2012)
Over and Under the Pond (Messner, 2017)
Being Frog (Sayre, 2020)
Can an Aardvark Bark? (Stewart, 2017)

Descriptive Verbs

To create a sense of the vibrancy and movement of the natural world, authors often employ lively descriptive verbs. Choose a mentor text, such as *Being Frog* (Sayre, 2020), and make a list of all the verbs used by the author. If students need a movement break, you could invite them to demonstrate some of these verbs by displaying the verbs on cards or on screen and asking students to move in the way that the verb suggests. Next, divide students into small groups, assign them an animal (or ask them to quickly choose their own), and ask each group to brainstorm a list of verbs they associate with that animal. If you have enough time, offer students the opportunity to observe their animal through a webcam (refer to the lists earlier in this chapter). Give the groups a chance to share their lists with the whole class, and add to their listings any other suggestions that come from the whole group. Invite your students to revisit a current piece of their own writing to see how it might be enlivened with descriptive verbs.

Wait, Rest, Pause: Dormancy in Nature (Atkins, 2020)
We All Play / kimêtawânaw (Flett, 2021)
Seashells, More Than a Home (Stewart, 2019)

MULTIMODAL RESPONSE

Murals

Collaborating on a mural is a wonderful way for students to share their observations and their learning. Engage your students in a discussion of a concept or topic related to a unit of study that they would like to represent visually by co-constructing a large work of art. For example, when studying geography or habitats, you could create a mural to represent a particular landscape. Students could also explore a concept such as beauty and create a mural that represents what is collectively beautiful to them. You also might choose to represent a cycle in nature in mural format. Consider engaging the support of your school art specialist or a local artist to explore mural arts. Students should spend time discussing what they would like to represent in the mural and how they will work together to create the work of art. Use a bulletin board, a hallway wall, or a community site as a location to display your mural so many people may enjoy it.

> *Maybe Something Beautiful* (Campoy & Howell, 2016)
> *Diego Rivera: His World and Ours* (Tonatiuh, 2011)
> *Hey, Wall!* (Verde, 2018)

Collages

The medium of collage offers students an opportunity to play with colors, textures, patterns, and images. Explore books that incorporate this art form, such as Micha Archer's *Wonder Walkers* (2021). On her website, Micha Archer includes a video that presents her process of creating collages, depicting the different materials and methods she uses to create papers that then become the media for her collages. Compare her style of collage with Patrick McDonnell's use of collage technique reminiscent of scrapbook entries, which incorporate engravings from the 19th and early 20th centuries, photographs, and images of journal entries. Using these methods and those of other collage artists (for example, Steve Jenkins and Robin Page, Bryan Collier, Ed Young, and Ekua Holmes), provide students with an opportunity to create collages, depicting images that create joy and curiosity in their lives.

> *Wonder Walkers* (Archer, 2021)
> *We Shall Overcome* (Collier, 2021)
> *Seeds Move!* (Page, 2019)

Photo Essays

There are an array of beautifully crafted photo essays that serve as wonderful invitations to consider how photographic images can document beauty and wonder in the world. Gather a collection of photo essays (see the list below and many are featured on The Classroom Bookshelf) and engage in a genre study. For middle-grade classrooms, include the photo essay series *Scientists in the Field,* published by Houghton Mifflin Harcourt. Guide your students to make observations about the roles the photographs play in the book: How are the text and the photographs related? How do the photographs move the narrative or expository text forward? How are the photographs placed within the book? After students learn about the techniques, structures, and composition strategies of the genre, engage them in the creation of original photo essays. Students might choose to document a place, a process, an event, or even patterns or a theme. Provide digital cameras or tablets and use an ebook composition tool like Book Creator to allow your students the opportunity to write and illustrate a book using photography.

> *It's Our Garden: From Seeds to Harvest in a School Garden* (Ancona, 2013)
> *Can We Help? Kids Volunteering to Help Their Communities* (Ancona, 2015)
> *Hatching Chicks in Room 6* (Arnold, 2017)
> *Handle With Care: An Unusual Butterfly Journey* (Burns & Harasimowicz, 2014)

Nature-Inspired Design

Observation of nature can lead to innovations in design. Engineers, scientists, and artists have developed inventions that transform the human experience based on watching, wondering, and noticing phenomena in the natural world. Share titles that describe such inventions and find ways to incorporate student making into your units of study. What problem needs to be solved? How can nature observation inform the problem? What can students design/invent based on their observations and wonderings?

> *Dreaming Up: A Celebration of Building* (Hale, 2012)
> *Wild Ideas: Let Nature Inspire Your Thinking* (Kelsey, 2015)
> *Welcome to the Neighborwood* (Sheehy, 2015)

SOCIAL-EMOTIONAL LEARNING

Listening to Nature

In her author's note in *The Wisdom of Trees,* Lita Judge (2021) describes sitting with her back against the trunk of a thousand-year-old oak tree in England. Her reflections in this spot led her to a life-altering career change. She poses the question: "Was it the tree's wisdom that seeped into my body, or the sanctuary it provided, allowing me to feel my own?" This experience speaks to the power nature holds for prompting reflection. Read this author's note aloud and offer your students the opportunity to sit and listen to the natural world. If it is not possible to be outside, this could even happen in the classroom when you play audio tracks from nature to offer moments of quiet stillness and contemplation. Notice that this may feel uncomfortable for some, since contemporary life is often filled with sound and media input at every moment. Following the experience, invite students to free write about what they heard and how it felt. Share with students additional titles that focus on nature, reflection, and mindfulness.

Tiny, Perfect Things (Clark, 2018)
The Wisdom of Trees (Judge, 2021)
Ideas Are All Around (Stead, 2016)

Mindfulness

The practice of mindfulness involves awareness of presence in the here and now. In recent years many children's book titles have been published that serve as a call to slow down, to observe, to be in the moment. Gather a collection of titles that inspire close observation and read these aloud as a preface to spending time in an environment where students can quietly observe nature. Help students practice close observation by inviting them to describe their sensory experiences: What do you hear? Smell? See? Feel?

Here and Now (Denos, 2019)
Dream Builder: The Story of Architect Philip Freelon (Lyons, 2020)
A Stone Sat Still (Wenzel, 2019)

CHAPTER 9

Invitations to Use Books to Cultivate Critical Consciousness Toward Creating a Better World

In Chapter 5, we described the many ways books can help us cultivate a critical consciousness to make the world more equitable and peaceful for all. These efforts can be deepened through teaching invitations that encourage students to consider issues of perspective, privilege, positioning, and power with children's literature, including questions about representation and identity; the power of words and illustrations; and matters of agency, equity, and justice. In this chapter, we offer a collection of such invitations to facilitate student responses. For a complete list of teaching invitations across purposes and practices, see our online materials under the download tab at https://www.tcpress.com/reading-with-purpose-9780807768501.

TEXT SETS

Herstories

Biographies and history textbooks have often omitted or ignored the vital role women played in a number of fields, even though their contributions were just as important, if not superior to, their male counterparts. Fortunately, the stories of these women are finally being told to children. With the help of your school or local librarian, gather a set of picture book and chapter book biographies about these remarkable women. As students read these texts, encourage them to think about why these women were hidden from history and to conduct further research about them.

> *Counting on Katherine: How Katherine Johnson Saved Apollo 13* (Becker, 2018)
> *The Girl Who Ran: Bobbi Gibb, the First Woman to Run the Boston Marathon* (Poletti & Yee, 2017)
> *Queen of Physics: How Wu Chien Shiung Helped Unlock the Secrets of the Atom* (Robeson, 2019)

Privilege and Perspective in Traditional Tales

Many of the traditional tales (i.e., fairy tales, fables, folk tales, myths, and legends) shared in classrooms derive from Western oral tradition. However, tales with similar plot lines, characters, and themes can be found in numerous other cultural traditions. Why, then, do these Westernized versions get shared over and over in our classrooms while versions from other cultures get limited time in the spotlight? Have students locate a wide variety of diverse cultural versions of popular traditional tales by searching local bookstores and libraries or searching online. Invite them to read aloud, act out, or create digital storytelling versions of the tales, and stage a classroom revue to share the tales with other students.

La Princesa and the Pea (Elya, 2017)
Over the Hills and Far Away: A Treasury of Nursery Rhymes (Hammill, 2015)
Beauty Woke (Ramos, 2022)

CONTENT CONNECTIONS AND DISCIPLINARY LITERACIES

Understanding and Expanding Identity

Another central theme found throughout children's and young adult literature is the question of identity. Often, the main characters seek to define who they are, attempting to shape their identity through categories and rules. Authors approach the question of identity from different angles, such as notions of homeland, family ancestry, nationality, and intersectionality. Have students work in partners or small groups to identify lines and examples in various books where the characters explore different facets of their identities. Ask students to consider their own identities in relation to the cultural communities they embrace, as well as the intersections of their multiple identities (e.g., gender, race, ethnicity, nationality, language, religion, and socioeconomic class). Encourage students to think about how they are so much more than the identity they think they hold or that they have been told they are. Help them cultivate their critical consciousness by extending that understanding about the identities of others around them. You might support their thinking with an anchor chart or a graphic organizer. Sometimes it takes facing adversity to realize this; other times it does not and we are able to expand our identity through profound learning experiences. Extend these conversations into multimodal response options where students can share their reflections via poetry, music, visual art, drama, etc.

Why Am I Me? (Britt, 2017)
Alma and How She Got Her Name (Martinez-Neal, 2019)
Where Are You From? (Méndez, 2019)

Dreamers (Morales, 2018)
Your Name Is a Song (Thompkins-Bigelow, 2020)

Power and Voice

Engage your students in an explicit discussion of power structures, using the experiences of the young activists featured in a book. Unpack the context of their activism. What were they working to change? Who had the power to change the situation? How did these activists work to be heard by those in power? How did they claim the power to make change? What did they do? What did they say? Who was involved? Invite students to discuss the broader question of what power they have in their own lives as young people. Connect with the ideas embedded in the Youth-led Participatory Action Research movement, which positions young people as researchers of their community with the goals of creating change toward equity and social justice.

Can We Help? Kids Volunteering to Help Their Communities (Ancona, 2015)
No Voice Too Small: Fourteen Young Americans Making History (Metcalf et al., 2020)
Our House Is on Fire: Greta Thunberg's Call to Save the Planet (Winter, 2019)
Malala's Magic Pencil (Yousafzai, 2017)

Peaceful Protests

What does it mean to engage in protest? What are some different ways to protest peacefully? What are the pros and cons of each? What are the goals of the protest? How can protests be effective ways of effecting social change and social justice? Learn more about the history of peaceful protest through children's literature. Collaborate with your school or local librarian to compile a text set of titles that feature peaceful protest.

Above the Rim: How Elgin Baylor Changed Basketball (Bryant, 2020)
Let the Children March (Clark-Robinson, 2018)
The Teachers March! How Selma's Teachers Changed History (Wallace & Wallace, 2020)

Building Awareness of Systemic vs. Individual -Isms

One challenge of addressing issues around any sort of socially oppressive or discriminatory -ism (e.g., racism, sexism, classism, ageism) is the difficulty of discerning its existence and consequences on a systemic level versus an individual level. Many people believe that oppression or discrimination does not exist if they don't observe or partake in it on an individual level in their everyday lives. Help students cultivate their critical consciousness to perceive and distinguish between systemic and individual forms of oppression and discrimination by exploring books specifically on these topics. Make sure to juxtapose any books that describe the -ism's impact on an individual character's life with the impact on a greater society. Ask questions such as: Why is this character being treated unfairly? Would others who look/sound/act like them be treated the same, and why? What else could be the cause of this unfair treatment? Would this source treat everyone unfairly, or just those who look/sound/act like this character? Why or why not? Engage students in research projects that help them find data about large populations of the same demographic versus individual experiences to help them develop further understanding about systemic and individual oppression and discrimination.

> *An Indigenous People's History of the United States for Young People* (Dunbar-Ortiz et al., 2019)
> *Fault Lines in the Constitution* (Levinson & Levinson, 2019)
> *Stamped: Racism, Antiracism, and You* (Reynolds & Kendi, 2020)
> *You Call This Democracy? How to Fix Our Government and Deliver Power to the People* (Rusch, 2020)

Community Service and Activism

Many children's books describe various forms of community service and activism designed to make a positive change at the local, national, or even global level. Additionally, social justice topics are often centered in realistic or historical fiction, but plenty of fantasy and science fiction books are grounded in social issues as well. Multigenre thematic units can provide the flexibility to explore a theme through the genre that an individual student might enjoy most. Have students identify all the examples of service and activism described in one such book, analyzing the goals, underlying philosophies, and values of each. How effective is each effort? What are the pros and cons of pursuing such lines of service and activism? After examining these examples, encourage students to identify ways they can participate in social justice, community service, and activism in their neighborhoods, towns, and counties, and explore how they can actually pursue such efforts.

> *The Tantrum That Saved the World* (Herbert & Mann, 2022)
> *Dictionary for a Better World* (Latham & Waters, 2020)
> *We Are Water Protectors* (Lindstrom, 2020)
> *No Voice Too Small: Fourteen Young Americans Making History* (Metcalf et al., 2020)

CRITICAL LITERACIES

Because the theme of Cultivating Critical Consciousness overlaps considerably with the practice of Critical Literacies, this section only offers teaching invitations that focus on deconstructing text, reconstructing text, and counterstorytelling.

Stereotypes in Series Books

By nature of their repeated characters and plot structures, many series books continue to perpetuate stereotypes about different populations of people. Invite students to engage in an inquiry about the series books on the classroom bookshelf and in the school library. What kinds of characters do they notice appear most in the series? What do students notice about the descriptions and illustrations in series books? Their plotlines? What patterns do students see regarding how similar-looking characters think, feel, and behave? How do those patterns correspond with or challenge what students know about those populations in the real world? Invite students to write to the school principal, curriculum administrator, and school board about these issues, advocating instead for adding new series and titles that celebrate the mosaic of human diversity, such as the titles below.

The Crossover series (Alexander, 2019a)
Anna Hibiscus series (Atinuke, 2007–)
Maybe Marisol series (Kelly, 2021a–)
Juana and Lucas series (Medina, 2016–)

Challenging Single Story/Single Voice Representations

View Chimamanda Ngozi Adichie's (2009) famed TED talk on the danger of a single story. Use this framing as a way of further discussing the dangers of relying on a single story for understanding groups of people or complex social issues. Discuss with students the power of narrative, either fictional or informational, to challenge single story/voice representations. Ask them to consider the book's content. What have they learned about the people or issue involved? What information is included? What is excluded? Why? Why have particular representations been privileged over time? How does the omission of certain material in a book shape readers' perspectives, as well as the inclusion of certain material? What language does each author use to talk about the issue? How do people use the language in similar and different ways, and why? How is language use possibly embedded in issues of power and privilege? Have your students determine which books provide the most accurate and comprehensive information and write reviews that can be shared with the school librarian and printed out and taped into the books' inside covers for future readers to consider.

Boy, Everywhere (Dassu, 2021)
Coronavirus: A Book for Children (Jenner et al., 2020)

The Seventh Wish (Messner, 2016)
Unspeakable: The Tulsa Race Massacre (Weatherford, 2021)

Rewriting History From Voices Unheard

American history is often told through the eyes of elected leaders, meaning that textbooks and historical accounts heavily lean toward the telling of history from White, male, economically and socially privileged positions. Interrogate your social studies textbook with your students. Whose voices are centered? Whose voices are missing? Encourage students to conduct research to find out more about the voices unheard, including women, children, and those from diverse cultural and ethnic backgrounds, and then rewrite a period of history from other points of view.

Efrén Divided (Cisneros, 2019)
Indian No More (McManis & Sorell, 2019)
Almost Astronauts: 13 Women Who Dared to Dream (Stone, 2009)
Unspeakable: The Tulsa Race Massacre (Weatherford, 2021)

READING PROCESS

Poetry: Power and Protest

Invite your students to reflect on poetry's power to convey human experience and to advocate for social change. Visit the Poetry Foundation's online collection "Poems of Protest, Resistance, and Empowerment," making sure to note whose voices are included in this collection and whose might be left out. For younger students, be sure to preview the collection to select poems that are developmentally appropriate. Ask your students to identify a contemporary (or perennial) social issue about which they feel passionate. Support your students to compose and share their own protest poems.

One Today (Blanco, 2015)
We Shall Overcome (Collier, 2021)
The Hill We Climb: An Inaugural Poem for the Country (Gorman, 2021b)
I, Too, Am America (Hughes, 2012)
Peace (Paul & Paul, 2021)

Social Justice Allusions

Identifying and understanding allusions can deepen students' overall meaning making of a text. Authors often will use descriptions that allude to social issues and social justice events to enhance the content of their text. Illustrators, too, will include images that are allusions to social issues and events. See which references

Invitations to Use Books to Cultivate Critical Consciousness 133

your students noticed in the text while reading. How does the author/illustrator use these allusions in their work? What layers of meaning do these references add to the text? How does this text in turn help cultivate critical consciousness about the social issue or event?

> *The Undefeated* (Alexander, 2019c)
> *Change Sings: A Children's Anthem* (Gorman, 2021a)
> *The Last Cuentista* (Higuera, 2021)

Who Can Tell This Story?

Conduct an author study with an eye toward critical consciousness and authentic voice. Have your students read the article "Who Can Tell My Story?" written by multiple-award-winning author Jacqueline Woodson (1998). Frame your author study with the question "Whose stories does this author tell?" Based on Woodson's article, what parts of the author's life *might* have been drawn upon to create the characters in her books? How does the author tell a character's story authentically?

> *The Last Cuentista* (Higuera, 2021)
> *Hello, Universe* (Kelly, 2017)
> *Ancestor Approved: Intertribal Stories for Kids* (Smith, 2021)

VISUAL LITERACIES

Picture Book Illustrations as Activist Statements

Engage students in a discussion about how to recognize activist illustrations in children's picture books. What are the pros and cons of such illustrations? What is or should be the goal of picture books? What picture books might be considered activist statements? How influential might these books be?

> *The Undefeated* (Alexander, 2019c)
> *The Patchwork Bike* (Clarke, 2018)
> *Change Sings: A Children's Anthem* (Gorman, 2021a)
> *Dreamers* (Morales, 2018)

WRITING DEVELOPMENT

Mentor Texts for Multigenre Writing

Review the different writing genres that students have been introduced to throughout the year, such as poetry, narrative, and expository/informational writing. Then review the purpose, content, organizational structure, and linguistic features of the various genres, discussing how each genre could be used to explore a particular social concern. How might the characteristics of each contribute a unique perspective when explaining the issues? How might each be used to cultivate critical consciousness and advocate for social justice? Have students explore a social issue by writing pieces in different genres to address it. You might want to have them work individually or in small groups to create multigenre writing portfolios.

Dictionary for a Better World (Latham & Waters, 2020)
Echo: A Novel (Ryan, 2015)

Rewriting Traditional Tales for Today's World

Many of your students are already familiar with fairy tales, folktales, myths, legends, and fables that have been reimagined and retold for modern audiences and issues because of their prevalence in films, television shows, and other popular media. Using the SurLaLune Fairy Tales website as your starting point, have students locate three picture book versions of a favorite traditional tale that has been rewritten and adapted for contemporary times. Have them analyze the different representations of the story, drawing upon details in the text and illustrations and explaining how 21st-century issues and settings have influenced the retelling. Next, have them write their own original retelling in short story format, incorporating issues, settings, and elements of today's world. Make sure they pay attention to the craft of fiction, including dialogue.

La Princesa and the Pea (Elya, 2017)
Far, Far Away (McNeal, 2014)
Beauty Woke (Ramos, 2022)
Echo Echo: Reverso Poems about Greek Myths (Singer, 2016)

Speechwriting as Social Action

Speeches are often effective ways to cultivate critical consciousness and inspire social action. Once students are knowledgeable about the qualities of a good speech, have them try their hand at speechwriting. Teach them the characteristics of oration and rhetoric, and encourage them to think about how those characteristics must be incorporated into speechwriting to be effective. For example, teach them the three different kinds of rhetoric—deliberative, judicial, and epideictic—so they can focus on the audience and purpose while they write and rehearse their speeches. Locate videos of famous speeches, and share them with students so they can both hear and see the qualities needed for being an effective orator and rhetorician. You may want to have students work in small groups or teams, and then have them deliver their final speeches before classmates, families, and community members.

What Do You Do With a Voice Like That? The Story of Extraordinary Congresswoman Barbara Jordan (Barton, 2018)
Strong Voices: Fifteen American Speeches Worth Knowing (Bolden, 2020)
Martin's Big Words: The Life of Dr. Martin Luther King, Jr. (Rappaport, 2001)
Voice of Freedom: Fannie Lou Hamer: The Spirit of the Civil Rights Movement (Weatherford, 2015)

Writing for Social Action

Many books include backmatter that provide information about ways readers can learn more about the social issues described. Have students use backmatter to conduct further research, and engage students in a few different writing activities:

- Write letters to the local paper urging the townspeople and local government officials to support a particular social cause.
- Write thank-you letters to the town leaders and community organizers for their hard work in supporting a particular social cause.
- Write plans for taking social action to support those in need within your community, such as holding a clothing drive, organizing a fundraiser, cleaning up a littered part of town, or establishing a free tutoring service, and then select one plan to follow up on.
- Create a class informational ("all-about") book about a particular social concern, and ask your school or local librarian to display it and add it to their collections.

Mama's Nightingale: A Story of Immigration and Separation (Danticat, 2015)
The Day the Crayons Quit (Daywalt, 2013)
The Red Pencil (Pinkney, 2014)

MULTIMODAL RESPONSE

Making Art as a Way of Making Sense and Helping

Have students illustrate and write about what they would want to do to help address a social inequity or issue. These efforts can range from collecting donations for a refugee center to volunteering at a soup kitchen. The initial drawing and prewriting will help students organize their ideas. After the presentations of the ideas are completed, make a class collage with the work and have the class create a title for their collage. Encourage students to act upon their ideas and to document their coming to life using video or photographs.

Maybe Something Beautiful (Campoy & Howell, 2016)
Luis Paints the World (Farish, 2016)
Hey, Wall! A Story of Art and Community (Verde, 2018)

Art as Advocacy

Many famous artists use art to express explicit social critique. Use Visual Thinking Strategies (Yenawine, 2013) to examine various art pieces designed for this purpose. Invite students to make connections between art and contemporary social challenges (Jean-Michel Basquiat's painting "The Irony of the Negro Policeman" and Diego Rivera's "Detroit Industry Murals" are particularly well-suited to this discussion). Introduce your students to artists who use/used their art as advocacy (Pablo Picasso, Diego Rivera, Kerry James Marshall, Banksy, and many others—please consult your school's art specialist and local librarians for additional suggestions). Extend this exploration by inviting your students to create a work of art (individually or collectively) that expresses a position on a social issue in your community.

Dave the Potter: Artist, Poet, Slave (Hill, 2010)
Radiant Child: The Story of Young Artist Jean-Michel Basquiat (Steptoe, 2016)
Diego Rivera: His World and Ours (Tonatiuh, 2011)

Music and Movement as Advocates and Healers

Music and movement provide their own kind of advocacy. Share with students different ways that music and movement have been used around the world to bring help and hope. Invite students to join you in an impromptu dance party to start the day, to make their own instruments, to play musical instruments for one another, and to create and share playlists. What are songs that energize them and bring them hope? What are songs that help them process strong feelings?

Drum Dream Girl: How One Girl's Courage Changed Music (Engle, 2015)
Ada's Violin: The Story of the Recycled Orchestra of Paraguay (Hood, 2016)
Josephine: The Dazzling Life of Josephine Baker (Powell, 2014)

SOCIAL-EMOTIONAL LEARNING

Microaggressions

The Merriam-Webster dictionary defines a *microagression* as a "comment or action that subtly and often unconsciously or unintentionally expresses a prejudiced attitude toward a member of a marginalized group." Have an open discussion about the impact microaggressions have on characters in books and what power and privilege have to do with who experiences microaggressions. Some students may experience microaggressions in their own lives, or they may realize that they have been perpetrating microaggressions they were not conscious of until encountering moments of microaggressions in texts. Consider as a class the actions students might take in their own lives as their consciousness is raised, such as coming together to commit to certain kinds of language or processes with one another when microaggressions occur. Support students with language they can use to address microaggressions openly, such as: "When you said _____, it made me feel _____" and "You may not be aware of what you just said/did. You _____. In the future, _____."

> *New Kid* (Craft, 2019)
> *Legacy: Women Poets of the Harlem Renaissance* (Grimes, 2021)
> *What Lane?* (Maldonado, 2021)
> *Cilla-Lee Jenkins: Future Author Extraordinaire* (Tan, 2018)

Allies and Coconspirators

An ally is someone who supports a cause and stands in solidarity with oppressed people. Select an appropriate book, and discuss with students whether they think the characters are allies or coconspirators—what evidence from the book makes them think that? Following this discussion, support students to have a plan for what they can do when they see discrimination or oppression occur. We recommend using the Teaching Tolerance Allies Discussion Activity, adapted from *Because We Can Change the World: A Practical Guide to Building Cooperative, Inclusive Classroom Communities* by Mara Sapon-Shevin (2010).

> *The Crossover* (Alexander, 2014)
> *New Kid* (Craft, 2019)
> *What Lane?* (Maldonado, 2021)
> *Separate Is Never Equal: Sylvia Mendez and Her Family's Fight for Desegregation* (Tonatiuh, 2014)

In Closing

We believe literature today holds an even more important place in our classrooms than ever before. The books we share with students, teachers, and with our own families excite us. They arrest us. They make us laugh aloud and sometimes cry from the deepest parts of ourselves. We cannot imagine teaching without books in our work with children and young adults and hold deep respect for the artistry of book creators.

Somewhere in the world right now an author and an illustrator are working to bring a new book into the world that has the potential to make your students' hearts more capacious and their minds more curious. Once in the hands of a reader, that book may inspire a student to be more compassionate to a friend who is hurting, to ask big questions about what happened and why, to pay attention to the natural world more closely, or to take on a new perspective that helps make a better world.

The world of children's literature will continue to challenge us as educators to rethink our assumptions about how we can use books to ignite learners in our classrooms. Our four purposes and the invitations we suggest are meant to serve as sites of possibility for the ways you may engage students with books. But, they are also meant to inspire you to see a world of possibility within the pages of each new book that enters your classroom. We invite you to seek out and champion new works of children and young adult literature and create new purposes for reading with your students.

We hope this book inspires you to think deeply about why you read and how you invite young people to engage with the world through books. Most of all, we hope this book helps you stay courageous and remain hopeful as you center books and the possibilities they create for the students in your care.

References

Adichie, C. N. (2009). *The danger of a single story* [Video]. TED Conferences. https://www.ted.com/talks/chimamanda_ngozi_adichie_the_danger_of_a_single_story/comments

Akpan, N. (2019). How to talk to your kids about climate change. PBS News Hour. https://www.pbs.org/newshour/science/how-to-talk-to-your-kids-about-climate-change

Alberta Council for Environmental Education (ACEE). (2017). What is excellent climate change education? AACE. https://www.abcee.org/what-excellent-climate-change-education

American Library Association (n.d.). Randolph Caldecott Medal. Retrieved on January 16, 2023 from https://www.ala.org/alsc/awardsgrants/bookmedia/caldecott

An, S. (2022). Teaching about the Vietnam War: Centering Southeast Asian refugee voices through children's literature. *Social Studies and the Young Learner, 34*(4), 13–18.

Anderson, D. (2014). Outliers: Elementary teachers who actually teach social studies. *The Social Studies, 105*, 91–100.

Ardoin, N. M., & Bowers, A. (2020). Early childhood environmental education: A systematic review of the research literature. *Educational Research Review, 31*(20), 100353. https://doi.org/10.1016/j.edurev.2020.100353

Arizpe, E. (2021). The state of the art in picturebook research from 2010 to 2020. *Language Arts, 98*(5), 260–272.

Au, W. (2009). Social studies, social justice: W(h)ither the social studies in high-stakes testing? *Teacher Education Quarterly, 36*(1), 43–58. https://www.jstor.org/stable/23479200

Bal, P. M., & Veltkamp, M. (2013). How does fiction reading influence empathy? An experimental investigation on the role of emotional transportation. *PLOS ONE, 8*(1), e55341. https://doi.org/10.1371/journal.pone.0055341

Baytas, M. O., & Schroeder, S. (2021). Cultivating civic engagement in the early grades with culturally appropriate children's literature. *Social Studies and the Young Learner, 33*(4), 3–8.

Bensusen, S. J. (2020). The power of observation. *Science and Children, 57*(5), 60–65.

Bird, E. (2018). Review of the day: The rabbit listened by Cori Doerrfeld [Blog]. A Fuse 8 Production. https://afuse8production.slj.com/2018/05/29/review-of-the-day-the-rabbit-listened-by-cori-doerrfeld/

Bishop R. S. (1990). Mirrors, windows, and sliding glass doors. *Perspectives, 6*(3), ix–xi.

Blanco, N. J., & Sloutsky, V. M. (2019). Adaptive flexibility in category learning? Young children exhibit smaller costs of selective attention than adults. *Developmental Psychology, 55*(10), 2060–2076. https://doi.org/10.1037/dev0000777

Boler, M. (2006). The risks of empathy: Interrogating multiculturalism's gaze. *Cultural Studies, 11*(2), 253–273. https://doi.org/10.1080/09502389700490141

Brooks, W., & Browne, S. (2012). Towards a culturally situated reader response theory. *Children's Literature in Education. 43*(1), 74–85. https://doi.org/10.1007/s10583-011-9154-z

Brophy, J., & VanSledright, B. (1997). *Teaching and learning history in elementary schools.* Teachers College Press.

Bryant-Davis, T., & Ocampo, C. (2005). The trauma of racism: Implications for counseling, research, and education. *The Counseling Psychologist, 33*(4), 574–578. https://doi.org/10.1177/0011000005276581

Burgess, S. R., Sargent, S., Smith, M., Hill, N., & Morrison, S. (2011). Teacher's leisure reading habits and knowledge of children's books: Do they relate to the teaching practices of elementary school teachers? *Reading Improvement, 48*(2), 88–102.

Cappiello, M. A., & Dawes, E. T. (2014). *Teaching to complexity: A framework for text evaluation.* Shell Education.

Cappiello, M. A., & Dawes, E. T. (2021). *Text sets in action: Pathways through content literacy.* Stenhouse.

Cappiello, M. A., & Hadjioannou, X. (2022). Exploring the purposes of backmatter in nonfiction picture books for children: A typology. *The Reading Teacher, 76*(3), 309–316. https://doi.org/10.1002/trtr.2154

Cervetti, G., & Pearson, D. P. (2012). Reading, writing, and thinking like a scientist. *Journal of Adolescent and Adult Literacy, 55*(7), 580–586. https://doi.org/10.1002/JAAL.00069

Chang, W-C., & Cochran-Smith, M. (2022). Learning to teach for equity, social justice, and/or diversity: Do the measures measure up? *Journal of Teacher Education*, 1–16. https://doi.org/10.1177/00224871221075284

Child and Adolescent Health Measurement Initiative. (2021). *National survey of children's health.* https://www.childhealthdata.org/learn-about-the-nsch/NSCH

Coleman, J. J. (2021). Affective reader response: Using ordinary affects to repair literacy normativities in ELA and English Education. *English Education, 53*(4), 254–276.

Collaborative for Academic, Social, and Emotional Learning. (2023). *2013 CASEL guide: Effective social and emotional learning programs—Preschool and elementary school edition.* https://casel.org/fundamentals-of-sel/

Comber, B. (2015). Critical literacy and social justice. *Journal of Adolescent & Adult Literacy, 58*(5), 362–367. https://doi.org/10.1002/jaal.370

Cooperative Children's Book Center. (2021). *Books by and/or about Black, indigenous, and people of color (all years).* [Statistics]. School of Education, University of Wisconsin–Madison. https://ccbc.education.wisc.edu/literature-resources/ccbc-diversity-statistics/books-by-about-poc-fnn/

Crenshaw, K. (1991). Mapping the margins: Intersectionality, identity politics, and violence against women of color. *Stanford Law Review, 43*(6), 1241–1299. https://doi.org/10.2307/1229039

Cunningham, K. E., Cappiello, M. A., Dawes, E. T., & Enriquez, G. (2021). The pitfalls and potential of anthropomorphism in children's literature. In *Animals are us: Anthropomorphism in children's literature: Celebrating the Peter J. Solomon collection* (pp. 17–28). Harvard University Press.

Dalal, M., Cazorla-Lancaster, Y., Chu, C. G., & Agarwal, N. (2022). Healthy from the start—Lifestyle interventions in early childhood. *American Journal of Lifestyle Medicine, 16*(5), 562–569. https://doi.org/10.1177/15598276221087672

References

Dávila, D. (2015). #WhoNeedsDiverseBooks?: Preservice teachers and religious neutrality with children's literature. *Research in the Teaching of English, 50*(1), 60–83. https://www.jstor.org/stable/24889905

Dawes, E. T., Cappiello, M. A., Magee, L., Bryant, J., & Sweet, M. (2019). Portraits of perseverance: Creating picturebook biographies with third graders. *Language Arts, 96*(3), 153–166. https://www.jstor.org/stable/26779051

Deheane, S. (2009). *Reading in the brain: The new science of how we read.* Penguin Books.

Deringer, S. A. (2017). Mindful place-based education: Mapping the literature. *Journal of Experiential Education, 40*(4), 333–348. https://doi.org/10.1177/1053825917716694

DiCamillo, K. (2014). Newbery medal acceptance speech. https://www.ala.org/alsc/sites/ala.org.alsc/files/content/awardsgrants/bookmedia/newbery-14.pdf

Duncan-Andrade, J. M. R. (2009). Note to educators: Hope required when growing roses in concrete. *Harvard Educational Review, 79*(2), 181–194. https://doi.org/10.17763/haer.79.2.nu3436017730384w

Dunn, M. B. (2022). When teachers lose loved ones: Affective practices in teachers' accounts of addressing loss in literature instruction. *Reading Research Quarterly, 57*(3), 1049–1064. https://doi.org/10.1002/rrq.460

Durlak, J. A., Dymnicki, A. B., Taylor, R. D., Weissberg, R. P., & Schellinger, K. B. (2011). The impact of enhancing students' social and emotional learning: A meta-analysis of school-based universal interventions. *Child Development, 82*(1), 405–432. https://doi.org/10.1111/j.1467-8624.2010.01564.x

Dutro, E. (2011). Writing wounded: Trauma, testimony, and critical witnesses in literacy classrooms. *English Education, 43*(2), 193–211. https://www.jstor.org/stable/23017070

Dutro, E. (2019). *The vulnerable heart of literacy: Centering trauma as powerful pedagogy.* Teachers College Press.

Edmundson, M. (2004). *Why read?* Bloomsbury Publishing.

Elledge, S. (1986). *E. B. White: A biography.* W. W. Norton & Company.

Enriquez, G. (2013). "But they won't let you read!": A case study of an urban middle school male's response to school reading. *Journal of Education, 193*(1), 35–46. https://doi.org/10.1177/002205741319300105

Enriquez, G. (2016). Reader response and embodied performance: Body-poems as performative response and performativity. In G. Enriquez, E. Johnson, S. Kontovourki, & C. Mallozzi (Eds.), *Literacies, learning, and the body: Putting theory and research into pedagogical practice* (pp. 41–56). Routledge.

Enriquez, G. (2021). Foggy mirrors, tiny windows and heavy doors: Beyond diverse books towards meaningful literacy instruction. *Language Arts, 75*(1), 103–106. https://doi.org/10.1002/trtr.2030

Enriquez, G. (2022). "I don't want to finish this book!", or a posthumanist view of affect, reader response, and children's literature. *Children's Literature in Education, 53*, 313–326. https://doi.org/10.1007/s10583-022-09501-z

Enriquez, G., Clark, S., & Calce, J. (2017). Using children's literature for dynamic learning frames and growth mindsets. *The Reading Teacher, 70*(1), 711–719. https://doi.org/10.1002/trtr.1583

Enriquez, G., & Wager, A. C. (2018). The reader, the text, the performance: Opening spaces for the performing arts as reader response. *Voices from the Middle, 26*(1), 21–25.

Epstein, T. (1993). Why teach history to the young? In M. Tunnell & R. Ammon (Eds.), *The story of ourselves: Teaching history through children's literature* (pp. 1–7). Heinemann.

Falter, M. M., & Bickmore, S. T. (Eds). (2018). *When loss gets personal: Discussing death through literature in the secondary ELA classroom.* Rowman & Littlefield.

Ferlazzo, L. (2020, January 28). Author interview with Dr. Gholdy Muhammad: 'Cultivating genius.' *EdWeek Blog.* https://www.edweek.org/teaching-learning/opinion-author-interview-with-dr-gholdy-muhammad-cultivating-genius/2020/01

Fitchett, P. G., Heafner, T. L., & Lambert, R. G. (2014). Examining elementary social studies marginalization: A multilevel model. *Educational Policy, 28*(1), 40–68. https://doi.org/10.1177/0895904812453998

Freebody, P., & Luke, A. (1990). Literacies programs: Debates and demands in cultural context. *Prospect, 5*(3), 85–94.

Freire, P. (1970). *Pedagogy of the oppressed.* Continuum.

Freire, P., & Macedo, D. (1987). *Literacy: Reading the word and the world.* Bergin & Harvey.

Friedman, J., & Johnson, N. F. (2022). *Banned in the USA: The growing movement to censor books in schools.* PEN America. https://pen.org/report/banned-usa-growing-movement-to-censor-books-in-schools/

Gallego, M. A., & Hollingsworth, S. (2000). *What counts as literacy: Challenging the school standard.* Teachers College Press

Goade, M. (2021, June 28). 2021 Caldecott acceptance speech by Michaela Goade. *The Horn Book Online.* https://www.hbook.com/story/2021-caldecott-medal-acceptance-by-michaela-goade

Graff, J. M., & Shimek, C. (2020). Revisiting reader response: Contemporary nonfiction children's literature as remixes. *Language Arts, 97*(4), 223–234.

Groce, E. C., & Gregor, M. N. (2020). Destination discrimination: Navigating the highways of segregated America with trade books. *Social Studies and the Young Learner, 32*(3), 26–31.

Harju, M. L., & Rouse, D. (2018). Keeping some wildness always alive: Posthumanism and the animality of children's literature and play. *Children's Literature in Education, 49,* 447–466. https://doi.org/10.1007/s10583-017-9329-3

Haudenosaunee Confederacy. (2023). *Values.* https://www.haudenosauneeconfederacy.com/values/

Heafner, T. L., & Fitchett, P.G. (2012). National trends in elementary instruction: Exploring the role of social studies curricula. *Social Studies, 103*(2), 67–72. https://doi.org/10.1080/00377996.2011.592165

Hertz, C., & Mraz, K. (2018). *Kids first from day one: A teacher's guide to today's classroom.* Heinemann.

Hetland, L., Winner, E., Veenema, S., & Sheridan, K. M. (2013). *Studio thinking 2: The real benefits of visual arts education* (2nd ed.). Teachers College Press.

Hilder, M. B. (2005). Teaching literature as an ethic of care. *Teaching Education, 16*(1), 41–50. https://doi.org/10.1080/1047621052000341617

Hillis, S., N'konzi, J. N., Msemburi, W., Cluver, L., Villaveces, A., Flaxman, S., & Unwin, H. J. T. (2022). Orphanhood and caregiver loss among children based on new global excess COVID-19 death estimates. *JAMA Pediatric, 176*(11), 1145–1148. doi:10.1001/jamapediatrics.2022.3157

Hoffman, M. (2000). *Empathy and moral development: Implications for caring and justice.* Cambridge University Press.

References

Holson, L. M. (2019, June 27). Climate change is scaring kids: Here's how to talk to them. *The New York Times.* https://www.nytimes.com/2019/06/27/science/climate-change-children-education.html

hooks, b. (1994). *Teaching to transgress.* Routledge.

hooks, b. (2001). *All about love: New visions.* William Morrow and Company.

Howard, T. C. (2013). How does it feel to be a problem? Black male students, schools, and learning in enhancing the knowledge base to disrupt deficit frameworks. *Review of Research in Education, 37*(1), 54–86. https://doi.org/10.3102/0091732X12462985

Jackson, I., Sealey-Ruiz, Y., & Watson, W. (2014). Reciprocal love: Mentoring Black and Latino males through an ethos of caring. *Journal of Urban Education, 49*(4), 1–24. https://doi.org/10.1177/0042085913519336

Janks, H. (2000). Domination, access, diversity and design: A synthesis for critical literacy education. *Educational Review, 52*(2), 175–186. https://doi.org/10.1080/713664035

Jiménez, L. M. (2021). Mirrors and windows with texts and readers: Intersectional social justice at work in the classroom. *Language Arts, 98*(3), 156–161.

Johnson, A. (2020, August 24). Teaching compassion—not empathy—and critical reading. *School Library Journal.* https://www.slj.com/story/Teaching-Compassion-Not-Empathy-and-Critical-Reading-Opinion-literacy-libraries

Jones, S. (2006). *Girls, social class, and literacy: What teachers can do to make a difference.* Heinemann.

Jones, S. (2012). Trauma narratives and nomos in teacher education. *Teaching Education, 23*(2), 131–152. https://doi.org/10.1080/10476210.2011.625087

Jones, S., Brown, J. L., & Aber, J. L. (2011). Two-year impacts of a universal school-based social-emotional and literacy intervention: An experiment in translational developmental research. *Child Development, 82*(2), 533–554. https://doi.org/10.1111/j.1467-8624.2010.01560.x

Jones, S., & Clarke, L. W. (2007). Disconnections: Pushing readers beyond connections and toward the critical. *Pedagogies: An International Journal, 2*(2), 95–115. https://doi.org/10.1080/15544800701484069

Jones, S., Clarke, L. W., & Enriquez, G. (2010). *The reading turn-around: A five-part framework for differentiated instruction.* Teachers College Press.

Kabat-Zinn, J. (2017, October 1). Too early to tell: The potential impact and challenges—ethical and otherwise—inherent in the mainstreaming of Dharma in an increasingly dystopian world. *Mindfulness, 8*(5), 1125–1135. https://doi.org/10.1007/s12671-017-0758-2

Kantor, E. (2020, February 7). Observations and conservation: PW talks with Sy Montgomery and April Pulley Sayre. *Publishers Weekly.* https://www.publishersweekly.com/pw/by-topic/childrens/childrens-authors/article/82373-observation-and-conservation-pw-talks-with-sy-montgomery-and-april-pulley-sayre.html

Kendi, I. X. (2016). *Stamped from the beginning: The definitive history of racist ideas in America.* Bold Type Books.

Kiefer, B. (1991). Envisioning experience: The potential of picture books. *Publishing Research Quarterly, 7*(3), 63. https://doi.org/10.1007/BF02678162

Kiefer, B. (1994). *The potential of picturebooks: From visual literacy to aesthetic understanding.* Prentice Hall.

Kiefer, B., & Tyson, C.A. (2010). *Charlotte Huck's children's literature: A brief guide.* McGraw-Hill.

Kirby, J. N., Tellegen, C. L., & Steindl, S. R. (2017). A meta-analysis of compassion-based interventions: Current state of knowledge and future directions. *Behavior Therapy, 48*(6), 778–792. https://doi.org/10.1016/j.beth.2017.06.003

Kirkland, D. E. (2019). More than words: Teaching literacy to vulnerable learners. *Literacy Today, 37*(2), 10–11.

Konrath, S. H., & Grynberg, D. (2013). The positive (and negative) psychology of empathy. In D. Watt & J. Panksepp (Eds.), *The psychology and neurobiology of empathy*. Nova Science Publishers.

Ladson-Billings, G. (2009). *The dreamkeepers: Successful teachers of African American children*. Jossey-Bass.

Langer, E. J. (2016). *The power of mindful learning*. Da Capo Press.

Lankshear, C., & Knobel, M. (2006). *New literacies: Everyday practices and classroom learning*. Open University Press.

Larsen, N., Lee, K., & Ganea, P. (2018). Do storybooks with anthropomorphized animal characters promote prosocial behaviors in young children? *Developmental Science, 21*(3), e12590. http://doi.org/10.1111/desc.12590

Leland, C., Lewison, M., & Harste, J. (2017). *Teaching children's literature: It's critical!* (2nd ed.). Routledge.

Levstik, L. (1998). "I wanted to be there:" The impact of narrative on children's historical thinking. In M. Tunnell & R. Ammon (Eds.), *The story of ourselves: Teaching history through children's literature* (pp. 65–78). Heinemann.

Levstik, L., & Barton, C. (2001). *Doing history: Investigating with children in elementary and middle school* (2nd ed.). Lawrence Erlbaum Associates.

Lewis, C., & Dockter Tierney, J. (2011). Mobilizing emotion in an urban English classroom. *Changing English, 18*(3), 319–329. https://doi.org/10.1080/1358684X.2011.602840

Lewis Ellison, T. (2014). An African American mother's stories as T.M.I.: M.N.I ethics and vulnerability around traumatic narratives in digital literacy research. *International Journal of Qualitative Methods, 13*, 255–274. https://doi.org/10.1177/160940691401300113

Louv, R. (2005). *Last child in the woods: Saving our children from Nature-Deficit Disorder*. Algonquin Books.

Luke, A. (2012). Critical literacy: Foundational notes. *Theory Into Practice, 51*(1), 4–11. https://doi.org/10.1080/00405841.2012.636324

Luke, A. (2018). *Critical literacy, schooling, and social justice: The selected works of Allan Luke*. Routledge

Luke, A., & Freebody, P. (1999). Further notes on the four resources model. *Reading Online, 3*, 1–6.

Madigan, S, Eirich, R., Pador, P., McArthur, B. A., & Neville, R. D. (2022). Assessment of changes in child and adolescent screen time during the COVID-19 pandemic: A systematic review and meta-analysis. *JAMA Pediatrics, 176*(12), 1188–1198. doi:10.1001/jamapediatrics.2022.4116

Mantzicopoulos, P., & Patrick, H. (2011). Reading picturebooks and learning science: Engaging young children with informational text. *Theory Into Practice, 50*(4), 269–276. https://www.jstor.org/stable/41331054

Martell, C. (2013). Learning to teach history as interpretation: A longitudinal study of beginning teachers. *The Journal of Social Studies Research, 37*, 17–31. https://doi.org/10.1016/j.jssr.2012.12.001

Mayer, D. A. (1995). How can we best use children's literature in teaching science concepts? *Science and Children, 32*(6), 16–43.

McCaw, C. T. (2020). Mindfulness 'thick' and 'thin'—A critical review of the uses of mindfulness in education. *Oxford Review of Education, 46*(2), 257–278. https://doi.org/10.1080/03054985.2019.1667759

Mehta, J. (2020, December 23). Make schools more human. *The New York Times*. https://www.nytimes.com/2020/12/23/opinion/covid-schools-vaccine.html

Miller, E., & Kissler, B. (2019). Vivian Vasquez, NCTE's 2019 outstanding elementary educator in the English language arts. *Language Arts, 97*(2), 72–77.

Moss, B. (2003). *Exploring the literature of fact: Children's nonfiction trade books in the elementary classroom*. The Guilford Press.

Muhammad, G. (2020). *Cultivating genius: An equity framework for culturally and historically responsive literacy*. Scholastic.

Muhammad, G. (2023). *Unearthing joy: A guide to culturally and historically responsive literacy teaching and learning*. Scholastic.

Müller, M. G. (2008). Visual competence: A new paradigm for studying visuals in the social sciences? *Visual Studies, 23*(2), 101–112. https://doi.org/10.1080/14725860802276248

Myers, C. (2013, August 6). Young dreamers. *The Horn Book*. https://www.hbook.com/2013/08/authors-illustrators/young-dreamers/

Myers, J. (2014). Digital conversations: Taking reader response into the 21st century. *English in Texas, 44*(1), 59–65.

Myers, W. D. (2014, March 15). Where are all the people of color in children's books? *The New York Times*. https://www.nytimes.com/2014/03/16/opinion/sunday/where-are-the-people-of-color-in-childrens-books.html

Nathanson, S., Pruslow, J., & Levitt, R. (2008). The reading habits and literacy attitudes of inservice and prospective teachers: Results of a questionnaire survey. *Journal of Teacher Education, 59*(4), 313–321. https://doi.org/10.1177/0022487108321685

Natarjan, A., Moslimani, M., & Lopez, M. H. (2022, December 16). *Key facts about recent trends in global migration*. Pew Research Center. https://www.pewresearch.org/fact-tank/2022/12/16/key-facts-about-recent-trends-in-global-migration/

National Academies of Sciences, Engineering, and Medicine. (2014). *Literacy for science: Exploring the intersection of the Next Generation Science Standards and Common Core for ELA Standards: A workshop summary*. The National Academies Press.

National Council for the Social Studies. (2010). *National curriculum standards for social studies: A framework for teaching, learning, and assessment*. National Council for the Social Studies.

National Council for the Social Studies. (2017). *Powerful, purposeful pedagogy in elementary school social studies* [Position statement.] https://www.socialstudies.org/position-statements/powerful-purposeful-pedagogy-elementary-school-social-studies

National Council for the Social Studies. (2019). *Early childhood in the social studies context* [Position statement]. https://www.socialstudies.org/position-statements/early-childhood-social-studies-context

National Council for the Social Studies. (2023). *College, career, and civic life (C3) framework for social studies state standards: Guidance for enhancing the rigor of K-12 civics, economics, geography, and history*. https://www.socialstudies.org/standards/c3

National Council of Teachers of English. (n.d). *Charlotte Huck award*. https://ncte.org/awards/ncte-childrens-book-awards/charlotte-huck-award/

National Institutes of Health Clinical Center. (2015). *Talking to children about death*. Author.

Nel, P. (2014). Was the cat in the hat black? Exploring Dr. Seuss's racial imagination. *Children's Literature, 42*, 71–98. https://doi.org/10.1353/chl.2014.0019

Neuman, S. B., & Moland, N. (2019). Book deserts: The consequences of income segregation on children's access to print. *Urban Education, 54*(1), 126–147. https://doi.org/10.1177/0042085916654525

NGSS Lead States. (2013). *Next Generation Science Standards: For states, by states.* National Academies Press.

Noddings, N. (2012). The caring relation in teaching. *Oxford Review of Education, 38*(6), 771–781. https://doi.org/10.1080/03054985.2012.745047

Nodelman, P., Hamer, N., & Reimer, M. (Eds.). (2017). *More words about pictures.* Routledge.

op de Beeck, N. (2018). Children's ecoliterature and the New Nature Study. *Children's Literature in Education, 49*(1), 73–85. https://doi.org/10.1007/s10583-018-9347-9

Pantaleo, S. (2018). Learning about and through picturebook artwork. *Reading Teacher, 71*(5), 557–567. https://doi.org/10.1002/trtr.1653

Pantaleo, S. (2020). Slow looking: "Reading picturebooks takes time." *Literacy, 54*(1), 40–48. https://doi.org/10.1111/lit.12190

Paris, D. (2012). Culturally sustaining pedagogy: A needed change in stance, terminology, and practice. *Educational Researcher, 41*(3), 93–97. https://doi.org/10.3102/0013189X12441244

Paris, D., & Alim, H. S. (2014). What are we seeking to sustain through culturally sustaining pedagogy? A loving critique forward. *Harvard Educational Review, 84*(1), 85–100. https://doi.org/10.17763/haer.84.1.982l873k2ht16m77

Patterson, T. J., & Shuttleworth, J. M. (2020). Teaching hard history through children's literature about enslavement. *Social Studies and the Young Learner, 32*(3), 14–19.

Pearson, P. D., Moje, E., & Greenleaf, C. (2010). Literacy and science: Each in the service of the other. *Science, 328*(5977), 459–463. https://doi.org/10.1126/science.1182595

Pendharkar, E. (2022, February 9). Efforts to ban critical race theory could restrict teaching for a third of America's kids. *Education Week, 41*(21), 8.

Proust, M., & Ruskin, J. (2011). *On reading.* Hesperus Press.

Quindlen, A. (1998). *How reading changed my life.* Ballantine Books.

Rosenblatt, L. (1938). *Literature as exploration.* D. Appleton-Century Company.

Rosenblatt, L. (1978/1994). *The reader, the text, the poem: The transactional theory of the literary work.* Southern Illinois University Press.

Royce, C. A., & Wiley, D. A. (1996). Children's literature and the teaching of science: Possibilities and cautions. *The Clearing House, 70*(1), 18–20. https://www.jstor.org/stable/30189226

Sanders, J. S. (2018). *A literature of questions. Nonfiction for the critical child.* University of Minnesota Press.

Santayana, G. (2011). *The life of reason or the phases of human progress: Introduction and reason in common sense* (Critical Edition, Volume VII, Book One). (M. S. Wokeck & M. A. Coleman, Eds.). MIT Press. (Original work published 1905).

Sapon-Shevin, M. (2010). *Because we can change the world: A practical guide to building cooperative, inclusive classroom communities.* Corwin Press.

Seligman, M. E. P., Ernst, R. M., Gillham, J., Reivich, K., & Linkins, M. (2009). Positive education: Positive psychology and classroom interventions. *Oxford Review of Education, 35*(3), 293–311. https://doi.org/10.1080/03054980902934563

Shanahan, T., Callison, K., Carriere, C., Duke, N. K., Pearson, P. D., Schatschneider, C., & Torgesen, J. (2010). *Improving reading comprehension in kindergarten through* 3rd

References

grade: A practice guide (Report No. NCEE 2010–4038). National Center for Education Evaluation and Regional Assistance, Institute of Education Sciences, U.S. Department of Education. https://ies.ed.gov/ncee/wwc/Docs/PracticeGuide/readingcomp_pg_092810.pdf

Shimek, C. (2021). "Let nature be your teacher": An ecocritical analysis of outdoor play in award-winning picturebooks in the United States. *Journal of Children's Literature, 47*(1), 51–61.

Shor, I. (1999). What is critical literacy? In I. Shor and C. Pari (Eds.), *Critical literacy in action: Writing words, changing worlds* (pp. 1–30). Boynton/Cook Publishers.

Sipe, L. R. (2002). Talking back and taking over: Young children's expressive engagement during storybook read-alouds. *The Reading Teacher, 55*(5), 476–483.

Snow, C. (2002). *Reading for understanding: Toward an R&D program in reading comprehension.* RAND Corporation. https://www.rand.org/pubs/monograph_reports/MR1465.html

Souto-Manning, M., & Yoon, H. S. (2018). *Rethinking early literacies: Reading and rewriting worlds.* Routledge.

Spencer, T. (2022). Using children's literature to advance anti-racist early childhood teaching and learning. *Issues in Teacher Education, 31*(2), 9–31.

Tavares, M. (2011, March/April). The reason for the picture. *The Horn Book, 87*(2), 49–55.

Teding van Berkhout, E., & Malouff, J. M. (2016). The efficacy of empathy training: A meta-analysis of randomized controlled trials. *Journal of Counseling Psychology, 63*(1), 32–41. https://doi.org/10.1037/cou0000093

Thomas, E. E. (2016). Stories still matter: Rethinking the role of diverse children's literature today. *Language Arts, 94*(2), 112–119. https://www.jstor.org/stable/i40203645

Tishman, S. (2018). *Slow looking: The art and practice of learning through observation.* Routledge.

Tyner, M. (2021, February 2). The CCBC's diversity statistics: New categories, new data. *School Library Journal.* https://www.hbook.com/story/the-ccbcs-diversity-statistics-new-categories-new-data

UNESCO. (2023). Literacy. United Nations Educational, Scientific and Cultural Organization. https://www.unesco.org/en/literacy

VanSledright, B. (2002). *In search of America's past: Learning to read history in elementary school.* Teachers College Press.

Varelas, M., Pieper, L., Arsenault, A., Pappas, C. C., & Keblawe-Shamah, N. (2014). How science texts and hands-on explorations facilitate meaning making: Learning from Latina/o third graders. *Journal of Research in Science Teaching, 51*(10), 1246–1274. https://doi.org/10.1002/tea.21173

Vasquez, V. M., Janks, H., & Comber, B. (2019). Critical literacy as a way of being and doing. *Language Arts, 96*(5), 300–309.

Wager, A. C., Clarke, L. W., & Enriquez, G., with Garcia, C., Lara, G. P., & Reynolds, R. (2019). *The reading turn-around with emergent bilinguals: A five-part framework for powerful teaching and learning (Grades K–6).* Teachers College Press.

Watson, W., Sealey-Ruiz, Y., & Jackson, I. (2014). Daring to care: The role of culturally relevant care in mentoring Black and Latino male high school students. *Race, Ethnicity, and Education, 19*(5), 980–1002. https://doi.org/10.1080/13613324.2014.911169

We Need Diverse Books. (2023). *About us.* https://diversebooks.org/about-wndb/

Wells, N. M. & Lekies, K. S. (2006). Nature and the life course: Pathways from childhood nature experiences to adult environmentalism. *Children, Youth and Environments, 16*(1), 1–24. https://www.jstor.org/stable/10.7721/chilyoutenvi.16.1.0001

Wells, R., & Zeece, P. D. (2007). My place in my world: Literature for place-based environmental education. *Early Childhood Education Journal, 35*(3), 285–291. https://doi.org/10.1007/s10643-007-0181-8

Welsh, K. M., Brock, C. H., Robertson, D. A., & Thrailkill, L. (2020). Disciplinary literacy in a second-grade classroom: A science inquiry unit. *Reading Teacher, 73*(6), 723–734. https://doi.org/10.1002/trtr.1881

Williams, J. A., Podeschi, C., Palmer, N., Schwadel, P., & Meyler, D. (2012). The human–environment dialog in award-winning children's picture books. *Sociological Inquiry, 82*(1), 145–159. https://doi.org/10.1111/j.1475-682X.2011.00399.x

Wineburg, S. (2010). Historical thinking and other unnatural acts: Debates about national history standards become so fixated on the question of "which history" that a more basic question is neglected: Why study history at all? *Phi Delta Kappan, 80*(4), 81–94. https://doi.org/10.1177/003172171009200420

Wineburg, S. (2021). The silence of the ellipses: Why history can't be about telling our children lies. *Phi Delta Kappan, 102*(5), 8–11. https://doi.org/10.1177/0031721721992558

Wissman, K. K., & Wiseman, A. (2011). "That's my worst nightmare": Poetry and trauma in the middle school classroom. *Pedagogies: An International Journal, 6*(3), 234–239. https://doi.org/10.1080/1554480X.2011.579051

Wolf, M. (2018). *Reader come home: The reading brain in a digital world.* Harper.

Wolfenbarger, C. D., & Sipe, L. (2007). A unique visual and literacy art form: Recent research on picturebooks. *Language Arts, 84*(3), 273–280.

Woodson, J. (1998, January 1). Who can tell my story. *The Horn Book Magazine, 74*(1), 34–38. https://www.hbook.com/story/who-can-tell-my-story

Wooten, D. A., & Clabough, J. (2014). Scientists in the field: Igniting the wonderment and value of science. *Journal of Children's Literature, 40*(2), 37–43.

Worth, K., Winokur, J., Crissman, C., Heller-Winokur, M., & Davus, M. (2009). *The essentials of science and literacy: A guide for teachers.* Educational Development Center and Heinemann.

Wright, T. S., & Gotwals, A. W. (2017). Supporting disciplinary talk from the start of school: Teaching students to think and talk like scientists. *Reading Teacher, 71*(2), 189–197. https://doi.org/10.1002/trtr.1602

Xiao, W., Lin, X., Li, X., Xu, X., Guo, H., Sun, B., & Jiang, H. (2021). The influence of emotion and empathy on decisions to help others. *SAGE Open, 11*(2). https://doi.org/10.1177/21582440211014513

Yenawine, P. (2013). *Visual thinking strategies: Using art to deepen learning across school disciplines.* Harvard Education Press.

Yeshurun, Y., Nguyen, M., & Hasson, U. (2021). The default mode network: Where the idiosyncratic self meets the shared social world. *Nature Reviews Neuroscience, 22*(3), 181–192. https://doi.org/10.1038/s41583-020-00420-w

Zapata, A. (2022). (Re)animating children's aesthetic experiences with/through literature: Critically curating picturebooks as sociopolitical art. *The Reading Teacher, 76*(1), 84–91. https://doi.org/10.1002/trtr.2128

Zarnowski, M. (2003). *History makers: A questioning approach to reading & writing biographies.* Heinemann.

Zarnowski, M. (2013). Reading for the mystery in nonfiction science books. *Journal of Children's Literature, 39*(2), 14–21.

Zarnowski, M. (2014). Shaping nonfiction: Making the facts "dance together." *Journal of Children's Literature, 40*(2), 6–14.

Zarnowski, M. (2019). "How one person sees another person": Focusing on the author's perspective in picturebook biographies. *Language Arts, 96*(3), 145–152. https://www.jstor.org/stable/26779049

Zarnowski, M., & Turkel, S. (2011). Nonfiction literature that highlights inquiry: How "real" people solve "real" problems. *Journal of Children's Literature, 37*(1), 30–37.

Zarnowski, M., & Turkel, S. (2012). Creating new knowledge: Books that demystify the process. *Journal of Children's Literature, 38*(1), 28–34.

Zarnowski, M., & Turkel, S. (2017). How history as mystery reveals historical thinking. *Language Arts, 94*(4), 234–243.

CHILDREN'S BOOKS

Alexander, K. (2014) *The crossover*. Houghton Mifflin Harcourt.

Alexander, K. (2019a). *The crossover* series. Houghton Mifflin Harcourt.

Alexander, K. (2019b). *How to read a book* (M. Sweet, Illus). HarperCollins.

Alexander, K. (2019c). *The undefeated* (K. Nelson, Illus.). Houghton Mifflin Harcourt.

Alston, B. B. (2021). *Amari and the night brothers*. Balzer & Bray.

Anand, S. (2021). *Laxmi's mooch* (N. H. Ali, Illus). Kokila.

Ancona, G. (2013). *It's our garden: From seeds to harvest in a school garden*. Candlewick Press.

Ancona, G. (2015). *Can we help? Kids volunteering to help their communities*. Candlewick Press.

Anderson, B. (2022). *Cloaked in courage: Uncovering Deborah Sampson, patriot soldier*. Calkins Creek.

Anderson, L. H. (2010). *Forge*. Atheneum Books for Young Readers.

Anderson, L. H. (2017). *Ashes*. Atheneum Books for Young Readers.

Applegate, K. (2012). *The one and only Ivan*. Harper.

Applegate, K. (2017). *Wishtree*. Feiwel & Friends.

Archer, M. (2021). *Wonder walkers*. Nancy Paulsen Books.

Armand, G. (2015). *Ira's Shakespeare dream* (F. Cooper, Illus.). Lee & Low Books.

Arnold, C. (2017). *Hatching chicks in room 6*. Charlesbridge.

Atinuke. (2007–present) *Anna Hibiscus* series (L. Tobia, Illus.). Candlewick Press.

Atkins, M. F. (2020). *Wait, rest, pause: Dormancy in nature*. Millbrook Press.

Averiss, C. (2018). *Joy* (I. Folath, Illus.). Quarto Publishing.

Bardoe, C. (2018). *Nothing stopped Sophie: The story of unshakable mathematician Sophie Germain* (B. McClintock, Illus.). Books for Young Readers.

Barnes, D. (2017). *Crown: An ode to the fresh cut* (G. C. James, Illus.). Agate Bolden Publishing.

Barnes, D. (2020). *I am every good thing* (G. C. James, Illus.). Nancy Paulsen Books.

Barnett, M. (2012). *Extra yarn* (J. Klassen, Illus.). Balzer & Bray.

Barton, C. (2018). *What do you do with a voice like that? The extraordinary Congresswoman Barbara Jordan* (E. Holmes, Illus.). Beach Lane Books.

Becker, H. (2018). *Counting on Katherine: How Katherine Johnson saved Apollo 13* (D. Phumiruk, Illus.). Christy Ottaviano Books.

Blanco, R. (2015). *One today* (D. Pilkey, Illus.). Little, Brown Books for Young Readers.

Bliss, Harry. (2018). *Grace for Gus*. Katherine Tegen Books.

Bolden, T. (2014). *Searching for Sarah Rector: The richest Black girl in America*. Abrams Books for Young Readers.

Bolden, T. (2020). *Strong voices: Fifteen American speeches worth knowing* (E. Velasquez, Illus.). HarperCollins.
Britt, P. (2017). *Why am I me?* (S. Qualls & S. Alko, Illus.). Scholastic.
Brown, D. (2015). *Drowned city: Hurricane Katrina and New Orleans*. Houghton Mifflin Harcourt.
Brown, D. (2021). *In the shadow of the fallen towers: The seconds, minutes, hours, days, weeks, months, and years after the September 11th attacks*. Houghton Mifflin Harcourt.
Brown, M. (2016). *Lesser spotted animals: The coolest creatures you've never heard of*. Scholastic.
Bryant, J. (2013). *A splash of red: The life and art of Horace Pippin* (M. Sweet, Illus.). Knopf Books for Young Readers.
Bryant, J. (2020). *Above the rim: How Elgin Baylor changed basketball* (F. Morrison, Illus.). Abrams Books for Young Readers.
Budhos, M. (2019). *The long ride*. Wendy Lamb Books.
Bulion, L. (2019). *Superlative birds* (R. Meganck, Illus.). Peachtree.
Burleigh, R. (2014). *Edward Hopper paints his world* (W. Minor, Illus.). Henry Holt.
Burns, L. G., & Harasimowicz, E. (2014). *Handle with care: An unusual butterfly journey*. Millbrook Press.
Campbell, C. (2014). *Mysterious patterns: Finding fractals in nature*. Boyd Mills Press.
Campoy, F. I., & Howell, T. (2016). *Maybe something beautiful* (R. López, Illus.). Houghton Mifflin Harcourt.
Cate, A. (2013). *Look up! Bird-watching in your own backyard*. Candlewick Press.
Chin, J. (2017). *Grand canyon*. Roaring Brook Press.
Cisneros, E. (2019). *Efrén divided*. Quill Tree Books.
Claire, C. (2017). *Shelter*. Kids Can Press.
Clark, M. H. (2018). *Tiny, perfect things* (M. Kloepper, Illus.). Compendium.
Clark-Robinson, M. (2018). *Let the children march* (F. Morrison, Illus.). Clarion Books.
Clarke, M. B. (2018). *The patchwork bike* (V. T. Rudd, Illus.). Candlewick Press.
Clements, A. (1997). *Big Al* (Yoshi, Illus.). Atheneum Books for Young Readers.
Cohn, D. (2002). *Si, se puede! Yes, we can! Janitor Strike in L.A.* (F. Delgado, Illus.). Cinco Punto Press.
Collier, B. (2021). *We shall overcome*. Scholastic.
Cordell, M. (2017). *Wolf in the snow*. Feiwel & Friends.
Cordell, M. (2021). *Bear island*. Feiwel & Friends.
Craft, J. (2019). *New kid*. HarperCollins.
Danticat, E. (2015). *Mama's nightingale: A story of immigration and separation* (L. Staub, Illus.). Dial Books for Young Readers.
Dassu, A. M. (2021). *Boy, everywhere*. Tu Books.
Davies, N. (2012). *Outside your window: A first book of nature* (M. Hearld, Illus.). Candlewick Press.
Davies, N. (2018). *The day war came* (R. Cobb, Illus.). Candlewick Press.
Daywalt, D. (2013). *The day the crayons quit* (O. Jeffers, Illus.). Candlewick Press.
de Arias, P. (2018). *Marwan's journey* (L. Borràs, Illus.). minedition.
de la Peña, M. (2015). *Last stop on Market Street* (C. Robinson, Illus.). G. P. Putnam's Sons.
de la Peña, M. (2018). *Love*. G. P. Putnam's Sons.
Denos, J. (2017). *Windows* (E. B. Goodale, Illus.). Candlewick Press.
Denos, J. (2019). *Here and now* (E. B. Goodale, Illus.). Candlewick Press.
dePaola, T. (1979). *Oliver Button is a sissy*. Voyager Books.

References

Diaz, J. (2018). *Islandborn* (L. Espinosa, Illus.). Dial Books for Young Readers.
DiCamillo, K. (2013). *Flora and Ulyssess: An illuminated adventure* (K. G. Campbell, Illus.). Candlewick Press.
DiCamillo, K. (2021). *The Beatryce prophecy* (S. Blackall, Illus.). Candlewick Press.
Doerrfeld, C. (2018). *The rabbit listened.* Dial Books for Young Readers.
Dunbar, E. A., & Van Cleve, K. (2019). *Never caught, the story of Ona Judge: George and Martha Washington's courageous slave who dared to run away.* Aladdin.
Dunbar-Ortiz, R., Mendoza, J., & Reese, D. (2019). *An Indigenous people's history of the United States for young people.* Beacon Press.
Elya, S. M. (2017). *La princesa and the pea* (J. Martinez-Neal, Illus.). G. P. Putnam's Sons.
Engle, M. (2015). *Drum dream girl: How one girl's courage changed music* (R. López, Illus.). Houghton Mifflin Harcourt.
Engle, M. (2019). *Dancing hands: How Teresa Carreño played the piano for President Lincoln* (R. López, Illus.). Atheneum Books for Young Readers.
Fan, T., & Fan, E. (2016). *The night gardener.* Simon & Schuster Books for Young Readers.
Fan, T., & Fan, E. (2018). *Ocean meets sky.* Simon & Schuster Books for Young Readers.
Fan, T., & Fan, E. (2021). *It fell from the sky.* Simon & Schuster Books for Young Readers.
Farish, T. (2016). *Luis paints the world* (O. Dominguez, Illus.). Carolrhoda Books.
Fleming, C. (2014). *The family Romanov: Murder, rebellion and the fall of Imperial Russia.* Anne Schwartz Books.
Fleming, C. (2016). *Giant squid* (E. Rohmann, Illus.). Roaring Brook Press.
Flett, J. (2021). *We all play / kimêtawânaw.* Greystone Kids.
Gidwitz, A. (2016). *The inquisitor's tale: Or, the three magical children and their holy dog* (H. Aly, Illus.). Dutton Children's Books.
Giovanni, N. (2018). *I am loved* (A. Bryan, Illus.). Atheneum Books for Young Readers.
Goodman, S. (2016). *The first step: How one girl put segregation on trial* (E. B. Lewis, Illus.). Bloomsbury Children's Books.
Gorman, A. (2021a). *Change sings: A children's anthem* (L. Long, Illus.). Viking.
Gorman, A. (2021b). *The hill we climb: An inaugural poem for the country.* Viking.
Gravett, E. (2012). *Wolf won't bite.* Simon & Schuster Books for Young Readers.
Griffith, E. (2021). *Secrets of the sea: The story of Jeanne Power, revolutionary marine scientist* (J. Stone, Illus.). Clarion Books.
Grimes, N. (2021). *Legacy: Women poets of the Harlem Renaissance.* Bloomsbury Children's Books.
Hale, C. (2012). *Dreaming up: A celebration of building.* Lee & Low Books.
Hammill, E. (2105). *Over the hills and far away: A treasury of nursery rhymes* (Various artists, Illus.). Candlewick Press.
Harrison, D. L. (2018). *A place to start a family: Poems about creatures that build* (G. LaRoche, Illus.). Charlesbridge.
Harvey, J. W. (2022). *Ablaze with color: A story of painter Alma Thomas* (L. Wise, Illus.). Harper.
Henkes, K. (1991). *Chrysanthemum.* HarperCollins Children's Books.
Herbert, M., & Mann, M. (2022). *The tantrum that saved the world* (M. Herbert, Illus.). North Atlantic Books.
Higuera, D. B. (2021). *The last cuentista.* Levine Querido.
Hill, L. C. (2010). *Dave the potter: Artist, poet, slave* (B. Collier, Illus.). Little, Brown Books for Young Readers.

Hillery, T. (2020). *Harlem grown: How one big idea transformed a neighborhood* (J. Hartland, Illus.). Simon & Schuster/Paula Wiseman Books.

Hiranandani, V. (2018). *The night diary*. Dial Books for Young Readers.

Ho, J. (2021). *Eyes that kiss in the corners* (D. Ho, Illus.). Harper.

Hood, S. (2016). *Ada's violin: The story of the recycled orchestra of Paraguay* (S. W. Comport, Illus.). Simon & Schuster Books for Young Readers.

Hopkinson, D. (2013). *The great trouble: A mystery of London, the blue death, and a boy called Eel*. Alfred A. Knopf.

Hopkinson, D. (2016). *A bandit's tale: The muddled misadventures of a pickpocket*. Alfred A. Knopf Books for Young Readers.

Hughes, L. (2012). *I, too, am America* (B. Collier, Illus.). Simon & Schuster Books for Young Readers.

Hunt, L. M. (2015). *Fish in a tree*. Nancy Paulsen Books.

Janeczko, P. B. (2014). *Firefly July: A year of very short poems* (M. Sweet, Illus.). Candlewick Press.

Jenner, E., Wilson, K., & Roberts, N. (2020). *Coronavirus: A book for children* (A. Scheffler, Illus.). Nosy Crow.

Johnson, V. (2018). *The Parker inheritance*. Arthur A. Levine Books.

Judge, L. (2012). *Bird talk: What birds are saying and why*. Roaring Brook Press.

Judge, L. (2021). *The wisdom of trees. How trees work together to form a natural kingdom*. Roaring Brook Press.

Keller, T. (2020). *When you trap a tiger*. Random House.

Kelly, E. E. (2017). *Hello, universe*. Greenwillow Books.

Kelly, E. E. (2021a). *Maybe Marisol* series. Greenwillow Books.

Kelly, E. E. (2021b). *Maybe maybe Marisol Rainey*. Greenwillow Books.

Kelsey, Elin. (2015). *Wild ideas: Let nature inspire your thinking* (S. Kim, Illus.). Owl Kids Books.

Kensky, J., & Downes, P. (2018). *Rescue and Jessica: A life-changing friendship*. Candlewick Press.

Kim, P. (2014). *Here I am* (S. Sanchez, Illus.). Picture Window Books.

Lakshmi, P. (2021). *Tomatoes for Neela* (J. Martinez-Neal, Illus.). Viking.

Latham, I., & Waters, C. (2020). *Dictionary for a better world: Poems, quotes, and anecdotes from A to Z* (M. Amini, Illus.). Carolrhoda Books.

Lawlor, L. (2012). *Rachel Carson and her book that changed the world* (L. Beingessner, Illus.). Holiday House.

Leannah, M. (2021). *Most days* (M. E. Barrata, Illus.). Tilbury House.

Lee, J. S. (2021). *Finding home: The journey of immigrants and refugees* (D. Shannon, Illus). Orca Books.

L'Engle, M. (2012). *A wrinkle in time* (50th anniversary commemorative special ed.). Farrar, Straus, & Giroux. (Original work published 1962)

Letria, J. J. (2011). *If I were a book* (A. Letria, Illus.). Chronicle Books.

Levinson, C., & Levinson, S. (2019). *Fault lines in the Constitution: The framers, their fights, and the laws that affect us today*. Peachtree Publishers.

Levy, D. (2016). *I dissent! Ruth Bader Ginsburg makes her mark* (E. Baddeley, Illus.). Simon & Schuster Books for Young Readers.

Lewis, J., & Aydin, A. (2016). *March: Book three* (N. Powell, Illus.). Top Shelf Productions.

Lindstrom, C. (2020). *We are water protectors* (M. Goade, Illus.). Roaring Brook Press.

Love, J. (2018). *Julián is a mermaid*. Candlewick Press.

References

Lyons, K. S. (2019). *Going down home with daddy* (D. Minter, Illus.). Peachtree Publishers.

Lyons, K. S. (2020). *Dream builder: The story of architect Philip Freelon* (L. Freeman, Illus.). Lee & Low Books.

Maillard, K. N. (2019). *Fry bread: A Native American family story* (J. Martinez-Neil, Illus.). Roaring Brook Press.

Maldonado, T. (2021). *What lane?* Nancy Paulsen Books.

Markel, M. (2013). *Brave girl: Clara and the shirtwaist makers' strike of 1909* (M. Sweet, Illus.). Balzer & Bray.

Martinez-Neal, J. (2019). *Alma and how she got her name*. Candlewick Press.

McManis, C. W., & Sorell, T. (2019). *Indian no more*. Tu Books, Lee & Low Publishers.

McNeal, T. (2014). *Far, far away*. Alfred A. Knopf.

Medina, J. (2016–present). *Juana and Lucas* series. Candlewick Press.

Medina, M. (2018). *Merci Suárez changes gears*. Candlewick Press.

Méndez, Y. S. (2019). *Where are you from?* (J. Kim, Illus.). Harper.

Messner, K. (2016). *The seventh wish*. Bloomsbury Children's Books.

Messner, K. (2017). *Over and under the pond* (C. S. Neal, Illus.). Chronicle Books.

Messner, K. (2021). *Dr. Fauci: How a boy from Brooklyn became America's doctor* (A. Bye, Illus.). Simon & Schuster Books for Young Readers.

Metcalf, L. H., Dawson, K. V., & Bradley, J. (2020). *No voice too small: Fourteen young Americans making history* (J. Bradley, Illus.). Charlesbridge.

Mills, D., & Alva, A. (2018). *La frontera: El viaje con Papá/My journey with Papa*. Barefoot Books.

Montgomery, S. (2020). *Becoming a good creature: A memoir in thirteen animals* (R. Green, Illus.). Houghton Mifflin Harcourt.

Morales, Y. (2018). *Dreamers*. Neal Porter Books.

Naidoo, B. (2004). *Making it home: Real-life stories from children forced to flee*. Puffin Books.

Nelson, K. (2011). *Heart and soul: The story of America and African Americans*. Balzer & Bray.

Nelson, M. (2022). *Augusta Savage: The shape of a sculptor's life*. Christy Ottaviano Books.

Nelson, V. M. (2015). *The book itch: Freedom, truth, and Harlem's greatest bookstore* (R. G. Christie, Illus.). Carolrhoda Books.

Nivola, C.A. (2012). *Life in the ocean: The story of oceanographer Sylvia Earle*. Farrar, Straus & Giroux.

Nobleman, M. T. (2018). *Thirty minutes over Oregon: A Japanese pilot's World War II story* (M. Iwai, Illus.). Clarion Books.

Novesky, A. (2102). *Georgia in Hawaii: When Georgia O'Keefe painted what she pleased* (Y. Morales, Illus.). Harcourt Children's Books.

Nye, N. S. (2020). *Everything comes next: Collected and new poems*. Greenwillow Books.

Oh, E. (Ed.). (2017). *Flying lessons & other stories*. Crown Books for Young Readers.

Orgill, R. (2016). *Jazz day: The making of a famous photograph* (Francis Vallejo, Illus.). Candlewick Press.

Orwell, G. (1946). *Animal Farm*. Harcourt, Brace and Company, Inc.

Page, R. (2019). *Seeds move!* Beach Lane Books.

Paul, M. (2015a). *One plastic bag: Isatou Ceesay and the recycling women of the Gambia* (E. Zunon, Illus.). Millbrook Press.

Paul, M. (2015b). *Water is water: A book about the water cycle* (J. Chin, Illus.). Roaring Brook Press.
Paul, M., & Paul, R. (2021). *Peace* (E. Meza, Illus.). NorthSouth Books.
Phelan, M. (2016). *Snow White: A graphic novel*. Candlewick Press.
Phi, B. (2017). *A different pond* (T. Bui, Illus.). Capstone Young Readers.
Pinkney, A. D. (2008). *Boycott blues: How Rosa Parks inspired a nation* (B. Pinkney, Illus.). Greenwillow Books.
Pinkney, A. D. (2010). *Sit-in: How four friends stood up by sitting down* (B. Pinkney, Illus.). Little, Brown Books for Young Readers.
Pinkney, A. D. (2014). *The red pencil* (S. W. Evans, Illus.). Little, Brown Books for Young Readers.
Pinkney, J. (2006). *The little red hen*. Dial Books for Young Readers
Pinkney, J. (2009). *The lion and the mouse*. Little, Brown Books for Young Readers.
Poletti, F., & Yee, K. (2017). *The girl who ran: Bobbi Gibb, the first woman to run the Boston marathon* (S. Chapman, Illus.). Compendium.
Powell, P. H. (2014). *Josephine: The dazzling life of Josephine Baker* (C. Robinson, Illus.). Chronicle Books.
Prevot, F. (2015). *Wangari Maathai: The woman who planted millions of trees* (A. Fronty, Illus.). Candlewick Press.
Rabinowitz, A. (2014). *A boy and a jaguar* (C. Chien, Illus.). Houghton Mifflin Harcourt.
Ramos, N. (2022). *Beauty woke* (P. Escobar, Illus.). Versify.
Rappaport, D. (2001). *Martin's big words: The life of Dr. Martin Luther King, Jr.* (B. Collier, Illus.). Little, Brown Books for Young Readers.
Reynolds, J., & Kendi, I. X. (2020). *Stamped: Racism, antiracism, and you*. Little, Brown Books for Young Readers.
Rhodes, J. P. (2016). *Towers falling*. Little, Brown Books for Young Readers.
Riley, S. (2021). *The floating field: How a group of Thai boys built their own soccer field*. Millbrook Press.
Robeson, T. (2019). *Queen of physics: How Wu Chien Shiung helped unlock the secrets of the atom* (R. Huang, Illus.). Union Square & Co.
Rockliff, M. (2015). *Mesmerized: How Ben Franklin solved a mystery that baffled all of France* (I. Bruno, Illus.). Candlewick Press.
Rumford, J. (2010). *Rain school*. Houghton Mifflin Books for Children.
Rusch, E. (2020). *You call this democracy? How to fix our government and deliver power to the people*. Houghton Mifflin Harcourt.
Ruzzier, S. (2018). *Fox + chick: The party and other stories*. Chronicle Books.
Ryan, P. M. (2015). *Echo: A novel*. Scholastic Press.
Sana, F. (2016). *The journey*. Flying Eye Books.
Sanders, R. (2019). *Stonewall: A building. An uprising. A revolution* (J. Christoph, Illus.). Random House.
Santat, D. (2014). *The adventures of Beekle: The unimaginary friend*. Little, Brown Books for Young Readers.
Santat, D. (2017). *After the fall: How Humpty Dumpty got back up again*. Roaring Brook Press.
Sayre, A. P. (2013). *Here come the humpbacks* (J. Hogan, Illus.). Charlesbridge.
Sayre, A. P. (2015). *Raindrops roll*. Beach Lane Books.
Sayre, A. P. (2020). *Being frog*. Beach Lane Books.
Schnell, L. K. (2015). *High tide for horseshoe crabs* (A. Marks, Illus.). Charlesbridge.

Scieszka, J. (1996). *The true story of the three little pigs* (L. Smith, Illus.). Viking.
Senzai, N. H. (2018). *Escape from Aleppo*. Paula Wiseman Books.
Sepahban, L. (2016). *Paper wishes*. Farrar Straus Giroux Books for Young Readers.
Sheehy, S. (2015). *Welcome to the neighborwood*. Candlewick Press.
Sheinkin, S. (2010). *The notorious Benedict Arnold: A true story of adventure, heroism, and treachery*. Roaring Brook Press.
Sheinkin, S. (2012). *Bomb: The race to build—and steal—the world's most dangerous weapon*. Roaring Brook Press.
Sidman, J. (2011). *Swirl by swirl: Patterns in nature* (B. Krommes, Illus.). Houghton Mifflin Harcourt.
Sidman, J. (2014). *Winter bees and other poems of the cold* (R. Allen, Illus.). Houghton Mifflin Harcourt.
Sidman, J. (2018). *Round* (T. Yoo, Illus.). Houghton Mifflin Harcourt.
Simon, S. (2002). *Animals nobody loves*. Chronicle Books.
Singer, M. (2010). *Mirror mirror: A book of reverso poems* (J. Masse, Illus.). Dutton Books for Young Readers.
Singer, M. (2013). *Follow follow: A book of reverso poems* (J. Masse, Illus.). Dial Books.
Singer, M. (2016). *Echo Echo: Reverso poems about Greek myths* (J. Masse, Illus.). Dial Books.
Slater, D. (2017). *The antlered ship* (T. Fan & E. Fan, Illus.). Beach Lane Books.
Smith, C. L. (Ed.). (2021). *Ancestor approved*. Heartdrum.
Smith, M. G. (2020). *When we are kind* (N. Niedhardt, Illus.). Orca Book Publishers.
Sorell, T. (2021). *We are still here! Native American truths everyone should know* (F. Lessac, Illus.). Charlesbridge.
Stanley, D. (2016). *Ada Lovelace, poet of science: The first computer programmer* (J. Hartland, Illus.). Simon & Schuster Books for Young Readers.
Stead, P. C. (2010). *A sick day for Amos McGee* (E. E. Stead, Illus.). Roaring Brook Press.
Stead, P. C. (2016). *Ideas are all around*. Roaring Brook Press.
Stead, R. (2015). *Goodbye stranger*. Wendy Lamb Books.
Steptoe, J. (2016). *Radiant child: The story of young artist Jean-Michel Basquiat*. Little Brown.
Stewart, M. (2013). *No monkeys, no chocolate* (N. Wong, Illus.). Charlesbridge.
Stewart, M. (2017). *Can an aardvark bark?* (S. Jenkins, Illus.). Beach Lane.
Stewart, M. (2019). *Seashells, more than a home* (S. Brannen, Illus.). Charlesbridge.
Stone, T. L. (2009). *Almost astronauts: 13 women who dared to dream*. Candlewick Press.
Stone, T. L. (2013). *Courage has no color: The true story of the Triple Nickles, America's first paratroopers*. Candlewick Press.
Sweet, M. (2016). *Some writer! The story of E. B. White*. Houghton Mifflin Harcourt.
Tan, S. (2018). *Cilla-Lee Jenkins: Future author extraordinaire* (D. Wulfekotte, Illus.). Square Fish.
Tarpley, N. (2017). *The Harlem charade*. Scholastic Press.
Temple, K., & Temple, J. (2019). *Room on our rock* (T. R. Baynton, Illus.). Kane Miller Books.
Thomas, I. (2019). *Moth: An evolution story* (D. Egnéus, Illus.). Bloomsbury Children's Books.
Thompkins-Bigelow, J. (2020). *Your name is a song*. The Innovation Press.
Tonatiuh, D. (2011). *Diego Rivera: His world and ours*. Abrams Books for Young Readers.
Tonatiuh, D. (2014). *Separate is never equal: Sylvia Mendez and her family's fight for desegregation*. Abrams Books for Young Readers.

Verde, S. (2018). *Hey, wall! A story of art and community* (J. Parra, Illus.). Simon & Schuster/Paula Wiseman Books.
Wallace, S. N., & Wallace, R. (2020). *The teachers march! How Selma's teachers changed history* (C. Palmer, Illus.). Calkins Creek.
Weatherford, C. B. (2014). *Sugar Hill: Harlem's historic neighborhood* (R. G. Christie, Illus.). Albert Whitman and Company.
Weatherford, C. B. (2015). *Voice of freedom: Fannie Lou Hamer: The spirit of the Civil Rights Movement* (E. Holmes, Illus.). Candlewick Press.
Weatherford, C. B. (2021). *Unspeakable: The Tulsa race massacre* (F. Cooper, Illus.). Carolrhoda Books.
Wenzel, B. (2019). *A stone sat still*. Chronicle Books.
White, E. B. (1952). *Charlotte's web*. Harper & Brothers.
Winter, J. (2011). *The watcher: Jane Goodall's life with the chimps*. Schwartz & Wade Books.
Winter, J. (2019). *Our house is on fire: Greta Thunberg's call to save the planet*. Beach Lane Books.
Woelfe, G. (2014). *Mumbet's declaration of independence* (A. Delinois, Illus.). Carolrhoda Books.
Woodson, J. (2012). *Each kindness* (E. B. Lewis, Illus.). Nancy Paulsen Books.
Woodson, J. (2022). *The year we learned to fly* (R. López, Illus.). Nancy Paulsen Books.
Yamada, K. (2018). *What do you do with a chance?* Compendium.
Yamasaki, K. (2021). *Dad bakes*. Norton Young Readers.
Yelchin, E. (2011). *Breaking Stalin's nose*. Henry Holt and Company.
Yolen, J., & Stemple, H. E. Y. (2021). *I am the storm* (K. Howdeshell & K. Howdeshell, Illus.). Rise Books.
Yousafzai, M. (2017). *Malala's magic pencil* (Kerascoët, Illus.). Little, Brown Books for Young Readers.
Yuksel, M. O. (2022). *One wish: Fatima Al-Fihri and the world's oldest university*. Harper Collins.

Index

Ablaze With Color (Harvey), 57, 69–70, 72, 117
Above the Rim (Bryant), 99, 129
action(s), 1, 5, 9, 30, 34–36, 42, 44, 48, 50, 56, 60, 64, 68, 74–75, 81, 84, 88–89, 91–92, 97–98, 106, 120, 137. *See also* Social action; collaborative, 54, 115
activism, 47, 56, 68, 74, 120, 129–130
Ada Lovelace (Stanley), 88, 112
Ada's Violin (Hood), 136
Adventures of Beekle, The (Santat), 96
After the Fall (Santat), 34, 88, 96, 98, 105
agency, 33–34, 44, 46, 50, 54, 79, 83–84, 88, 91–93, 98, 120
Alma and How She Got Her Name (Martinez Neal), 128
Almost Astronauts (Stone), 132
Amari and the Night Brothers (Alston), 98
Anna Hibiscus series (Atinuke), 131
Ancestor Approved (Smith), 110, 133
animal(s), 20, 25–26, 32, 33–34, 50, 58, 65, 74, 76, 116, 118–120, 123
Animals Nobody Loves (Simon), 76
anthropomorphized animals, 33–34
Antlered Ship, The (Slater), 96
art, 11, 23, 45, 49, 55, 57, 59, 61, 68–72, 87, 117, 124, 135–126. *See also* Illustration(s); visual, 119, 128
artist(s), 26, 49, 57, 61, 68–69, 74, 107, 117, 124–125, 136, 138. *See also* illustrator(s)
artistic choices, 99
artistic design, 68
artistic expression, 69, 104
artistic techniques, 76
artistry, ix, 6, 121
artwork, 26, 33, 69, 97, 103, 117, 122
Ashes (Anderson), 108, 114
assess, 24, 39, 56, 74, 92. *See also* Informal assessment
assessment tools, 84
assumption(s), 16, 18–19, 22, 78–80, 86–88, 92, 138
Augusta Savage (Nelson), 111
author(s), 3–4, 11, 15–17, 28–29, 44, 46–49, 51, 54–55, 61, 75–76, 80, 85, 88, 95, 97, 99, 104, 108–109, 113, 120–123, 128, 131–133, 138. *See also* Writer(s); authentic, 20; author's note, 33, 65, 82, 85, 125–126; identity, 68, 80; student, 23; visible, 47
autobiography(ies), 12, 24
award(s), 60; AAAS/Subaru SB&F Prize for Excellence in Science, 60; Caldecott, 2, 41, 52, 60, 67–68; Charlotte Huck, 26, 32; Coretta Scott King, 2; Ezra Jack Keats, 60; Green Earth, 60; National Book Award, 48; Newbery, 19, 35, 67; *The New York Times* Notable Children's Book, 32; winning author, 7, 19, 85, 133; winning book(s), 23, 60

backmatter, 46–49, 58, 108–109, 112–113, 121, 135
Bandit's Tale, A (Hopkinson), 54–55
Bear Island (Cordell), 29, 38, 103–105
Beatryce Prophecy, The (DiCamillo), 54–55, 99
Beauty Woke (Ramos), 78, 86, 128, 134
Becoming a Good Creature (Montgomery), 104, 118
Being Frog (Pulley Sayre), 23, 65, 118, 123
belonging, 1, 5, 12, 14, 21, 36, 87, 113
Big Al (Clements), 76
biodiversity, 59–60
biography(ies), 20–21, 23, 45, 49, 56, 65, 69, 74, 88, 90, 98, 111–112, 114, 116–117, 127. *See also* Autobiography(ies)
Bird Talk (Judge), 123
blog, 3–4, 7, 101, 121. *See also* Classroom Bookshelf, The
Bomb (Sheinkin), 113
book bans, 30, 44
book bias, 17–20
book conversations, 12, 21–23, 25, 41
book club, 17, 25, 55
book desert, 14
Book Itch, The (Nelson), 111
book review(s), ix, 3, 95, 115, 131
book selection, ix, 1, 4, 9, 12, 18–19, 21–24, 66, *See also* Choice: book; Text selection
Boy and a Jaguar, A (Rabinowitz), 99
Boy, Everywhere (Dassu), 86, 131
Boycott Blues (Pinkney), 89

157

Brave Girl (Markel), 79, 89, 102
Breaking Stalin's Nose (Yelchin), 81

Can an Aardvark Bark? (Stewart), 123
Can We Help? (Ancona), 89, 106, 125, 129
care, ix, 9, 21, 24–29, 31–32, 35–36, 38–39, 78, 93, 96–97, 103, 108; about others, 6, 21, 34, 39, 95, 103; about self, 6, 21, 34, 38, 39, 95; capacity for, 33–34; medical, 47; to select books, 55–56, 74, 86
censorship. *See* Book bans
change, x, 13, 23, 26–29, 31, 41, 43–44, 52–54, 58, 64, 77, 79, 89, 91, 106, 115, 129, 130; character, 93; social, 36, 84, 89, 92, 129, 130
Change Sings (Gorman), 79, 106, 133
changemaker(s), 56; changemaking, 74
character(s), 3–4, 14, 18–21, 32–36, 38–39, 50, 55–56, 74, 76, 85, 86–88, 95–96, 99, 101–103, 105, 128, 130–131, 133, 137; change, 98; diverse, 34–35, 60; dynamic, 38, 98; realistic, 31, 34; traits, 2, 23, 34
Charlotte's Web (White), 28–29
childhood, 14, 21, 23, 29, 32, 54, 82, 90
children's books, 5, 9, 12, 22, 45, 61, 63, 122, 130, 133. *See also* Children's literature; Literature
children's literature, ix, xi, 3, 5–6, 12, 17, 19, 26–31, 33, 41, 44–46, 52, 61, 63–64, 79, 81, 83–85, 87, 95, 97, 120, 138. *See also* Children's books; Literature
choice(s), ix, 9, 24, 55, 99, 108; author, 48, 75, 121; book, 2, 14, 55; instructional, x, 1; student, 57, 108
Chrysanthemum (Henkes), 76
Cilla-Lee Jenkins (Tan), 137
citizen(s), 51, 110; global, 9, 36; scientists, 74; senior, 107
citizenship, 30, 42
civil rights, 88, 115; Civil Rights Era, 45; Civil Rights Movement, 20, 40
classroom(s), ix, xi, 1–6, 9, 11–20, 22–25, 28, 31, 34, 39–40, 42–44, 46–47, 56–57, 61–62, 72, 74–75, 77, 86–87, 92, 104, 107, 110, 114, 118–119, 121, 125, 128, 138. *See also* Community; bookshelf(ves), 4, 33–34, 102, 131; community, 21, 23, 43, 103; library(ies), 12, 18–20, 23, 35, 55, 101; practice, x, 18
Classroom Bookshelf, The, ix, 3–5, 7, 21, 36, 45, 93, 121, 125
climate change, 53, 59, 97
climate justice, 59, 75, 120
Cloaked in Courage (Anderson), 46, 109
close observation, ix, 5, 9, 22, 24, 57–59 61–64, 66–71, 73–74, 78, 93, 97, 119, 122–123, 126
close reading, 65, 99, 120
community, 6, 15, 17, 21–23, 40–43, 53, 55, 66, 69, 76, 83, 89, 103–104, 107, 110–111, 115, 124, 129, 130, 135–136

compassion, x, 3, 9, 21, 26, 29, 34–36, 38–39, 95, 101, 138; self-compassion, 36, 38
comprehension, ix, 2, 16, 26, 31, 64, 77–78, 81. *See also* Meaning
conference, ix, 12, 14
connect(ion), 21, 23, 29–32, 39–43, 47, 49–50, 61, 64–65, 68–70, 72, 74, 90, 104, 106, 108–109, 116, 118, 121, 129, 136. *See also* Disconnect(ion); Interconnectedness; Reconnect(ion); content, 2, 96, 108, 117, 122, 128; to characters, 21, 39, 102; to nature, 59, 61, 72; to past, ix, 5–6, 9, 21, 24, 40, 43, 45, 54–56, 78, 93, 96, 107; to present, 41, 55; with books, 7, 12
conscientização, 78–79
content, 2–4, 16, 19–20, 26, 30, 66, 78, 80, 84–85, 121–122, 131–132, 134; area(s), 20, 24, 100, 123; standards, 116
context(s), ix–x, 5–7, 12, 16–17, 22, 35, 44–45, 47, 50, 54, 66, 129. *See also* Classroom
conversation(s), 3, 12, 21–23, 26, 35, 41–42, 45, 53, 59–60, 63, 75, 86, 96–97, 104–105, 128
Cooperative Children's Book Center, 17
Coronavirus (Jenner et al), 131
counterstorytelling, 88, 131
Counting on Katherine (Becker), 78, 112, 115, 127
courage, 13, 29, 31–33, 68, 138
Courage Has No Color (Stone), 109, 113
creativity, 2, 11, 35, 112
critical consciousness, 5–6, 22, 24, 39, 75–81, 83–85, 87–88, 90–93, 127–128, 130–131
critical hope, 28
critical literacy(ies), 80–81, 97, 111, 119, 131, 133–134
critical love, 39
critical race theory, 30
critical thinking, 43
Crossover, The (Alexander), 105, 131
Crossover, The (series), (Alexander), 131
Crown (Barnes), 78–79, 87, 103
culture, 2, 4, 19, 28, 34, 39, 42, 44, 50, 54–56, 68–69, 78, 85–87, 110–111, 128. *See also* Sociocultural; classroom, 13, 16; popular, 82
cultural awareness, 10, 78
cultural backgrounds, 4, 132
cultural differences, 96
cultural identity(ies), 16, 22, 81
cultural norms, 40, 110
culturally relevant pedagogies, 36
culturally sustaining practices, 36
curiosity, 3, 11, 22, 61, 97, 124
curriculum, ix, 1, 2, 4, 5, 10, 12, 14, 23, 43, 45, 57, 63, 76, 85, 97, 122

Dad Bakes (Yamasaki), 104
Dancing Hands (Engle), 99

Index

Dave the Potter (Hill), 49, 109, 136
Day the Crayons Quit, The (Daywalt), 135
Day War Came, The (Davies), 79
Day You Begin, The (Woodson), 33
decoding, 13, 77–78, 81
deficit, 21, 61, 87
democracy, 9
developmental milestones, 54
developmental readiness, 131
developmentally appropriate, 45, 132
Dictionary for a Better World (Latham & Waters), 79, 106, 130, 134
Diego Rivera (Tonatiuh), 124, 136
Different Pond, A (Phi), 79
digital, 59, 99; cameras, 125; nonfiction, 15; resource, 3; storytelling, 128; technology, 79; world, 60
disciplinary literacy(ies), 45, 59, 61, 64–65, 96, 108, 117, 128
disconnect(ion), 12–14, 20, 59, 61
diverse, 67, 73, 85–87, 128, 132; authors, 4; books, 22, 24, 86; classroom(s), 34; identity(ies), 20, 81; individuals, 17; representations, 4, 20–22; society(ies), 18, 33, 36, 56, 74; text(s), 84–86; world, 31, 33, 36, 38
diversity, 1, 5, 7, 9, 12, 16, 20, 35, 42, 56, 68, 74, 86, 131
Dr. Fauci (Messner), 119
Dream Builder (Lyons), 126
Dreamers (Morales), 52, 108, 129, 133
Dreaming Up (Hale), 125
Drowned City (Brown), 112
Drum Dream Girl (Engle), 97, 136
dynamic learning frame, 33, 105

Each Kindness (Woodson), 76
ebook(s), 15, 125
Echo (Ryan), 134
Echo Echo (Singer), 87, 134
education, 12, 18, 44, 52, 58, 60, 69, 71, 75, 79, 84. *See also* Literacy(ies)
Edward Hopper Paints His World (Burleigh), 117
Efrén Divided (Cisneros), 132
emotion, 2, 4, 9, 16, 26–27, 30, 32–33, 35, 38–39, 54, 68, 95–97, 99–103, 105, 114, 120–122.
emotionally transport(ing), 9, 21, 31–33, 46
emotionally vulnerable, 28
empathy, 30–31, 35–36, 38, 47
engagement, x, 1, 3, 5, 12, 14, 17, 22, 24, 26, 29–31, 34, 44, 46, 49, 56–61, 67, 69–73, 75, 78, 87–89, 93, 105, 107, 116
environment, ix, 6, 9, 16, 57, 60, 65, 66, 71, 73–74, 116, 119, 120, 128; environmental stewardship, 59–60
equity, 1, 5, 9, 12, 22, 30, 32, 47, 56, 60, 78–79, 83–84, 88, 102, 127, 129, 111; equitable representations, 21; equitable world, 31, 33, 77–78, 127; inequity, 31, 78, 84–85, 89, 91, 95, 98, 135
Escape From Aleppo (Senzai), 108
Everything Comes Next (Nye), 100
Extra Yarn (Barnett), 95
Eyes That Kiss in the Corners (Ho), 78, 87, 103–104

Family Romanov, The (Fleming), 50, 109, 114
fantasy, 98, 130
Far, Far Away (McNeal), 134
Fault Lines in the Constitution (Levinson & Levinson), 108, 113, 130
fiction(s), 1, 4, 6, 19, 23, 25–26, 32, 41, 45, 50–54, 63, 89, 98, 100, 107–108, 131, 134; contemporary realistic, 98; fictionalized (fictionalization), 47, 49; graphic, 15; historical, 21, 49–50, 53–55, 81, 108, 114; science, 130
Finding Home (Lee), 89
Firefly July (Janeczko), 102
First Step, The (Goodman), 110, 114
Fish in a Tree (Hunt), 103
Floating Field, The (Riley), 99
Flora and Ulysses: The Illuminated Adventures (DiCamillo), 28, 101
Flying Lessons & Other Stories (Oh), 103
Follow Follow (Singer), 88
Forge (Anderson), 108
four purposes framework, 5–7, 21, 57, 93, 138. *See also* Purpose: four purposes
Fox + Chick (Ruzzier), 96, 101
framework, 1, 5, 7, 9, 12, 23–24, 47, 54, 57, 93. *See also* Four purposes framework; antiracist, 43; College, Career, and Civil Life (C3) Framework, 45; Historically Responsive Literacy Framework, 43
Frederick (Lionni), 95
Frog and Toad (Lobel), 95
Fry Bread (Maillard), 110

genre, 2, 4, 6, 15, 20, 23–24, 44, 49, 54, 66, 78, 85, 98, 111–112, 134; multigenre, 64, 130, 133; study, 69, 120, 125
Georgia in Hawaii (Novesky), 117
Giant Squid (Fleming), 119
Girl Who Ran, The (Poletti & Yee), 127
Going Down Home With Daddy (Lyons), 100, 104
Goodbye Stranger (Stead), 88
government, 40, 48, 81–82, 135
Grace for Gus (Bliss), 100
Grand Canyon (Chin), 109, 113, 119
graphic books, 19, 49, 112. *See also* Graphic novel; Text: graphic text
graphic novel(s), 18–19, 34, 99. *See also* Graphic books; Text: graphic
graphic organizer(s), 63, 70, 128
Great Trouble, The (Hopkinson), 50, 114

Handle With Care (Burns &Harasimowicz), 125
Harlem Charade, The (Tarpley), 111
Harlem Grown (Hillery), 57–58, 61–62, 72
Hatching Chicks in Room 6 (Arnold), 125
Heart and Soul (Nelson), 97
Hello, Universe (Entrada Kelly), 86, 102, 133
Here and Now (Denos), 118, 126
Here Come the Humpbacks (Pulley Sayre), 123
Here I Am (Kim), 102
Hey, Wall! (Verde), 124, 136
High Tide for Horseshoe Crabs (Schnell), 116
Hill We Climb, The (Gorman), 132
history, 6, 41–49, 52–56, 68–69, 81, 88–89, 92, 97, 109–111, 114–115, 127, 129, 132. See also Social studies
hope(s), 31, 38, 68, 91, 97, 99, 104, 106, 120, 136
How Reading Changed My Life (Quindlen), 6
How to Read a Book (Alexander), 100, 102

I Am Every Good Thing (Barnes), 26–27, 36–38, 100, 103
I Am Loved (Giovanni), 104
I Am the Storm (Yolen & Stemple), 100
Ideas Are All Around (Stead), 126
I Dissent! (Levy), 112
identity(ies), 4, 16–18, 20, 22, 26, 32, 44, 54, 68, 78–81, 85–88, 91, 102, 115, 127; intersectional, 22, 36, 43, 80, 91; multiple, 34, 127; sociocultural, 22, 80
If I Were a Book (Letria & Letria), 11–12
Illustration(s), 3, 11, 21, 35, 38, 45, 49, 51, 53, 55, 63, 68–70, 72, 74–75, 97, 99, 101–102, 107, 112–113, 121, 127, 131, 133–134
illustrator(s), 2–3, 16, 38–39, 48–50, 54, 67–68, 76, 80, 85, 95, 97, 99, 101, 104–105, 109, 112–113, 121–122, 132–133, 138. See also Artist
imagination, xi, 1, 17, 26, 28, 33, 45, 50, 53, 101
inclusion, 1, 5, 9, 12, 21–22, 30–34, 55, 87–88, 131
informal assessment, 12
In the Shadow of the Fallen Towers (Brown), 112, 115
Indian No More (McManis & Sorrell), 96
Indigenous People's History of the United States for Young People, An (Dunbar-Ortiz et al), 110, 130
informational book, 63, 135. See also Text: informational
injustice, 25–26, 28, 31, 36, 39, 41, 42, 56, 79, 84–85, 87, 89, 91–92, 96–97
inquiry, 17, 22, 24, 26, 42–43, 45–46, 62–66, 75, 98, 114, 118, 121
Inquisitor's Tale, The (Gidwitz), 54, 114

instruction, ix–x, 1–4, 14–15, 20, 24, 28–29, 35, 39, 56, 83, 92–93, 95; literacy, 1, 26, 44, 102; literature-based, 31–32, 35; reading, 20, 34; remedial, 24; social studies, 44; trauma-sensitive, 71; writing, 34
interconnectedness, 65–66, 68
Ira's Shakespeare Dream (Armond), 107
Islandborn (Diaz), 52–53, 102, 108
I, Too, Am America (Hughes), 132
It Fell From the Sky (Fan & Fan), 99, 105, 122
It's Our Garden (Ancona), 125

Jazz Day (Orgill), 111
Josephine (Powell), 111, 136
Journey, The (Sana), 108
joy, xi, 1–2, 26–29, 31, 33, 36, 39, 48, 54, 65, 69, 87, 95, 106, 124
Joy (Averiss), 29, 103–104, 106
Juana & Lucas series (Medina), 131
Julián Is a Mermaid (Love), 78
justice, 9, 36, 78–79, 83–84, 88, 127. See also Injustice; climate, 59, 74, 120; environmental, 68; social, 10, 129–130, 132, 134

La Frontera (Mills & Alva), 108
La Princesa and the Pea (Elya), 128, 134
language(s), 3–4, 13, 17, 23, 30, 32, 35, 39–40, 42, 46–49, 68, 78, 82, 85, 87, 91–92, 100, 102–104, 109, 120–122, 128, 131, 137; home, 1, 19–20
language arts, 6, 23, 45, 53
Last Cuentista, The (Higuera), 98, 133
Last Stop on Market Street (de la Peña), 67, 118
Laxmi's Mooch (Anand), 87
Legacy (Grimes), 111, 137
Lesser Spotted Animals (Brown), 120
lesson(s), 1, 5, 13, 42, 75, 77, 90, 121
Let the Children March (Clark-Robinson), 89, 129
library(ies), ix–x, 3, 20, 30, 44, 109, 111, 128–129, 131, 135. See also Classroom: library(ies)
librarian(s), 19, 114, 116, 127, 136
Life in the Ocean (Nivola), 117
Lion and the Mouse, The (Pinkney), 34
literacy(ies), ix–x, 1, 12–14, 18, 22–24, 29, 31, 45, 62, 64, 77–79, 81, 95, 105. See also Critical literacy(ies); Disciplinary literacy(ies); Instruction: literacy; Visual literacy; education, 79, 81, 88; environmental, 130; learning, ix, 30–31; racial, 36; science, 64; scholar(s), 16–17, 31, 43; skills, 26, 79, 87, 91; specialist(s), 1, 81
literature, ix–x, 1–4, 22, 26–30, 31–33, 46, 58–59, 63, 85, 138. See also Children's literature; Young; adult literature; circle(s), 4, 53, 55; literature-based, 1, 3, 30–31; response, 32

Index

Little Red Hen, The (Pinkney), 78
lived experiences, 13, 16, 20, 22, 42, 78
Long Ride, The (Budhos), 55, 96, 110
Look Up! (Cate), 118, 122
Love (de la Peña), 104
Luis Paints the World (Farish), 136

Making It Home (Naidoo), 89
Malala's Magic Pencil (Yousafzai), 129
Mama's Nightingale (Danticat), 135
March: Book Three (Lewis & Aydin), 101, 112
Martin's Big Words (Rappaport), 135
Marwan's Journey (DeArias), 79, 86, 107
Matthew's Dream (Lionni), 95
Maybe Marisol series (Entrada Kelly, 131
Maybe Maybe Marisol Rainey (Entrada Kelly), 34–35, 96
Maybe Something Beautiful (Campoy & Howell), 124, 136
meaning(s), x, 2, 13, 16–18, 22, 30–32, 64, 68, 78, 95, 112, 132–133. *See also* Comprehension
Merci Suárez Changes Gears (Medina), 102
Mesmerized (Rockliff), 108
mindfulness, 22, 59, 61, 72, 74 126
mirror(s), 17, 19–20, 39, 55, 66, 87, 96
Mirror Mirror (Singer), 88
multimodal resources, 108
multimodal response, 100, 114, 124, 135
modality(ies), 16, 23
Most Days (Leannah), 106
Moth (Thomas), 120
Mumbet's Declaration of Independence (Woelfe), 108
Mysterious Patterns (Campbell), 119

narrative, 32, 35, 43, 48, 54, 68, 88, 131. *See also* Fiction; Text: narrative
National Council of Teachers of English, 26
National Science Teachers Association, 64
nature, 22, 57, 60, 65, 69–70, 72–73, 97, 103–104, 117–121, 123–124, 126; human, 27; interpretive, 44
natural curiosity, 3, 22, 61
natural world, 5–6, 9, 22, 59, 61, 64–65, 66, 68–69, 74, 97, 116–117, 119, 121, 123–124, 126, 138
naturalist(s), 64, 116, 118–119
neuroscience, 31
Never Caught (Dunbar & Van Cleve), 48, 97, 108–109
New Kid (Craft), 19, 34, 99–101, 137
Night Diary, The (Hiranandani), 53, 98, 108
Night Gardener, The (Fan & Fan), 122
No Child Left Behind, 44
No Monkeys, No Chocolate (Stewart), 116
No Voice Too Small (Metcalf et al), 79, 89, 106, 120, 129–130

nonfiction, 1, 4, 15, 19, 21, 23–24, 41, 45–51, 54, 61, 63–64, 66, 76, 89, 98, 106–109, 111–114, 118, 120–121.
Nothing Stopped Sophie (Bardoe), 88
Notorious Benedict Arnold, The (Sheinkin), 108
novel, 15, 35, 53–55, 81–82, 86, 88. *See also* Graphic novel

observation, 57–59, 61–65, 67–70, 73, 114, 116–117, 121–122, 125. *See also* Close observation
Ocean Meets Sky (Fan & Fan), 105
Oliver Button Is a Sissy (dePaola), 79
One and Only Ivan, The (Applegate), 25–26, 33, 105
One Plastic Bag (Paul), 106
One Today (Blanco), 132
One Wish (Yuskel), 90–91, 110, 115
Our House Is on Fire (Winter), 129
Outside Your Window: A First Book of Nature (Davies), 23, 121
Over and Under the Pond (Messner), 123
Over the Hills and Far Away (Hammill), 128

Paper Wishes (Sepahban), 97
Parker Inheritance, The (Johnson), 88
Patchwork Bike, The (Clarke), 133
Peace (Paul & Paul), 132
pedagogy(ies), 31, 58–59. *See also* Culturally relevant pedagogies; Instruction
pedagogical purpose, 21
pedagogical structures, 24
People Could Fly, The (Hamilton), 33
perspective(s), 2, 16, 29–30, 32, 34, 43
picture book(s), ix, 23, 26, 29, 32–33, 40–41, 45–46, 49, 53–55, 57, 60–61, 63, 65–69, 71–73, 76, 68, 89–90, 97, 99–100, 102, 111–112, 117, 122, 127, 133–134. *See also* Fiction; Nonfiction
Place to Start a Family, A (Harrison), 121
podcast(s), 23, 85, 114–115
poem(s), 66, 87–88, 98, 121, 132. *See also* Poetry
poetry, 4, 23, 53–54, 61, 89, 107, 120–121, 126, 132–133. *See also* Poem
positioning, 80, 84–85, 127
power, 2–5, 12–13, 26–28, 33, 35, 41–42, 44, 72, 75–76, 78–85, 87–88, 91–92, 98, 105, 120, 126–127, 129, 131–132, 137; empowerment, 56
praxis, 88, 90
primary grades, 40, 75
primary source(s), 47, 49, 55, 108–109, 111, 113
primary text, 49
privilege, 4, 26, 34, 41, 60, 84–90, 127–128, 131–132, 137
protest(s), 41, 89, 129, 132

purpose(s), ix–x, 1–2, 4–7, 9–18, 21–24, 29–31, 38–39, 45, 59, 71, 77, 83, 87, 93, 95, 97–98, 114, 134, 138. *See also* Four purposes framework; braided, ix, 16; four purposes, 6–7, 21, 57, 93, 138; purposeful teaching, 85; purposefulness, ix–x

Queen of Physics (Robeson), 127

Rabbit Listened, The (Doeerfeld), 32–33, 95, 99, 101, 103–105
race, 19, 35, 44, 128. *See also* Critical race theory
racism, 27, 31, 40, 44, 96, 129. *See also* Critical race theory
Rachel Carson and Her Book That Changed the World (Lawler), 23, 117
Radiant Child (Steptoe), 99, 136
Rain School (Rumford), 110
Raindrops Roll (Pulley Sayre), 97
RAND, 16
read-aloud(s), 4, 14, 23, 26, 34–35, 40–41, 55, 64, 76, 85, 89, 93
selections, 18–19
reader(s), ix–x, 1–7, 11–17, 19–22, 24, 26, 28–29, 32–39, 45–51, 53–56, 60–61, 65–70, 72–73, 75–76, 78, 80–81, 84–85, 88–89, 91, 93, 96, 98, 102, 104–105, 108–109, 113–114, 121–123, 131, 135, 138; critical, 112; developing, 4; elementary, 35; engaged, 44–45; enthusiastic, 12; lifelong, 2; middle-grade, 35, 48; proficient, 2–3; reluctant, 15; struggling, 15, 18
reader response, 16, 39, 56, 68, 76, 83. *See also* Literature: response; Transaction; Transactional theory
reading, xi, 1–3, 12–21, 23–24, 31–32, 45, 47, 76, 78, 81, 106–107, 112; activities, 64; benchmarks, 79; curricular-based, 14; experience(s), ix, 5, 14, 16, 24, 106; identity(ies), 17. *See also* Identity; independent, 20, 23, 93, 99, 101; interests, 20; intervention, 24; lesson, 13; life, 1, 13; material, 4, 16; practices, 2, 14–15, 19; preference(s), 12, 15; process, 32, 98, 112, 120, 132; program(s), 2, 24; skill(s), 18, 49, 112; "testimonial reading," 36; transactions, 6. *See also* Reader response; Literature; Transactional theory
reading the world, 13, 79, 88
reconnect(ion), 60
Red Pencil, The (Pinkney), 135
relationship(s), 16, 23, 29–30, 64, 67, 81, 91, 97, 102. *See also* Connection(s); sound-letter, 78; to the text, 80; with books, 11–12; with nature, 60
representation(s), 4, 17, 21–22, 34, 55–56, 60, 70, 72, 74, 78, 80, 87–88, 96, 116–117, 127, 131, 134

research, 2–3, 9, 16, 30–31, 33, 35, 43–47, 49, 51, 64–66, 69, 85, 110–113, 130, 132, 135; author's, 49; educational, 45, 83; historical, 109; process, 112; Youth Participatory Action, 129
researcher(s), 2, 12, 50, 58–60, 129
Rescue and Jessica (Kensky & Downes), 96
resilience, 30–31, 38–39, 53–54, 104
rewriting, 2, 13, 132, 134. *See also* Counterstorytelling; Text reconstruction
Room on Our Rock (Temple & Temple), 78
Round (Sidman), 119

science, 6, 23, 58–66, 70, 88, 90, 116–117
Scientists in the Field (Houghton Mifflin Harcourt), 64–65
Searching for Sarah Rector (Bolden), 109
Seashells, More Than a Home (Stewart), 123
Secrets of the Sea (Griffith & Stone), 65, 118
Seeds Move! (Page), 116
self-portrait collages, 26–27
Separate Is Never Equal (Tonatiuh), 110, 113, 137
series bin, 35,
series book(s), 125, 131
Seventh Wish, The (Messner), 132
Shelter (Claire), 103
Si se puede! Yes We Can! (Cohn), 89
Sick Day for Amos McGee (Stead), 96
Sit In (Pinkney), 89
sliding glass door(s), 17, 20, 86–87
Snow White (Phelan), 101, 112
social action, 79, 85, 88, 90, 134–135
social and emotional learning (SEL), 29–30, 102, 115, 125, 136
social-emotional growth, 59
social responsibility, 34
social studies, 6, 23, 41–46, 52 132. *See also* History
Some Writer! (Sweet), 102
Splash of Red, A (Bryant), 69, 113, 117
Stamped (Reynolds & Kendi), 40, 130
Stamped From the Beginning (Kendi), 43
stereotype(s), 18, 20, 34, 80, 82, 86, 119, 131
Stone Sat Still, A (Wenzel), 104, 126
Stonewall (Sanders), 79, 97
Sugar Hill (Weatherford), 111
Superlative Birds (Bulion), 120
summer slump, 24
Swirl by Swirl (Sidman), 119

Tantrum That Saved the World, The (Herbert & Mann), 99, 106, 120, 130
teacher(s), ix–x, 1–6, 12–14, 16–20, 23–24, 27–30, 34, 36, 44–45, 48, 52–54, 57–58, 64, 72, 88, 90, 93, 138
teacher education, 12

Index

teacher educators, ix, 1, 9, 28
teaching invitation(s), x, 3, 7, 21, 93, 95, 107, 116, 127, 131
Teachers March, The (Wallce & Wallace), 113–114, 129
technology, 12, 79, 88. *See also* Digital
testing, 43, 131
text(s), ix–x, 2–7, 11–12, 16–17, 19, 22–24, 26, 28, 31–36, 38–39, 41, 43–44, 46–49, 51–52, 54–55, 62–65, 68–69, 78–81, 84–88, 93, 96, 99, 102, 107–113, 117, 120–121, 125, 127, 132–135. *See also* Fiction; Nonfiction; authentic, 84–85; diverse, 84–85; emotionally transporting, 31–32, 36; expository, 66, 121, 125; features, 112; graphic, 101. *See also* Graphic books; Graphic novel; informational, 15, 65. *See also* Informational book; leveled, 26; mentor, 6, 38, 51, 69, 113, 123, 133; multigenre, 64; multimodal, 64; narrative, 42, 125; structure, 13
text deconstruction, 84, 87–88, 131
text reconstruction, 85, 88. *See also* Counterstorytelling
text selection(s), 22, 27–28, 30, 34, 36, 87. *See also* Book selection; Read-aloud: selections
text set(s), 53, 55, 64, 85–86, 95, 107–108, 112, 116–117, 127, 129; multimodal, 64
textbook(s), 23, 44, 47, 127, 132
Thirty Minutes Over Oregon (Nobleman), 110, 115
Tiny, Perfect Things (Clark), 72, 106
Tomatoes for Neela (Lakshmi), 99, 104
Towers Falling (Rhodes), 53, 55
transaction(s), ix, 6, 16, 17. *See also* Reader response; Transactional theory
transactional theory, 16. *See also* Reader response; Transaction(s)
True Story of the Three Little Pigs, The (Scieszka), 75
trauma, x, 26, 29, 31–32, 71, 104

unit(s), 75, 86, 124; history 41, 52; literacy, 64
Undefeated, The (Alexander), 79, 96, 102, 133
Unspeakable (Weatherford), 49, 79, 115, 132

visual literacy(ies), 68, 99, 112, 121, 133
voice(s), 19, 25, 51, 66, 73, 78, 85–86, 88, 92, 103, 106, 129, 131–133; student, 57, 101
Voice of Freedom (Weatherford), 135

Wait, Rest, Pause (Atkins), 123
Wangari Maathai (Prevot), 106, 117
Water Is Water (Paul), 121
We Are Still Here! (Sorell), 40–41, 47, 110
We All Play (Flett), 123
We Are Water Protectors (Lindstrom), 41, 68, 97, 110, 120, 130
We Shall Overcome (Collier), 124, 132
Welcome to the Neighborwood (Sheehy), 116, 125
What Do You Do With a Chance? (Yamada), 105
What Do You Do With a Voice Like That? (Barton), 135
What Lane? (Maldonado), 137
When We Are Kind (Smith), 100
When You Trap a Tiger (Keller), 86, 98
Where Are You From? (Méndez), 102, 128
Why Am I Me? (Britt), 102, 128
Winter Bees and Other Poems of the Cold (Sidman), 121
Wisdom of Trees, The (Judge), 66, 97, 120–121, 125–126
Wishtree (Applegate), 106
whole child, 29, 30, 38
Wild Ideas (Kelsey), 125
window(s), 17, 19–20, 39, 53–54, 86
Windows (Denos), 118
Watcher, The (Winter), 108, 122
Wolf in the Snow (Cordell), 99, 120
Wolf Won't Bite (Gravett), 75
Wonder Walkers (Archer), 65, 97, 106, 119, 122, 124
worldview(s), 2, 16, 84
writer(s), 23, 51, 93, 100, 111
writing, x, 2, 4, 13, 15, 23–24, 26, 30, 34, 45, 50–51, 54, 97, 100, 103, 105, 109, 111, 114, 120–123, 133, 136; activity(ies), 64, 77, 136; affirmation, 37–38; benchmarks, 79; descriptive, 50–51; development, 100, 113, 122, 133; multigenre, 123, 133–134; narrative, 133; portfolios, 134; styles, 47, 49

Year We Learned to Fly, The (Woodson), 32–33, 97, 101
You Call This Democracy? (Rusch), 130
young adult literature, 3, 5, 85, 128, 138
Your Name Is a Song (Thompkins-Bigelow), 103

Zoom, 110, 119

About the Authors

Erika Thulin Dawes is a professor and chair of the Language and Literacy Department in the Graduate School of Education at Lesley University, where she teaches courses in children's literature and early childhood literacy. She is the coauthor of several books, including *Teaching with Text Sets* (Shell, 2013), *Teaching to Complexity* (Shell, 2015), and *Text Sets in Action* (Stenhouse, 2021) and is a former chair of NCTE's Charlotte Huck Award for Outstanding Fiction for Children.

Katie Egan Cunningham is an associate professor of teacher education at Sacred Heart University, where she teaches courses in literacy methods and children's literature. She is the author of several books, including *Start With Joy: Designing Literacy Learning for Student Happiness* (Stenhouse, 2019) as well as coauthor of *Shifting the Balance: 6 Ways to Bring the Science of Reading to Upper Elementary Classrooms* (Stenhouse, 2023). Katie studies and supports schools to humanize education.

Grace Enriquez is a professor of language and literacy in the Graduate School of Education at Lesley University, where she teaches courses in children's literature, writing, and literacy research. She is coauthor of *The Reading Turn-Around* (Teachers College Press, 2010), *The Reading Turn-Around for Emergent Bilinguals* (Teachers College Press, 2019), and coeditor of *Literacies, Learning, and the Body* (Routledge, 2016). She is the children's literature editor of *The Reading Teacher* and former children's literature editor of *Language Arts*.

Mary Ann Cappiello is a professor of language and literacy in the Graduate School of Education at Lesley University, where she teaches courses in children's literature, content literacy, and more. She is coauthor of *Teaching with Text Sets* (Shell, 2013), *Teaching to Complexity* (Shell, 2015), and *Text Sets in Action* (Stenhouse, 2021), and former chair of NCTE's Orbis Pictus Award for Outstanding Nonfiction for Children.

Printed and bound by CPI Group (UK) Ltd, Croydon, CR0 4YY
31/07/2025
14712036-0005